T0348638

The Changing Landscape of
China's Consumerism

CHANDOS
ASIAN STUDIES SERIES

Series Editor: Professor Chris Rowley,
Centre for Research on Asian Management, Cass Business School,
City University, UK; HEAD Foundation, Singapore
(email: *c.rowley@city.ac.uk*)

Chandos Publishing is pleased to publish this major Series of books entitled *Asian Studies: Contemporary Issues and Trends*. The Series Editor is Professor Chris Rowley, Director, Centre for Research on Asian Management, City University, UK and Director, Research and Publications, HEAD Foundation, Singapore.

Asia has clearly undergone some major transformations in recent years and books in the Series examine this transformation from a number of perspectives: economic, management, social, political and cultural. We seek authors from a broad range of areas and disciplinary interests covering, for example, business/management, political science, social science, history, sociology, gender studies, ethnography, economics and international relations, etc.

Importantly, the Series examines both current developments and possible future trends. The Series is aimed at an international market of academics and professionals working in the area. The books have been specially commissioned from leading authors. The objective is to provide the reader with an authoritative view of current thinking.

New authors: we would be delighted to hear from you if you have an idea for a book. We are interested in both shorter, practically orientated publications (45,000+ words) and longer, theoretical monographs (75,000–100,000 words). Our books can be single, joint or multi-author volumes. If you have an idea for a book, please contact the publishers or Professor Chris Rowley, the Series Editor.

Dr Glyn Jones
Chandos Publishing
Email: *g.jones.2@elsevier.com*

Professor Chris Rowley
Cass Business School, City University
Email: *c.rowley@city.ac.uk*
www.cass.city.ac.uk/faculty/c.rowley

Chandos Publishing: Chandos Publishing is an imprint of Elsevier. The aim of Chandos Publishing is to publish books of the highest possible standard: books that are both intellectually stimulating and innovative.

We are delighted and proud to count our authors from such well-known international organisations as the Asian Institute of Technology, Tsinghua University, Kookmin University, Kobe University, Kyoto Sangyo University, London School of Economics, University of Oxford, Michigan State University, Getty Research Library, University of Texas at Austin, University of South Australia, University of Newcastle, Australia, University of Melbourne, ILO, Max-Planck Institute, Duke University and the leading law firm Clifford Chance.

A key feature of Chandos Publishing's activities is the service it offers its authors and customers. Chandos Publishing recognises that its authors are at the core of its publishing ethos, and authors are treated in a friendly, efficient and timely manner. Chandos Publishing's books are marketed on an international basis, via its range of overseas agents and representatives.

Professor Chris Rowley: Dr Rowley, BA, MA (Warwick), DPhil (Nuffield College, Oxford) is Subject Group leader and the inaugural Professor of Human Resource Management at Cass Business School, City University, London, UK, and Director of Research and Publications for the HEAD Foundation, Singapore. He is the founding Director of the multi-disciplinary and internationally networked Centre for Research on Asian Management (*http://www.cass.city.ac.uk/cram/index.html*) and Editor of the leading journal *Asia Pacific Business Review* (*www.tandf.co.uk/journals/titles/13602381.asp*). He is well known and highly regarded in the area, with visiting appointments at leading Asian universities and top journal Editorial Boards in the UK, Asia and the US. He has given a range of talks and lectures to universities, companies and organisations internationally with research and consultancy experience with unions, business and government, and his previous employment includes varied work in both the public and private sectors. Professor Rowley researches in a range of areas, including international and comparative human resource management and Asia Pacific management and business. He has been awarded grants from the British Academy, an ESRC AIM International Study Fellowship and gained a 5-year RCUK Fellowship in Asian Business and Management. He acts as a reviewer for many funding bodies, as well as for numerous journals and publishers. Professor Rowley publishes extensively, including in leading US and UK journals, with over 370 articles, books, chapters and other contributions.

The Changing Landscape of China's Consumerism

EDITED BY
ALISON HULME

AMSTERDAM • BOSTON • CAMBRIDGE • HEIDELBERG • LONDON
NEW YORK • OXFORD • PARIS • SAN DIEGO
SAN FRANCISCO • SINGAPORE • SYDNEY • TOKYO
Chandos Publishing is an imprint of Elsevier

Chandos Publishing
Elsevier Limited
The Boulevard
Langford Lane
Kidlington
Oxford OX5 1GB
UK
store.elsevier.com/Chandos-Publishing-/IMP_207/

Chandos Publishing is an imprint of Elsevier Limited

Tel: +44 (0) 1865 843000
Fax: +44 (0) 1865 843010
store.elsevier.com

First published in 2014

ISBN: 978-1-84334-761-3 (print)
ISBN: 978-1-78063-442-5 (online)

Library of Congress Control Number: 2014931607

© The editor and contributors, 2014

Project management by Neil Shuttlewood Associates, Gt Yarmouth, Norfolk, UK

Contents

List of abbreviations

CCP	Chinese Communist Party
CASS	Chinese Academy of Social Science
CAA	Chinese Advertising Association
CCP	Chinese Communist Party
CITS	China International Travel Service
CTS	China Travel Service
CYTS	China Youth Travel Service
IPR	Intellectual Property Rights
IV	IntraVenous
KPMG	Professional services company
PLA	People's Liberation Army
PRC	People's Republic of China
PWC	PriceWaterhouseCoopers
SARS	Severe Acute Respiratory Syndrome
SAC	Shanghai Advertising Corporation
SAIC	State Administration for Industry and Commerce
SARFT	State Administration of Radio, Film and Television
SOE	State-Owned Enterprise
TAR	Tibet Autonomous Region
TCM	Traditional Chinese Medicine
TNAA	TransNational Advertising Agency
TNC	TransNational Corporation
UN WTO	United Nations World Tourism Organization
WM	Western Medicine

Acknowledgements

I would like to thank Dr. Glyn Jones and the editors and support staff at Chandos, not forgetting George Knott's initial championing of the concept of this book, without which it would not exist. Thanks too to project manager Neil Shuttlewood for clear guidance and thought-provoking questions. I would also like to acknowledge the hard work of all the chapter authors and to thank them for sharing their originality of thought and dedication to their subject area. It was a pleasure working with all of you. Without the assistance of these and many other peole, the completion of this work would not have been possible. Many sincere thanks.

About the editor

Alison Hulme is an Associate Lecturer at Goldsmiths College, University of London, from where she gained her PhD in Cultural Studies in 2011 and her MA in Anthropology in 2006. She also has a BA in Media Studies from the University of Sussex. She has previously taught intensive courses in contemporary China at the University of Iceland and Beijing Foreign Studies University and also lectures part-time on contemporary China at University College Dublin. Her work focusses on media culture with an emphasis on China (film, TV, state-produced poster campaigns, imagery of cities, etc.), the history of entrepreneurialism in China, and material culture. These strands are linked by a concern with theories of the commodity and consumption. Prior to entering academia, Alison was a radio and TV presenter for many years. In her spare time she jointly runs a film club and has a particular interest in 1930s' Chinese leftist cinema and the French films of Jacques Tati. She runs a blog at *www.commodity tactics.wordpress.com*

About the contributors

Andreas Steen is Associate Professor of Modern Chinese History and Culture at Aarhus University, Denmark. He studied Sinology, English Philology, and Modern Chinese Literature at the Free University of Berlin and Fudan University, Shanghai. His main fields of research concentrate on various aspects of China's popular culture, modern Chinese history, and Sino-German relations from the nineteenth century until 1945. Among his publications are *Zwischen Unterhaltung und Revolution: Grammophone, Schallplatten und die Anfänge der Musikindustrie in Shanghai, 1878–1937* (Wiesbaden: Harrassowitz-Verlag, 2006), the edited volume *Deutsch-chinesische Beziehungen 1911–1927: Vom Kolonialismus zur 'Gleichberechtigung' – Eine Quellensammlung* (Berlin: Akademie-Verlag, 2006), and several articles on recent trends in the world of Chinese pop.

Calvin Hui is Assistant Professor of Chinese Studies in Modern Languages and Literatures at the College of William and Mary, Virginia. In May 2013, he received his PhD in Literature at Duke University, after completing his dissertation 'The People's Republic of Capitalism: the making of the new middle class in post-socialist China, 1978–present' under the supervision of Rey Chow, Michael Hardt, and Fredric Jameson. He has also obtained graduate certificates in East Asian Studies and Feminist Studies at Duke. Calvin's research and teaching focus on modern Chinese humanities (literature, film, and media), critical theory, and cultural studies, with an emphasis on Marxist theory, gender and sexuality studies, and postcolonial and ethnic studies.

Gabriel Lafitte taught Asian Studies and Public Advocacy at various Australian universities. He organized and led culture tours through China to Mongolia, and (briefly) considered a business partnership with China's Ministry of Culture, which promised access to assets under their control, including Dunhuang caves (off limits to foreigners), and the last living member of the Qing dynasty. He has spent 35 years working with

Tibetans, on the impacts of official policies on economic development, biodiversity, pastoral nomads, mining, and tourism. His chapter in this book was presented to the 13th Seminar of the International Association of Tibetan Studies, 2013; and an extended, graphically illustrated, online version is published by *www.savetibet.org* Updates are available from his blogspot *www.rukor.org* His book on mining and Tibet's sacred mountains, *Spoiling Tibet: China and Resource Nationalism on the Roof of the World*, was published by Zed Books, London, September 2013. He is now retired, growing a garden of native flowers in a village close to a major Australian city. His next book will be on the pastoral nomads of the Tibetan Plateau.

Geir Sigurðsson studied Chinese at the University of Kiel in Germany and Renmin University of China in Beijing, before receiving his PhD in comparative Chinese–Western philosophy from the University of Hawaii in 2004. He is currently Associate Professor in Chinese Studies at University of Iceland, has been head of the Chinese Studies programme since its establishment in 2007, and was director of the Northern Lights Confucius Institute 2008–2012. While regularly teaching courses on Chinese history, philosophy, religion, cinema and modernization, as well as on Western intellectual history, he focusses in his research in particular on Confucian and Daoist philosophical views on ethics, environmental issues, and meaningful living, and the resurgence of Chinese philosophical and religious traditions in contemporary China. His book, *Confucian Propriety and Ritual Learning: A Philosophical Interpretation* (forthcoming with SUNY Press, 2014) is a constructive hermeneutical study of the Confucian 'project' from the point of view of education and the important Confucian notion of *li*, often translated as 'ritual', 'ceremonies', or 'propriety'.

Giovanna Puppin is a Lecturer in International Promotional Cultures at Middlesex University. Her previous posts include a post-doctoral fellowship on the project 'The Chinese consumer between global aspirations and tradition' at Ca' Foscari University, and a visiting fellowship at the Communication and Media Research Institute, University of Westminster. She holds a BA in Chinese interpreting and a MA in Chinese translation, and in 2009, she obtained a PhD in Chinese Studies from Foscari University with a thesis entitled 'What's in a name? On China's search for 'public service advertising'.' In addition she has extensive experience as a freelance consultant for institutions and companies interested in the Chinese market. Her research interests include: China's promotional culture (advertising, branding, marketing); Chinese media, popular culture, and creative industries; identity, nationalism, and soft power in contemporary China. In her free time, she takes pictures of advertisements and blogs at *http://advertisingchina. blogspot.com*

Karen Tam is an artist whose research focuses on the various forms of constructions and imaginations of seemingly opposing cultures and communities, through her installation work in which she recreates spaces such as the Chinese restaurant, karaoke lounges, opium dens, and other sites of cultural encounters. She has exhibited her work in Canada, Ireland, the UK, Austria, and the US since 2000. Past residencies include RONDO Studio Residency (Austria), Djerassi Resident Artist Program (California), *Breathe* Chinese Arts Centre (Manchester, UK), Irish Museum of Modern Art (Dublin), Atelier Circulaire (Montréal), Southern Alberta Art Gallery (Lethbridge), Centre A (Vancouver), and 501 Artspace (Chongqing, China). She has received grants and fellowships from the Canada Council for the Arts, Conseil des arts du Québec, Fonds de recherche sur la société et la culture de Québec, Fonds pour la Formation de Chercheurs et l'Aide à la Recherche, and Social Sciences & Humanities Research Council of Canada, and has been longlisted for the Sobey Art Award 2010. Recent exhibitions were held at Plymouth City Museum & Art Gallery (UK), University of Toronto, RONDO Studios (Austria), Wilfred Laurier University (ON), Third Space (NB), Victoria & Albert Museum (London), CUE Art Foundation (New York), Chelsea Art Museum (New York), Musée d'art contemporain de Montréal, and New Art Gallery of Walsall (UK). Tam lives and works in Montréal (Québec) and London (UK) where she is a doctoral candidate at Goldsmiths' Centre for Cultural Studies (University of London). Her work can be seen at: *http://www.karentam.ca*

Qingyan Ma is a sociocultural anthropologist whose work investigates how people articulate understandings of medicine, body, and ethnicity in relation with the state, and in the everyday life of medical practice and consumption. Her primary focus is on the process, effect, and conceptualization of modernity in the era of neoliberal globalization in contemporary China. She has a BA in English and Economics from the South-western University of Finance and Economics in China and an MA in Anthropology from Sun Yat-sen University. She is currently completing her doctoral studies in the Department of Anthropology at Temple

University in Philadelphia, PA. Her thesis is titled 'The cultural politics of reproduction in the multi-ethnic borderland of P. R. China' and explores the impact of the changing public health policy on the reproductive practice for multi-ethnic populations in southwest China's Yunnan province. It reveals how national population policies were/are experienced at the local level in different time periods and analyzes how culture informs medical decisions and clinical realities, the influence of structural factors such as economics and accessibility, and how globalized biomedical definitions of reproduction are being adopted by the Chinese state and interpreted at the local level. Qingyan's research interests include biopolitics, modernity, history, and contemporary China studies.

Xin Wang is Associate Professor of Chinese Studies and serves as the Director of the Asian Studies program at Baylor University. He was born in Xi'an, China, and completed his Master's and doctorate at Baylor. In addition to his recent book *Higher Education as a Field of Study in China: Defining Knowledge and Curriculum Structure*, his publications have mainly focussed on the civic culture of the emerging middle class in China. His recent research projects include China's newly emerged urban art communities. Besides teaching and research at Baylor, he directs and leads the Baylor in China – Baylor Study Abroad – program every summer.

Introduction

Iron rice bowls and plastic money: the push and pull of consumerism's rise in capitalist/ communist China

Alison Hulme

As the plane takes off the girl next to me gently rustles the bag nestled between her feet, eager to explore its contents. She looks about 20, but it is difficult to tell. She wears some fashionably distressed jeans and a sports top. This is the flight from Shanghai to Kunming, the provincial capital of rural Yunnan province in Southwest China. I am the only non-Chinese face on board. Once we have reached our cruising height the girl leans down and pulls the bag onto her lap, opening it and taking out a blue Adidas zip-up top, a pale pink T-shirt with the words 'cool life' scrawled on it in glittery silver, and a Hello Kitty pencil case. She holds each of the things in front of her, examining them from different angles, turning them over in her hands, and feeling their insides and edges. Her face is at times tense, as if fearing potential regret at her own error of judgement or taste in buying them, and at times serene. Finally, seeming pleased with her purchases, she turns to me and smiles, asking where I am from – "Meiguo?" she says. I reply that I am not American, but English. "Ah Yinguo! David Beckham, Big Ben, Red Bus," she reels off gleefully, citing the global signs that have in recent years become those most attributed to the UK.

She informs me that nearly everyone on the flight is returning to Yunnan from shopping trips to Shanghai. It is the end of one of the government's new 'golden week' holidays, created expressly to encourage consumption – especially on the part of the rural masses. If the shopping contents of this plane are anything to go by, golden weeks are working. Looking around it is clear that almost everyone on the flight has at least one glossy carrier bag.

'It's expensive to fly though, isn't it?' I ask. 'Yes,' she replies, 'quite expensive, but we don't have much holiday, so the train takes too long.' Here, as elsewhere across the globe, time has come to mean money. The quicker the rural inhabitants can get to Shanghai and consume, the quicker they can get back to Yunnan to work and earn. A train would be a false economy. 'What do people buy?' I ask. Mainly clothes and presents, she says – things that are not as easy to find in Yunnan, such as Western designer labels. She explains that this is probably a rare trip to Shanghai for most people on board and that they would have saved money especially for it.

As we disembark from the plane at Kunming, I watch the long line of Chinese make their way across the tarmac, clutching their shiny bags, and shielding their faces against the driving drizzle. At the terminal building, they seem to suddenly and quietly disperse, getting into dusty, patched-up cars, strangely at odds with the glossy commercialism of their purchases. These are the rural inhabitants that the Chinese government is so keen to encourage to spend, hoping it can unlock their spending power in order to maintain economic growth, especially following the global downturn and hence falling demand from Europe and the US. The intention is effectively to create a reserve army of consumers, who can soak up the over-production necessary if China is to maintain its growth rate. A fall in growth, such as has happened in recent years, is a concern not only in the pure economic sense, but also socially, as it inevitably means loss of employment which in turn has led to civil unrest in recent years.

Government campaigns to encourage spending are vigorous – especially outside the coastal provinces where people are less well off and more likely to feel the necessity of maintaining savings. Therefore, it is in rural provinces such as Yunnan that the 'iron rice bowl' most incongruously meets the plastic credit card. Iron rice bowl (*tiefanwan*) is a term from the Mao era which describes the stability of one's position and income if one worked in a civic role for the Party or the government. It also came to be used as a way of describing the way in which, under communism, there was (at least in theory) a general provision for all. The iron rice bowl was therefore connected to the notion of the social guarantee (*baoxialai*) as providing all that was necessary for daily survival. When Deng Xiao Ping took leadership in 1978, encouraging innovation and entrepreneurship, many of the public sector jobs that had been considered iron rice bowl jobs were phased out or simply abolished and the concept itself was given short shrift in the new 'open-door' China. Being self-sufficient and entrepreneurial was now seen as key. For the first time in China's history, emphasis was unabashedly placed on individuals 'getting rich', albeit it (purportedly anyway) to aid the nation's attempt to develop at lightning pace. Getting rich was 'glorious' according to Deng and making money became part of a pseudo-Maoist rhetoric in which the pursuit of individual wealth was re-contextualized as part of an immense national effort to 'catch up' with levels of development in the West following the years of the Cultural Revolution.

Along with this new focus on wealth creation came the acceptability of new forms of finance. As Kelle Tsai (2002: 176–7) argues, localized informal micro-finance, or 'back-alley banking' became crucial to China's business culture, often relying upon network relations from the Mao era, such as shared *danwei*[1] experience . In addition, the borrowing of start-up costs for small businesses from friends and family also became commonplace. In fact Deng encouraged family lending as part of a large-scale re-appropriation of neo-Confucianism[2] put towards economic interests. In complete contrast to Mao's fears about the family unit as a productive profit-making entity, Deng's vision for China relied upon precisely that; in fact the Wenzhou model[3] based on small businesses eventually became the official paradigm for China's business development and remains so to this day (Hulme, 2014).

Gradually, as the 1980s progressed, emphasis began to be placed not only on making money and 'getting rich' in order to help the nation, but also on enjoying the fruits of labour (i.e., spending). Such was the desire on the part of the state to see the population spend that, in a momentous historical turnaround, China began to create its own credit cards and eventually allowed in the big credit card brands from the West. In the country that has eschewed all forms of ownership for 30 years, consuming with borrowed money was slowly but surely being encouraged in increasingly virulent ways. The journey from provision for all to credit for all was (apparently) complete. The vision of 'the good life' was no longer one of smiling peasants in extended family scenarios who were free of cares due to having 'enough' thanks to the kind and just provision of the State; but, rather, was one of a one-child family in an outward-looking global scenario in which pleasure was to be gained from the fact that their purchasing power was comparable with that of those in the West.[4]

This encouragement to spend has of course had a huge impact, with the Chinese populace buying products that simply would not have existed 30 years ago – luxury brands, fashionable designer label clothes, expensive wine, art, property, and non-tangible goods such as online products, travel, entertainment, and services. Such goods are the domain of the new middle class in China – the *xiaokang*; a term meaning 'basically' or 'functionally' well off or middle class but without huge wealth, living comfortably but ordinarily. Originally a Confucian term used to describe a society of modest means which sees the need for economic growth to provide prosperity, while making sure that prosperity is broadly distributed, the concept of *xiaokang* was re-appropriated by Deng and posited as the ultimate goal of Chinese modernization. More recently, Hu Jintao built it into his ideas on China's 'harmonious society'. To place this emergent consumerism of the *xiaokang* within a wider global context, it is necessary to recognize that as capitalism becomes an increasingly global phenomenon, consumer society is *the* mode of organization desired by nation states. Developing countries, such as China, aim to move as quickly as possible from small consumer goods to larger consumer 'durables', to services and intellectual goods, and to fully fledged consumer society status. However, while China's *xiaokang* is making consumerism an increasingly important part of China's economy and society, State encouragement alone is not sufficient to turn a *consuming* society into a consumer society (i.e., one in which the buying and selling of goods and services is *in reality* the most important social and economic activity).

Many rural provinces of China see very few of the changes that have come about due to the entrance of market economics. There are still vast (and growing) inequalities between the rural and urban areas. Perhaps not surprisingly therefore, the reserve army of consumers were, and are, not as easily mobilized as might have been hoped by the Chinese authorities. Despite changes in patterns of consumption, the cultural attitudes of generations of Chinese in regard to the necessity to save cannot be undone overnight or without evidence of serious welfare reform. In fact the relaxation of *hukou*, or household registration,[5] was in large part an attempt to address this by enabling more members of rural populations to live and work in coastal areas in order to provide them with the opportunity to become part of the urbanized army of consumers. Similarly, the creation of new welfare facilities since the late 1990s – such as unemployment insurance, medical insurance, workers' compensation insurance, maternity benefits, pension funds, and healthcare – had the same aim. Yet, it is far from the case that a credit culture has been able to pervade. In fact, what reigns is a rather awkward transition, a kind of power-sharing arrangement between Maoist and capitalist dreams, in which the lack of an iron rice bowl causes careful saving, alongside reliance upon credit. While consumption may certainly have become a way of life for the urban well off, amongst the poorer sections of Chinese society who are less confident of their earning ability, it is the careful spending of careful saving. Culturally too, as we will see throughout the book, consumption occupies an awkward position between ideas of a 'modern' China and more traditional notions of mutuality (or at least non-association with Western-style individualism).

In fact, in many ways this book is about what has emerged as a result of the meeting of capitalism (and therefore consumerism) and communism in China. It is about the changing sets of ideas and practices that have emerged as a result, and the ways in which the Chinese subject manages to make sense of new responsibilities as part of a society increasingly preoccupied with consumption at both the State and the individual level and yet contemporaneously determined to cling to older non-consumer values. It is about the ways in which the shift towards becoming a consumer society entails economic changes which impact upon political and cultural attitudes and behaviour and vice versa. Yet, it is also about the means by which traditional modes of thinking and ethical systems continue to have a place in twenty-first century China and become reconfigured to the capitalist–communist model.

Crucially, this constantly re-negotiated conundrum of capitalist–communist consumerism differs from any yet seen in global development and creates new questions for established theories of consumerism. Whilst the Chinese path to consumerism may share many aspects in common with those of Western countries, it is in fact unique to China, emerging from a specific set of desires and motivations born from various aspects of Chinese history and culture. The almost three-decade-long rule of a communism that removed itself from Moscow's influence relatively early on; the decidedly nationalistic tendency of Chinese rhetoric from 1912[6] onwards; the specific mode of operation of the Chinese official economic paradigm (the Wenzhou model); the continued importance of *guanxi* networks and 'face' (now often aided by conspicuous consumption) all these factors provide the basis for a consumerism that, despite surface appearances, cannot simplistically be likened to that of the West. The implication of this is that the direction Chinese consumerism will take, although perhaps predictable in many ways, cannot be fully known. What the chapters of this book explore is precisely the ways in which specific forms of consumption are riddled with awkward contradictions and cultural attitudes are in constant flux.

In Chapter 1 **Xin Wang** uses consumerism as a lens through which to interpret middle-class identity, culture, and values. He charts the rise of the middle class in China as a section of society most concerned with material wealth and a consumer lifestyle, exploring how middle-classness is realized through consumerism and cultural practices in everyday life. Wang points out how discussions surrounding middle-classness, from both the popular media and the business sector, tend to construct it on purely economic grounds despite the way in which middle-class identity is increasingly defined by cultural associations. He draws upon the work of Pierre Bourdieu, particularly underlining Bourdieu's argument that everyday practices and subcultures that make class identities possible and reproduce inequality depend not so much on economic assets *per se* but rather on the accumulation of social and cultural capital. Taste and lifestyle become huge indicators of class; therefore certain types of consumption are crucial 'hangers' upon which to place one's identity.

Through an analysis of the findings of his own survey into consuming in China, Wang finds that the middle class in China is concerned with consuming in a manner that increases personal *suzhi* – human quality of character – through edifying activities such as visiting art galleries and museums, travelling, and reading classic texts. It is also painfully aware of its own self-perpetuation and spends large amounts of money making sure its children gain an education and cultural capital that can enable them to remain middle class. Contemporaneously, however, they are also keen consumers of self-improvement books that hark back to the teachings of Confucius and other ancient Chinese schools of thought, especially those offering practical advice for work and life aimed at sharing apolitical lessons about interpersonal relationships, self-awareness, and the pursuit of happiness. In addition, Wang explains, the image of the middle class has become a popular subject for cultural consumption in Chinese popular media. In fact, construction of the social identity of the middle class has become a field of intense symbolic struggle for its members and non-members alike.

In Chapter 2 **Calvin Hui** explores how the consuming of fashion has affected China and what is at stake in the revisionist narrative of adopting a positive attitude towards the consumption of fashion. He argues that the way the consumption of fashion is represented in contemporary China reveals the historical contradictions of the early stage of the country's economic reforms and opening up. Key here is a (in Hui's view false) understanding of the revisionist narrative as a modernization project allowing freedom of choice for women through the consumption of more 'feminine' clothes. In a fervent polemic, Hui debunks the revisionist argument by deconstructing ideas surrounding what constitutes choice. He asks: Why must we choose individuality but not uniformity? Can we choose not to choose? Is choice always free? Is choice liberating a desire that has been repressed, or is it simply creating new desire? Is the person who does the choosing liberated or imprisoned by his or her own choice? For Hui, while the revisionist attutude towards the consumption of fashion has perhaps provided new choices (or at least widened existing ones) for women, it has also eradicated certain choices when it comes to gendered ways of being.

Gabriel Lafitte, in Chapter 3, critiques the way in which the contemporary Chinese citizen is taught to consume tourism as part of a set of practices that are seen to provide the individual with *suzhi* (as also mentioned by Xin Wang). Lafitte particularly focusses on Tibet as a destination heavily promoted to Chinese due to its accessibility yet 'difference'. He argues that consuming Tibet is a way of making oneself, the consumer, a model of modernity. This is, according to Lafitte, quite a reversal of older attitudes towards Tibet, which saw it as cold, remote, poor, and backward. However, more recently Tibet has been re-imagined as a safe comfortable family-friendly destination, and along with this has come a determined effort on the part of the State to promote a narrative of the long-standing and deep friendship between Tibet and Han China. For Lafitte, consumption of Tibet is the consumption of a myth: that of an (apparently) ahistoric timeless mystical place in which mainland Chinese can experience themselves as 'enlightened' global citizens.

Karen Tam's chapter is instrumental in illustrating how the new Chinese consumer is aware of Western brands and adopts practices that creatively re-imagine or re-appropriate such brands through the consumption of *shanzhai* (fake) products. She explores how copying has long been a part of Chinese manufacturing, basing her argument on seventeenth and eighteenth century art practices as well as current-day artists such as Michael Wolf, Christian Jankowski, Liu Ding, Leung Mee-ping, Xu Zhen, and Ai Weiwei. As Tam points out, *shanzhai* products are not simply direct copies of existing products, but rather are goods creatively produced as part of a disruptive grassroots business model. *Shanzhai* therefore, says Tam, can be seen as a method of re-appropriation, resistance, subversion, and critique which runs contrary to mainstream (and/or Western) consumer culture and is indicative of the historical cultural differences between China and the West.

In Chapter 5 **Qingyan Ma** takes another major trend in consumerism— that of medical consumerism – and explores the attitudes surrounding it of those on the margins of the state in rural Yunnan province. Drawn from her own fieldwork, Ma's analysis focusses on the individual's agency in choosing medical services, and the extent to which it is possible to actively engage with market reforms by taking on, reconfiguring, or resisting state public health discourse. Ma's chapter provides a wealth of anthropological insight into medical pluralism – including biomedicine, local herbal medicine, traditional Chinese medicine, and 'witchcraft'. She argues that the transition into market economy and the expansion of neoliberal globalization has impacted upon local people's view of their ethnic identity and their relationship with the state. More specifically, the rural consumer of healthcare desires medical products (such as IV drips) that he or she perceives as 'modern' and connects with 'scientific' progress. Interestingly though, this desire often sits alongside latent and loosely held beliefs in more traditional forms of medicine.

These first five chapters illustrate the way in which consumerism has taken off in China and the new practices of consumption that can be seen as a result. However, this move towards consumerism has not come about, and indeed still does not exist, without severe concerns to the contrary in Chinese society. There is a general concern, from public, Party, and government, that the onset of consumerism has led to a moral vacuum when it comes to certain aspects of society. As a result, traditional ethical codes and philosophical modes of thought retain much of their popularity. Furthermore, despite encouraging and facilitating consumption, State intervention is also used in efforts to maintain the cultural attitudes associated with *non*-consumerist society. In different ways, the final three chapters all explore this quandary.

Geir Sigurðsson's chapter explores classical Chinese philosophical views of consumption – Confucianism, Mohism, and Daoism. He identifies a consistent tendency to view material wealth as subordinate to virtue and morality in Confucian thinking, and a distinct aversion to consumption in the ethical codes of Mohism and Daoism. Furthermore, Sigurðsson argues, traditional Chinese philosophy is still an integral part of Chinese societal attitudes, and this in turn can be seen as an explanation for societal behaviour that appears to push back against the new consumerist mentality. He agrees with Weber's classic analysis that Chinese philosophy overall – at least not in its unappropriated form – is unlikely to stimulate consumption, and its presence alongside capitalism may partly explain why, despite huge economic growth, China has not yet become a consumer society.

In Chapter 7 **Andreas Steen** examines the phenomenon of Lei Feng – the 'model soldier' – and explores the ways in which the State is keen to keep the values attached to Lei Feng alive in Chinese society. Mao introduced the 'Learn from Lei Feng' campaign in 1963 and, as Steen argues, in many ways he embodied the values of the Maoist era with his helpfulness and modesty, obedience and self-restraint, and willingness to be a small 'screw' in the big 'machine' of communism. Fifty years on, official rhetoric is still keen to promote the Lei Feng spirit, especially in the light of incidents in recent years which have worried and outraged the general public in the selfishness of their nature. These cases of apparent moral decline inspire debates about the 'Lei Feng spirit' and fuel State attempts to keep it alive. Steen points out, however, that for many in China today the meaning of a Maoist model soldier does not sit easily with the globalized individualized commercialized reality of everyday life.

Strangely, as part of the attempt to promote Lei Feng and the values of a less commercial age, State campaigns encourage the promotion of Lei Feng merchandise such as computer games, films, souvenirs, hats, and shoes. The fact that he is at the centre of the debate on morality has increased his commercial value, so, despite being part of an attempt to limit individualistic attitudes (including in the pursuit of wealth and material things), Lei Feng himself has been commodified and sold as part of consumer society.

Finally, **Giovanna Puppin**'s chapter concentrates on the role of advertising in reforming China and the way in which its existence has been legitimized at State level by a practice of ensuring it has the requisite 'Chinese characteristics'. She explains how, from 1979, as part of the opening-up process, the Chinese authorities needed to find a set of rhetorical strategies in order to explain the return of a practice long accused of being capitalistic. 'Socialist advertising' or 'socialist advertising with Chinese characteristics' was a way of attaching Marxism to the practice of advertising – albeit perhaps rather dubiously we might argue. Puppin goes on to explain how the requirements of advertising with Chinese characteristics proved ambiguous and contradictory and indeed continue to be a difficult balancing act up to the present day. China wants to encourage consumerism, but contemporaneously does not want to encourage 'Western values' – in many ways advertising is the *mise-en-scène* of the struggle between the era of consumerism and the era of socialist provision. Desire is required of the potential consumer, yet recognized as highly problematic.

What these chapters show us is that, despite the government encouraging spending, the various new forms of spending, and the rise of a new middle class in China, there is also a strong awareness on the part of the general public and the State that the consumerist mentality is best kept in check. Chinese leaders are concerned with the potential for a moral breakdown in society and therefore, alongside the huge pull towards consumerism (the policies freeing up rural consumers, the encouragement to spend, the normalizing of 'plastic money'), there is a contemporaneous pushback both from the government and the people. This can be witnessed in the continuing popularity of traditional thinkers, the national outrage when a story of unethical actions hits the headlines, and the desperate attempts on the part of the State to maintain the popularity of 'moral' figures such as Lei Feng. The ideology of the plastic credit card has not yet won out over that of the iron rice bowl. What is more, this divide is born out geographically and generationally, with the rural population and the older generations being least keen to accept new attitudes towards consuming.

In fact today's consumer/subject in China is an embodiment of the conflicting ideologies behind the iron rice bowl and the plastic credit card – the revolutionary and revisionist eras. As Xiaobing Tang argues, certain revolutionary features can offer themselves as alternatives in the post-revolutionary era – 'when everyday life is affirmed and accepted as the new hegemony, when commodification arrives to put a price tag on human relations and even private sentiments, participatory communal action may offer itself as an oppositional discourse and expose a vacuity underlying the myriad of commodity forms' (Xiaobing Tang, 2002: 125). Indeed it is because of the continuing existence of certain elements of communism *within* the capitalist/market socialist era that, Tang argues, the Chinese subject can be seen as somehow schizophrenic in his or her attitudes towards capitalism and way of coping within it (Xiaobing Tang, 2002: 125).

This 'schizophrenia' is of course not specific to China – far from it. The West has its own version of the schizophrenic consumer who is no more or less detrimental to society. However, the Chinese version can certainly be seen in the determination to promote spending while curtailing individualism; to continue high rates of economic growth while attempting to build a more solid welfare state and provide a compassionate society; to depict China as at once modern *and* deeply historical. It can also be seen in the outright rejection, then re-appropriation, then return to the orginal form of historical philosophies such as Confucianism. And it can be seen in the uneasy line between modernism and 'functional' wealth and its fall into all things bourgeois – a line often blurred by fuzzy concepts such as 'Chinese characteristics' which allows bourgeois products and services to be legitimized and made part of an allegedly specifically Chinese (and therefore 'revolutionary') path. In fact, despite the differing historical circumstances and cultural nuances of Chinese consumerism compared with that of the West, its path through competing ideologies is proving no less problematic for the Chinese subject or indeed for China as a whole.

Notes

1. *Danwei* can be translated as 'work unit' and was the principal method of implementing party policy in Maoist China. The *danwei* was actually far more than a work unit though, binding workers to it for life, providing housing, food, clinics, childcare, schools, and therefore identity and social responsibility or face (*miazi*) too.
2. Technically neo-Confucianism began in the Tang (772–841) dynasty when Han Yu and Li Ao strove to empty it of its more mystical elements that had come from Buddhism and Daoism and place emphasis on the creation of rules for an ethical life. It became prominent during the Song and Ming dynasties.
3. The Wenzhou model comes from Wenzhou, an area with a specific economic history tied to the Yonjia School of thought which, unlike traditional Confucianism, respected traders and merchants as much as farmers and scholars.
4. Taken from a paper presented by the author at the University of Alberta (2013) entitled 'Projecting the good life at home and abroad: lineages of the Chinese revolutionary image from 1949 to the present.'
5. Under the Household Registration System, Chinese citizens are registered according to their home province and given rural or urban *hukou*. The roots of *hukou* stem back to Ancient China, to 2100 BCE, when the Huji system was in place. However, in its present form, it was introduced by the communist party in 1958, in an attempt to control the movements of workers.
6. It was in this year that Dr. Sun Yat Sen's Nationalist Party created the Republic of China, formally ending dynastic rule.

Notes

In pursuit of status: the rising consumerism of China's middle class

Xin Wang

Abstract: China is growing into an enormous market for global products and services and Chinese consumers are destined to take centre stage in the global bazaar. China's middle class has started showing its hunger for consumer goods and products, and both Chinese and international companies are betting on the rise of middle-class consumers in China. This chapter examines the consumer behaviour of China's middle class. It discusses how the consumption of commodities and cultural products creates middle-class identity. It illustrates the ways in which middle-class consumers assert their status through consumption of commodities and cultural products.

Key words: middle class, conspicuous consumption, economic aspirations, self-perpetuating, petite bourgeoisie, cultural capital.

Introduction

Since the inception of the economic reforms in 1978, China has become one of the world's fastest growing economies. According to China's National Bureau of Statistics, it has experienced economic growth with an average GDP of 9 per cent every year since 1990. Its GDP per capita doubled to $6100 (38,354 yuan) from 2009 to 2012, confirming its status as a middle-income nation, according to the World Bank's standards set in 2011. In 2012 its GDP reached 51.93 trillion yuan (US$8.28 trillion) – the second largest in the world (China National Bureau of Statistics).

After years of rapid growth generated by investment and exports, more recently China has been looking to restructure its economy. In May 2012, the government shifted its top priority from taming inflation to stabilizing growth by encouraging domestic spending and consumption. The focus on domestic economic growth has driven a dramatic rise in consumer spending. Retail sales for 2012 increased to 20.7 trillion yuan (US$3.3 trillion). Urban residents spent 17.9 trillion yuan in 2012 while rural residents spent 2.8 trillion yuan (China National Bureau of Statistics).

This rapid economic growth has resulted in a transformation of consumer behaviour, and the subsequent rise of consumerism in China has garnered worldwide attention, particularly from business and marketing. The world's leading research and consulting companies have released a number of reports on China's rising consumerism, particularly on China's newly emerged middle class.[1] These reports highlight China's growing middle class and expanding consumerism, suggest potential strategies for global corporations to tap into the Chinese market, and predict sales growth in China. The middle class is hailed as the new and growing market force for both Chinese and global markets. According to a PriceWaterhouseCoopers (PWC) report, China was the world's second-largest online retail market, after the United States, in 2011, with sales totalling $120 billion (MGI, 2013). Meanwhile, the term 'middle class' has become ubiquitous in popular media, with discussions of 'being middle class' primarily focusing on the economic aspirations of the middle class themselves. The media and business sector's fascination with China's middle class has also constructed it on economic grounds.

A small number of studies about Chinese consumer behaviours have noted that professional middle-class status and identity are increasingly shaped around a new set of collective interests related to access to resources and modes of consumption.[2] This chapter examines consumer behaviour among the middle class from the findings of a survey initially conducted by the author in Beijing in 2005 and continued in subsequent years.[3] It discusses how consumption of commodities and cultural products enables the display of a middle-class identity. The study does not argue that consumerism is the sole factor in defining cultural and social practices and the attributes of middle-classness; rather it explores how middle-classness is constructed *through* rising consumerism and middle-class consumption of specific commodities.

The primary concern of this chapter therefore is the role consumerism plays in the lives of the middle class through everyday practices and experiences. Consumerism is used as a lens through which to interpret middle-class identity, culture, and values. Following this broad line of inquiry, this chapter specifically raises the following questions: What factors decide the consumption of middle-class consumers? What particular patterns do they show in consumption? Has a consumer culture formed among the middle class? If so, will consumerism allow middle-class individuals and groups to create their identities? Though consumption is not the sole factor through which to interpret and understand China's middle class, it sheds light on everyday practices and experiences that shape people's culture. Ultimately, through discussions of middle-class consumption of print media, cultural productions (e.g., television programmes, films, exhibitions), commodities, and housing, this chapter intends to understand how consumerism (in addition to family, cultural, social, and economic values) shapes the collective identity of the middle class and their articulation of middle-classness. How is middle-classness realized through consumerism alongside cultural practices and everyday life? How does access to global goods and commodities shape discourses on middle-class ways of life? And how and why has being middle class become desirable and possible?

By way of setting the scene, it is important to note that China's emerging middle class, which numbers around 100 million people, is borne out of the recent economic reforms and the restructuring of the labour market, and represents a wide range of professions (Lu Xueyi, 2004). However, it primarily includes intermediate-level business professionals, mid-level managers, and private business owners. Business professionals, also known as the so-called 'white collars' (*bailing*), are office workers of businesses and enterprises in China. They often have a high level of education and professional training, and a high standard of living. The middle class also includes a public servant stratum, which consists of government employees, who exert a strong influence in public and social sectors as a result of administrative reform in the Chinese government system. Some government cadres have transferred from administrative positions to managerial positions in business and the economic arena. They are referred as the 'quasi middle class' due to their employment status and their social ties with the state and the ruling party (Li Qiang, 1999). Some of them are senior managerial staff of state-owned enterprises (SOEs) who gained income and control over state properties and production materials as a result of the privatization of state enterprises. Often regarded as 'red capitalists', they are shareholders of transformed state enterprises and control the production materials of the SOEs (Dickson, 2003). Meanwhile, a wide spectrum of professions has emerged in the transition towards a market-oriented economy. New professionals with knowledge in special areas, such as certified public accountants, lawyers, biotech and IT engineers, judicial workers, and medical staff, are regarded as the typical middle class. They have a stable income, a high level of education and professional training, and promising career prospects. In addition, China's intellectuals, including university professors, writers, and artists, are recognized as middle class (Zhou Xiaohong, 2005: 6, 16, 227). In the post-Mao reform era, this intellectual group has gained political recognition and social prestige as well as financial privileges.

What can be noted is that China's new middle class represents a wide range of people, all of whom are part of the middle class due to different factors – their occupations, economic capital (income, business ownership, and property ownership) and social capital (education, and social and political network). Chinese scholars agree that occupation is indicative of income levels and socioeconomic status and, therefore, can be used as the main denominator by which to identify the middle class.[4] In contrast to the lower-income stratum, which includes rural residents, the urban working class, and laid-off labourers, China's middle class possesses a relatively high level of education and professional skills and a relatively stable and high income. Chinese Academy of Social Sciences (CASS) research shows that about 73 per cent of respondents have post-secondary education or above, which gives this group an advantage in acquiring other social, economic, cultural, and political capital (quoted in Lu Xueyi, 2004). The 216 respondents of my own survey reflect a diverse range of professions defined as middle-income occupations, including civil servants, school teachers, researchers, technology and computer engineers, business professionals, administrators and managers, medical and legal professionals, small business owners, and independent freelancers such as actors and writers.

Tastes, symbols, and lifestyles: consumers of media

In contrast to Weberian approaches to middle-class formation through education, occupation, and social networks and Weberian interests in social mobility, Pierre Bourdieu studied the middle class as a social formation through everyday practices and experiences (Bourdieu, 1984). Bourdieu shows how everyday practices and subcultures that make class identities possible and reproduce inequality depend not so much on economic assets per se but rather on the accumulation of different kinds of capital, including social and cultural capital. With regard to the middle class, Bourdieu points out three important aspects which have made the middle class different from other social classes: the role of culture as a set of differentiated 'tastes', and socialization as a set of consciously differentiating practices; the importance of everyday practices; and the different kinds of capital available to the middle class (Bourdieu, 1984: 86). Bourdieu's perspective recognizes that economic, social, and cultural capital is making middle-class subjectivities and lifestyles possible, and that the lack of one or the other makes specific class positions appear to be always antagonistic, even if they are objectively characterized by shared interests.

For Bourdieu, class positions are not only determined by the relations of production (i.e., a worker's relation to the company owner), but depend on cultural traits, values, skills, expertise, tastes, manners, and other embodied attributes. His class theory uses tastes, rather than economic and financial indicators, to define social classes. He argues that all tastes are acquired according to and based on social class. He explains that 'taste classifies, and it classifies the classifier. Cultural subjects, classified by their classifications, distinguish themselves by the distinctions they make, between the beautiful and the ugly, the distinguished and the vulgar, in which their position in the objective classifications is expressed or betrayed' (Bourdieu, 1984: 6). Thus Bourdieu presents taste as an individual and collective resource used to mark social distinctions.

Sociologists have long argued that cultural choices can be associated with social and economic status. In Western society 'good taste' is the symbol appropriated by economic and social status and educational levels. In Paul Fussell's (1992) book on class, he describes how social class status could be revealed by symbols, styles, and intellectual proclivities. Fussell points out that class in America is not decided exclusively upon finances; rather, it is also a matter of taste, what one does with one's recreational time, what one reads, what schools one has attended, and how well one speaks. In his seminal work, *The American Middle Classes* (1951),[5] American sociologist C. Wright Mills used the term 'white collar' to refer to office workers as the new middle class. He observed the shift in the American labour force and argued that office workers – 'white collar' people on salary – were the new middle class of the mid-twentieth century. He explained that the white-collar middle class has new 'styles of life', which form a middlebrow culture in American society.

The term 'white collar' was adopted by Chinese scholars and citizens in the late 1980s to refer to those Chinese office workers who work for foreign companies, who have higher English proficiency and educational levels, and who can afford a 'petite bourgeoisie' lifestyle (*xiaozi*). A number of studies have contributed to the discussion about China's middle class and revealed some attributes of the middle class.[6] As beneficiaries of the economic reform, middle-class individuals and families are primarily concerned with their careers and personal wealth and show a strong inclination towards a materialistic lifestyle. Their interests in personal and family well-being represent a strong utilitarian and pragmatic culture within China's middle class. The findings of my research suggest that, with its increasing purchasing power, the middle class is reshaping China's urban consumerist and popular culture. For example, white-collar business professionals have become the target population group and primary consumers of popular media and entertainment productions. Newspapers are the leading medium in the public lives of middle-income citizens, with about 48 per cent of respondents reading newspapers daily. Television in China is the most preferred entertainment medium, and around 56 per cent of respondents watch TV every day. People with lower income levels tend to watch TV and radio more than those with higher income levels. In addition, respondents over 50 years old tend to use newspapers more frequently than the younger age groups.

Regarding print media, my findings show that the middle class is highly interested in reading books about individual development and career management. When asked what genres of books they frequently read, about 32 per cent of the respondents said they frequently read books on self-help and personal development. This can be seen as part of the trend for the middle class to seek new ways of thinking and living and their desire to develop individual potential and capabilities – factors often neglected by their parents' generations. As a result, the middle class is becoming more pragmatic in terms of learning and self-cultivation. The second most popular books are those on management and that provide advice on career and professional development. Middle-class business professionals often agree that they have to learn new business practices in order to survive and succeed in the business world as the pressure from work has intensified. The self-help genre also includes books on the teachings of Confucius and other ancient Chinese schools of thought, especially those offering practical advice for work and life. One such bestseller is Yu Dan's (2009) book on Confucianism,[7] over ten million copies of which have been sold throughout China. The success of Yu's book is attributed to its simple feel-good nature and apolitical lessons and stories about interpersonal relationships, self-awareness, and the pursuit of happiness. Her success shows that the well-to-do Chinese middle class is interested in self-development, but often through lessons drawn from traditional Chinese virtues.

In addition, historical fiction has received popularity among middle-class readers. Unlike traditional history books, the new genre of historical fiction portrays biographic accounts and anecdotes of historical figures, especially monarchs of various dynasties. This genre has dominated the dramatic programming on prime time TV since the mid-1990s. Fiction writer Er Yuehe's historical fictions on the three Qing emperors (Kangxi, Qianlong, and Yongzheng) were adapted to make popular TV dramas. This can be seen as an indication of the way in which the middle class has created a market for nostalgic accounts of Qing emperors' lives in the Forbidden City. Zhu Ying (2005) examines the factors leading to the rise of Qing drama and the ideological positioning of these dramas. She explains that these dramas depict heroic acts of emperors and patriots who fight against internal corruption and social injustice as well as external threats. With their strong and exemplary leaders, such dramas fit the ideological, political, and cultural framework of the 1990s, as the narratives of historic rulers in the popular media fed the public's desire and interest for a strong state against corruption and social injustice. As Dai Jinhua argues, the increasing popularity of historical fiction can be attributed to an imagined nostalgia of historical culture among the Chinese middle class (Dai Jinhua, 1997: 143–61). Strong leaders are embedded in the popular imagination and this fascination with heroic figures has led to a greater number of cultural productions of dynasty dramas for the middle-class audience.

What is noticeable in the research findings is that an interdependent relationship has emerged between print media and middle-class consumption culture. On the one hand, the publishing industry is driven by the need and reading habits of the middle class, which becomes the primary pool of readership. On the other hand, the reading interests, habits, and tastes of the middle class are shaped and fed by the publishing industry. As the Chinese media has shifted from being a pure social and political propaganda organ of the state to being a market-oriented business entity, media content targets the middle class, pandering to its lifestyles and materialistic and commercial values – a trend that represents the newly formed pragmatic and realistic culture of the middle class. In addition, urban lifestyle newspapers and publications, such as *Modern Weekly*, are emerging to appeal to well-to-do urban residents and their tastes.

Popular media and other state cultural apparatus, including the television and film industry, have also played a pivotal role in shaping the middle class's cultural consumption. In cultural and imaginary space, the media and entertainment industry has targeted the middle class as the primary consumers of popular cultural and entertainment products. Meanwhile, the image of the middle class has become a popular subject for cultural consumption in Chinese popular media, film, and literature. In fact, the middle class has been reimagined as the targeted audiences and consumers of state and popular media, and the construction of the social identity of the middle class has become a field of intense symbolic struggle.

TV shows and films have not only created and sold the image and lifestyles of the middle class, but also have helped shape leisure practices and popular culture among the middle class. Some recent popular films and TV dramas based on the middle-class lifestyle have generated keen interest among middle-class citizens. For example, the film *Go Lala Go*[8] (*Du Lala Shengzhi ji*), adapted from a bestselling book, tells an inspiring story about how an ordinary white-collar office worker gains success through her hard work in the corporate world. The film accentuated the significance of career mobility and lifestyle as a means of class distinction of the urban middle class. It inspires young white-collar Chinese to procure a 'good job' and climb the corporate ladder.

What the film indicates is how the middle class espouses Western cultural predispositions and consumption as its lifestyle. The emerging middle class is portrayed as consumers of global brands and luxury goods, primarily Western products. The film makes significant use of product placement in which, as McChesney explains, 'the product is woven directly into the story so it is unavoidable and its messages can be smuggled in when the viewer's guard is down' (McChesney, 2004: 147). Over 20 different brands are written into the plot to exhibit values and distinctions in tastes and lifestyles of the social elite and the middle class. Most product placements are Western luxury brands and commodities. Thus, the film serves as an inducement, functioning 'as a lure or bait to catch and keep people paying attention to advertising messages' (Smythe, 1994: 246). The chief aim of this inducement is to reproduce the formation of the middle class through the labour performed by the show's targeted viewers as its active 'audience commodity' (Smythe, 1994: 246). The labour of the audience and the class containment function of the film eventually turn the audience into both cultural and materialistic consumers. The media, including cinema and television, as simultaneously a commodity and an artefact, present ideology and culture manufactured and created for consumption and interpretation by a specific audience.

Luxury brands such as Gucci, Dior, Chloé, Chanel, Valentino, and many others, have become symbols of the middle class's newly acquired socioeconomic status and lifestyles. Even urban space has been classified to indicate the cultural and consumption predispositions of the well-to-do middle class. For example, the public places frequented by the middle class are coffee houses, clubs, and modern shopping malls filled with international brands; their vacation places are overseas resorts; their work places are glistening glass skyscrapers. It is within and through these spaces that the middle class is produced and reproduced. Eating, drinking, consuming, and working at these spaces become symbols of the middle-class lifestyle. Going to these places is as much an expression of middle-class identity as it is a consumption choice.

So, the middle class is a socioeconomic group defined by cultural products its members share. Sociologists have argued that consumption practices and choices are closely associated with social and economic status. In his famous book *The Theory of the Leisure Class* (1994 [1899]), the economist and sociologist Thorstein Veblen first introduced the concept of *conspicuous consumption*. He argued that people pursue and assert their social status through conspicuous consumption. Veblen defined conspicuous consumption as the use of money or other resources by people to display a higher social status than others. In his famous trickle-down theory, he argued that fashion is a process of emulation by which new fashion passes from the upper class to the lower, and people of lower classes copy the styles of those in higher classes as obviously as possible. This is exactly how *Go Lala Go* intends to portray the middle class and the ways in which it asserts its social status through its tastes, including fashion.

This echoes the theory developed by economist Herbert Blumer. In his seminal work, *Fashion: From Class Differentiation to Collective Selection* (Blumer, 1969), he argued that fashion is a social process. What people wear becomes a symbol of their identity and socioeconomic status. Fashion becomes the shared symbol of identity, whether through self-identity or through status and group membership. *Go Lala Go* shows how class status and identity are strongly represented and shaped by fashion. For example, each time the female protagonist receives a promotion at work, she buys shoes with even higher heels and a line of text appears on the film screen to indicate her new positions and salary. This upward mobility in her career and increase in her earnings match her upward consumption and her distinction when it comes to taste and lifestyle.[9] Lala's clothing marks out her class status, not only through her material status, but also through her tastes and symbols of identity.

The film also shows how the lifestyles of the middle class are closely associated with levels of consumption. On her first day of work, the chief secretary tells Lala, 'By the way, this company has really different personnel levels. People below manager level are small potatoes. This means they are poor, making less than 4,000 yuan. The managers are the middle class. They have their own cars, and an annual salary of over 200,000. Directors are upper class. Their annual incomes are over 500,000. They take their vacations abroad ... The CEO of the company, typical upper class, makes more than a million a year.' This quote reveals how the identity of the middle class is defined by its mode of consumption.

Cultural and social consumers

The findings of the research I undertook also show how the middle class are not only the primary consumers of commodities, but also of cultural activities – in other words, they are a class keen on leisure. The figures show a strong inclination for more individual or self-enrichment activities, such as travel, job-related training and education, sports, and cultural activities, as opposed to community-oriented or associational social activities. Only 1 per cent of my sample engaged in charitable activities and 6 per cent in neighbourhood and community activities, compared with 12 per cent who engaged in sports activities, 13 per cent in cultural activities, 20 per cent in continuing education and training, and 20 per cent in travel. This explains why the middle class tends to spend more resources on travel and education, including children's education.

Middle-class Chinese have developed an interest in leisure activities, including travel and vacations. These leisure activities are also ways of manifesting middle-class lifestyle and distinctive taste. *Go Lala Go* shows that such leisure activities are also the result of state policy that attempts to increase domestic consumption. For example, in addition to the Spring Festival holiday, the state created two Golden Week holidays in 1999 – the May Day holiday and the National Day holiday in October – with the intention of encouraging public spending in order to boost the domestic economy. The two Golden Week holidays have boosted China's tourist industry and retail sector. It is estimated about 50–80 million Chinese went on holiday during each Golden Week break in 2012.[10] The tourism industry has embraced the middle class by offering various travel products. The rise of tourism has instigated cultural consumption and urged tourist sites to create newly packaged cultural programs to accommodate the tastes of well-off middle-class tourists. For example, the most acclaimed Chinese filmmaker Zhang Yimou created his

Impression series at scenic sites to entertain middle-class travellers with cultural entertainment performances.

Additionally, a relaxation of visa restrictions on Chinese travellers by many destination countries also gives Chinese middle-class tourists an opportunity to visit European countries and the United States in order to learn about elite and popular culture in the West as well as Western middle-class lifestyles. China has officially become the world's largest outbound source market, overtaking Germany and the U.S. last year, with an estimated 83 million overseas trips made by Chinese citizens. Travel spending represents a significant proportion of global luxury goods spending. Chinese are the biggest single group of tax-free shoppers in the world, accounting for a rising chunk of global sales. Chinese tourists spent US$102 billion offshore in 2012. Furthermore, the primary products Chinese tourists purchase are luxury brands.[11] In a recent survey by KPMG, about 72 per cent of respondents said they purchase luxury items during overseas trips, with cosmetics, watches, and bags being the most purchased items.[12] Overseas luxury brands with a presence in China are benefitting from this trend and gaining more market recognition in China. Travel also helps Chinese consumers distinguish brands among countries of origin and associate certain countries with particular products. Chinese consumers particularly like Switzerland for luxury watches, France for cosmetics, perfumes, and bags, and the United States for clothes, bags, and cosmetics. However, overseas travel is more than just consumption for the Chinese middle class. According to the China Outbound Tourism Research Institute, the motivations of Chinese outbound travellers include increasing their self-esteem, gaining social capital, self-learning, and personal prestige. Outbound travel is also regarded as an investment in terms of the business opportunities it may offer up (Arlt, 2012).

Consumption of education

China's new middle class is also preoccupied with its children's education as it understands that middle-class status and standing can only be reproduced through education. Therefore, upwardly mobile middle-class parents tend to invest heavily in their children's education and qualifications as they do not want their children to 'lose at the starting line'. Education is regarded as a means of social mobility and is being sought for the prestige it confers. My research reveals that middle-class families spend more effort and money on their children's education than rural and low-income families. Education, regarded as a part of social capital, is sought in order to assert middle-class status. Urban middle-class households send their children to extracurricular programs to learn English, piano, violin, painting, calligraphy, and other subjects. To parents, the primary reason of this comprehensive extracurricular program is to raise the child's future competitiveness and give the child more advantages across the board. It is evident that the middle class hopes to acquire and transfer cultural capital through its children's education.[13] Parents provide their children with cultural capital by transmitting the values and knowledge needed to succeed in the current educational system. Chinese middle-class families are concerned about their children's success in education and their future careers. As far as middle class families are concerned, it is education that has helped them achieve their economic and professional success. Through acquiring educational capital and then a middle-class job, they have risen to middle-class status. They also see their educational attainment as the cultural capital which distinguishes them from other social classes. The 2011 Report on Educational Consumption in China by Market Probe China points out that the typical middle-class family spent an average of one seventh of their household income on education in 2011.[14]

China's middle-class consumption occurs around its specific patterns of socializing. For the majority of middle-class Chinese, this socializing takes place at home and in public spaces, such as restaurants, tea houses, and karaoke bars – places of consumption. The middle class places its career and professional life at the centre of its social life. Consumption is used to develop the middle class's social network around its profession and strengthen its social capital. As the middle class focuses on career and profession, it spends 54 per cent of its annual household educational expenditure on job-related training and certification, according to the 2011 Report on Educational Consumption in China.

Pierre Bourdieu's social capital theory explains why the middle class uses consumption to develop and strengthen its social network and social capital. Bourdieu defines social capital as 'the aggregate of the actual or potential resources which are linked to possession of a durable network of more or less institutionalized relationships of mutual acquaintance and recognition – or in other words, to membership of a group – which provides each of its members with the backing of the collectively-owned capital, a "credential" which entitles them to credit, in the various senses of the word' (Bourdieu, 1997: 51). In Bourdieu's view, 'the volume of the social capital possessed by a given agent ... depends on the size of the network of connections he can effectively mobilize and on the volume of the capital (economic, cultural or symbolic) possessed in his own right by each of those to whom he is connected' (Bourdieu, 1997: 51). Social capital is a resource in social networks that can be mobilized and utilized by individuals for their own ends. Bourdieu's concept of social capital is connected with class position and social status. For China's middle class, consumption for social networks and social capital will allow them to achieve their social and economic goals and status.

Consumers of technology and online shopping

The Internet and other new mobile technologies facilitate the consumption of commodities by offering new possibilities for socializing and consuming. The Internet provides the necessary social basis for communication and interaction as well as consumption. Online social-networking users have increased from 1.1 million in 1999 to 16 million in 2006.[15] Such sites enable Chinese professionals to post, share, and update their personal information, and to socialize in virtual communities. Users often build social networks based on their professional as well as their social and cultural interests. These sites have various theme boards, ranging from politics, social issues, business, and marketing to arts, history, and literature. Their popularity shows a burgeoning online civil society is emerging (see Hockx, 2005 and Yang, 2005).

Weibo, a new medium based on microblogging in much the same way as Twitter is, has emerged as the newest means of popular communication in China in the past few years, especially among the middle class. In fact, it was after Twitter was blocked in China in July 2009, that Sina.com released the trial version of its Chinese equivalent, Sina Weibo (Sina Microblog), in August 2009. Sina Weibo immediately became popular among Chinese netizens. It is one of the largest social-networking websites in China with 300 million users.[16] The majority of China's microblog accounts belong to urban middle-class users. Another medium is WeChat (*Weixn*, or micromessage), which is a mobile text and voice-messaging communication service developed by Tencent in China. It was first released in January 2011 and had 300 million users by the end of January 2012.[17]

The rise of digital and social media is having a significant impact on consumption. It has also helped to increase exposure for luxury brands in China. Chinese consumers are using online forums to discuss and research luxury brands. KPMG's survey shows that around 70 per cent of potential consumers search for luxury brands on the Internet at least once a month.[18] Meanwhile, it is worth noting that Chinese consumers also seek entertainment and pop culture on the Internet, which provides opportunities for luxury brand advertisers to establish their presence online and in the mobile world using social media and mobile applications. In its 2010 China Consumer Survey, McKinsey & Company reports that Chinese consumers are using mobile and online technologies to search for the best value products – a consumer behaviour connected with the Chinese traditional virtue of thrift. Social networking media also enable Chinese consumers to buy products endorsed through 'word of mouth' – a phenomenon which requires strong peer and family approval of the purchasing decision.[19]

Home ownership

The Chinese white-collar middle class has various means of asserting its social and economic status as well as its cultural tastes. Home ownership is one of the essential characteristics of the middle class. It is usually the largest consumption item for Chinese middle-class families and has become a symbol of social and economic status for the middle class. In this research, 78 per cent of respondents own their homes due to the fact their annual income has increased and urban living standards have improved. The neighbourhoods surveyed in this research exemplify three types of middle-class neighbourhoods of the time: an apartment house community, an apartment residential community built by the *danwei* ('work unit'), and a complex with both high-rise and low-rise apartments, condominiums, and townhouses. The size of the apartments ranges from 60 to 150 square metres of usable space. A typical apartment has two or three bedrooms, a kitchen, a dining room, a living room, one or two bathrooms, and one or two enclosed balconies. As subway lines and light rails have undergone extensive construction and as middle-class families have their own cars, more and more families are buying apartments in the suburbs as the apartment complexes in suburbs are less costly.

The most fundamental change I observed during the period I surveyed the respondents was the interior design and furnishing of middle-class families' homes. Twenty years ago, most Chinese living space was provided by *danwei* and limited in size, decoration, and comfort. The new privately owned apartments are spacious, bright, and Western in design. They are sold as concrete shells. Homeowners need to purchase every single thing to make their new apartment a home. The remodelling and decorating cost is usually about 10 to 20 per cent of the purchasing price of the apartment. Middle-class families emphasize the comfort and pleasure of their home by incorporating fashionable new designs from the West. Modern European furniture design fits the room layout and middle-class family budgets as well as middle-class family lifestyles and visions. Families usually borrow the design ideas of prototypes and models when designing their new apartments. A mixture of traditional and modern elements can be found within individual households. Though middle-class households intend to manifest pleasure, freedom, individuality, and choice through their home-owning experience, ironically, the newly renovated homes of the middle class represent similar tastes and similar designs, and convergent interests.

The home-centered consumption of the middle class reflects the state discourse on improving people's living standards in the tenth Five-Year Plan. The Plan was intended to expand domestic demand and boost domestic consumption, especially in such sectors as tourism, higher education, cars, housing, and financial services. Such a policy on accelerating domestic consumption continued during the recent global financial crisis as China's exports declined sharply. Stimulating domestic consumption became the focal point of the state's economic recovery strategy to move from an export-led economy to a consumption-led economy.[20] The strategies of the central government to boost domestic demand include increasing people's income, encouraging them to buy cars, getting on to the property ladder, and stabilizing the real estate market. Such state-promoted and media-espoused consumption has facilitated and accelerated the formation of the consumer culture of the middle class. Middle class consumption behaviours reflect their collective identity, convergent interests, and their lifestyles and preferences. As Bourdieu (1984) argues, household goods, the behaviour associated with their use, and the type and even location of residence can all be indicators of class status.

The identity of the middle class is closely related to its materialistic possessions and economic success. The middle-class obsession with home ownership and the desire for materialistic possessions is reflected in the hit TV series *Dwelling Narrowness (woju)*. The TV drama reveals the middle class in big cities has become the new class of *fangnu* (house slaves) with high mortgage payments for housing, cars, social security, and health care, etc. Middle-class individuals are being oppressed by the 'three new

15

mountains' – housing, healthcare, and their children's education. This reality faced by the middle class is backed by evidence from various research studies. According to the report from the China Index Academy, a domestic real estate research institute, as of 2009 the average house price in Beijing reached 16,057 yuan per square meter, a 54 per cent increase from the average price of 10,403 yuan in January 2009. In Shanghai, the average residential price for October 2009 was 16,954 yuan per square meter, up 22 per cent since January 2009.[21]

However, in addition to these 'mountains', the middle class is also obsessed with the consumption of luxury goods as well as the global middle-class lifestyle and status. As in the film *Go Lala Go*, the TV drama also employed product placement to implant the advertisement of luxury brands in the story. Such explicit advertising is a way of exhibiting the values and lifestyles of the middle class and eventually shaping their class identity and consciousness. The infomercials in the TV drama *Living Narrowness* feature luxury brands from the West. For example, the built-in infomercial about Land Rover (*Luhu*) describes the car as 'the British royal family's designated vehicle'. This infomercial is still having significant impact on the auto market in China. It is reported that sales of Land Rovers went up by 100 per cent in 2010 following the airing of the TV show (Chen Ming, 2011).

Popular media and entertainment productions have targeted middle-class viewers and turned them into consumers of certain types of commodities. The bourgeois lifestyle including leisure, luxury living, home ownership, and consumer culture created by the media is strongly espoused by the middle class. Yet, the image of 'house slaves' created by the entertainment industry is widely accepted by society. In an online survey conducted by the Chinese Internet portal Sina.com, about 59 per cent of 46,000 voters agreed with the statement that the drama reflects the public's sentiment on 'house slaves'.[22] Such widely accepted images created by the media and entertainment industry demonstrate how the media have acted as agents of socialization in the class identity acquisition of the newly emerged middle class.

Images of the 'explosive rich' versus the 'cultured'

Consumption practices enable insight into how consumers purchase products in order to signify their tastes and lifestyles. As Zukin and

Smith-Maguire (2004) assert, consumption is often viewed as a means to assert self-identity and communication of social status. As the economic and social status of China's middle class is not inherited, conspicuous consumption has become an important means of asserting status. China's middle-class consumers often view the purchase of brand name commodities as a manifestation of their economic and social status. Many middle-class consumers see tastes as related to their social and monetary status and perceive them to be acquired by their education and wealth. These consumers see themselves as perceived and judged on the tastes displayed through their consumer behaviours and ownership of material objects. Middle-class consumers often confuse cultural activities with social activities and consumerist activities, such as shopping, travel, dining, and clothing. They tend to purchase things that symbolize their newly acquired middle-class lifestyle and emphasize their distinctive tastes. A large number of these newly rich consumers use their material affluence to impress their friends, family, and colleagues as well as to distinguish themselves from lower-income groups. Studies have also noted that luxury brands and products have become symbols of financial success, which are deeply rooted in Chinese traditional values of *mianzi* (one's honour).[23] The formation of consumer culture in China has led to the development of 'hedonic values' among the middle class. Hedonic values are understood by Chinese consumers as being about having fun, pursuing instant gratification, and spending expressively or symbolically (Wang and Lin, 2009: 404). Chinese consumers look to luxury brands to provide physical evidence that they are both highly economically productive and enjoying life.

However, Chinese middle-class consumers are highly conscious of the social and cultural image of 'being cultured' and the economic status of 'being conspicuously rich'. The perceived image of the *nouveau riche* is often portrayed and referred to as *baofa hu* ('explosively rich'); people who have gained their financial successes overnight, a denigrating connotation of being uncultured and without cultural worth. To the middle class, 'being cultured' often means ownership of certain Western commodities because of the perceived prestige and modernity frequently attached to such products. For middle-class consumers, the West represents being modern and being tasteful. China's middle-class consumers follow the cultural tastes and styles of the West. They are not only consumers of Western products but also consumers of Western culture and lifestyles. Their consumption behaviours manifest their pursuit of a *xiaozi* (petite bourgeoisie) lifestyle. This shows that the middle class is a 'connected class', not only in terms of their connections to Western markets, products, cultures, languages, ideologies, and values, but also due to their ability to tap into opportunities to participate in globalisation in the realms of both production and consumption. Its participation in globalisation also makes China's middle class part of the *global* middle-class consumer class and allows it to share a similar consumer culture as the rest of the global middle class.

During intensive interviews with Chinese middle-class consumers carried out as part of this research, respondents often described the *xiaozi* (petite bourgeoisie) lifestyle as consisting of activities such as attending Western classical concerts and Broadway shows, listening to Western music, watching foreign films, drinking coffee, and consuming foreign products. It is also noted that many middle-class individuals embrace and appreciate Western high culture – such as opera, art, and classical music – as they swarm to exhibitions of French Impressionists, Italian Renaissance, and American Art in China.[24] The inclination for materialistic possession and cultural consumption of middle-class cultural forms confirms their social status and cultural tastes.

While demonstrating hedonic values and lifestyles in the consumption of Western commodities, Chinese middle-class consumers are showing strong interest in products and brands with distinctive Chinese characteristics and designs, as is witnessed in the decoration of middle-class households. Furthermore, as Thompson (2010) argues, businesses and products that incorporate 'Chinese Elements' are in the ascendency. Large corporations in China are beginning to show greater sensitivity to Chinese traditional values in their business operations and practice, especially those in the consumer market. In the last several years, Chinese media and netizens have launched online protests against several foreign companies for engaging in business practices that do not sufficiently recognize cultural and social sensitivities in China. Examples include a Starbucks store in the Forbidden City, Apple's low-quality service to its Chinese customers, and Gucci's workplace abuses in Shenzhen. Chinese netizens have expressed outrage on the popular microblogging site Sina Weibo, criticising these companies for taking advantage of Chinese consumers and being culturally insensitive. Meanwhile, some luxury brands have strengthened their communication efforts with consumers by actively showcasing culture and heritage. For example, Louis Vuitton organized the 'Louis Vuitton Voyages' Exhibition about iconic travel pieces and handbags with a history of travel, which took place at the National Museum of China, Beijing between May and August 2011. Chanel organized the 'Culture Chanel' Exhibition, showing 400 pieces from Chanel's past and present, including paintings, and drawings, which took place at the National Art Museum of China between November and December 2011.

Conclusion

As a beneficiary of China's economic reform, the middle class is an economically and socially advanced group in China's urban areas. Due to their financial well-being, the middle class is able to acquire new hobbies, new lifestyles, and new commodities. Research shows that as the middle class has been accumulating wealth and pursuing personal financial well-being, a strong consumer culture has been nurtured among its members. The middle class has embraced consumerism because consumption is extremely important in the pursuit of social status and lifestyle.

However, the question that remains is whether the growing consumer culture will aid the formation of a middle-class identity? Some scholars have documented the ways in which consumption allows individuals and groups to create new identities. For example, Liechty (2003) argues that the very act of buying reflects the cultural process and choice of consumption of an individual. Economic status is manifested and expressed through cultural aspects of consumption and lifestyle, and in this way consumption contributes to the formation of class. Thus, consumption is among the cultural processes through which an emerging middle class actually creates itself as a sociocultural entity. Middle-class individuals are those who are 'carving out a new cultural space which they explicitly locate, in language and material practice, between their classes "others" above and below' (Liechty, 2003: 30). Through lifestyles and consumption, people manifest a kind of class consciousness in a very practical way. Consumption patterns and lifestyle mainly serve as new performative mediums (Liechty, 2003: 115). Therefore, wearing a certain brand of clothing or driving a certain brand of car constitutes an important part of middle-class membership. Through consumption of certain goods, commodities, and services, middle-class identity is produced and reproduced. In other words, middle-class consumption exemplifies the processes by which the middle class in China is produced (and reproduces itself). This analysis of Chinese consumers has shown that the identity of China's middle class is closely associated with commodity consumption and the social practices of taste. The construction of the middle class is in continuous production and reproduction through cultural practices. As consumption is often a cultural choice, an expression of middle-class identity becomes a consumer choice. In the same way, consumption becomes a way of articulating and expressing identity for the middle class, as well as a symbol of lifestyle.

As China's middle class is still in the making, the subjective identity of the middle class is still being formed and fostered both individually and collectively. The middle class is conscious of its socioeconomic position. It shows its dispositions, tastes, and lifestyles through consumption. It tends to choose different ways and means to assert its newly acquired social and economic status. The middle class asserts its status by conspicuously spending money on housing, home furnishing, travel, and luxury brands. Regardless of which means they choose, members of the middle class participate in the 'game of distinction' (Bourdieu, 1984: 57). It is through consumption of various goods and commodities that the contemporary middle class is in pursuit of its social status and demonstrates its distinction from both the upper class and the lower class.

Notes

1. For example: Bain & Company (2011); Bain & Company and Kantar Worldpanel (2012); KPMG (2013); FBIC (2013); McKinsey & Company (2006, 2009, 2010).
2. For example: Davis (2000), (2005); Tomba (2004).
3. A total of 216 surveys were collected from households in Beijing in summer 2005. The average annual income per capita in 2006 was 17,653 RMB (US$2053) in Beijing, which is higher than the national average annual income per capita 11,663 RMB (US$1505), according to the National Statistic Bureau. The average size of households was three people. Official standards of income were used as the defining class. These identify the middle-income stratum as households with an annual income ranging from 60,000 RMB (US$7250) to 500,000 RMB (US$62,000).
4. A study by the Chinese Academy of Social Science (CASS) in 2001 used occupation as the primary indicator to define Chinese middle-income stratum. The estimated number of middle-class households in China was 80 million. The CASS report adopted the term *zhongchan jieji*, which means 'the middle property stratum', to de-emphasize the income and ownership of private assets and properties but used occupational characteristics as the criteria for the new social class. Some scholars define the middle class as the socioeconomic group with annual household earnings of 30,000 RMB ($3600) (see Yang

Yiyong, Ed., 1997). China's National Bureau of Statistics posits the annual income of middle-income households in a range from 60,000 RMB (US$7500) to 500,000 RMB (US$62,000) in its 2005 report (CNBS, 2005). Li Chunling used multiple factors to define the middle class: the middle class would constitute 15.9 per cent of the whole population when using professions and occupations, 24.6 per cent when using income, 35 per cent when using consumption, 46.8 per cent when using self-identification (subjective cognition). *Sources*: Li Chunling (2003) and Xin Wang (2008, 2009).

5. Mills' book was translated into Chinese and published in China by Zhejiang People's Press in 1987 and by Nanjing University Press in 2006.

6. For more information see Goodman (1999); Lu Xueyi (2002); Li Chunling (2004).

7. Yu Dan, a professor of mass media at Beijing Normal University, gained her fame from a series of lectures on Confucianism she presented on CCTV's *Lecture Room*. Her book became a bestseller in China. The new English edition of her book *Confucius from the Heart: Ancient Wisdom for Today's World* was published by Macmillan in 2009.

8. *Go Lala Go!* (2010), formerly called *Du Lala's Promotion*, an urban romance film, is directed by Xu Jinglei and co-stars Xu Jinlei, Stanley Huang, Karen Mok, Li Ai, and Pace Wu.

9. The costume designer of the film is the celebrated American costume designer Patricia Field, who has won several awards for designing costumes for the television series *Sex and the City*.

10. See *China Tourism Review 2012*, China Tourism Academy. Available from: *http://eng.ctaweb.org*

11. See *Annual Report of China Outbound Tourism Development 2012*, China Tourism Academy. Available from: *http://eng.ctaweb.org/* [accessed 24 July 2013].

12. KPMG (2013).

13. Bourdieu defines cultural capital as the forms of knowledge, skills, and education that give families or individuals a higher status in society. He points out that cultural capital is initially passed down by the family (Bourdieu, 1997).

14. Available from: *http://www.morningpost.com.cn/zhoukan/jyzk/2011-01-20/98301.shtml* [accessed 24 July 2013].

15. CNNIC Internet Development Report.

16. See the report on China Internet Watch on 29 February 2012. Available from:

http://www.chinainternetwatch.com/1395/sina-weibo-users-2011/ [accessed 24 July 2013].

17. See the report in *China Daily* on 17 January 2013. Available from: *http://www.chinadaily.com.cn/cndy/2013-01/17/content_16128915. htm* [accessed 24 July 2013].

18. KPMG (2013).

19. McKinsey (2010).

20. China's Prime Minister Wen Jiabao stated that China would focus on domestic demand, particularly consumer demand, as the driving force of economic growth in his government work report at the opening of the second session of the 11th National People's Congress (NPC) on 5 March 2009. Available from: *http://news.xinhuanet.com/english/ 2009-03/05/content_10945808.htm* [accessed 24 July 2013].

21. Data available from *http://fdc.soufun.com/Report/CIAReport.aspx* [accessed 24 July 2013].

22. Data available from *http://survey.ent.sina.com.cn/result/39451.html* [accessed 20 July 2010].

23. See Wang and Lin (2003); Zhou and Hui (2003).

24. The first large-scale exhibition of French Impressionist paintings was held in Beijing, Shanghai, and Guangzhou in 2004. The exhibition included 51 representative works from the Musée d'Orsay by 14 classical impressionist painters, including famous pieces by Edgar Degas, Edouard Manet, and Pierre Auguste Renoir. This is the highest level exhibition of its kind ever held in China to reveal the beginning and development of Impressionists in France; the Italian Renaissance Art Exhibition was held at the Millennium World Art Museum in Beijing in 2006. The work of Renaissance masters, including Leonardo da Vinci, Raphael, and Titian, was on display at the art exhibition. *Art in America: Three Hundred Years of Innovation*, the largest and most comprehensive exhibition of American art, was held in Beijing and Shanghai in 2007.

2

Mao's children are wearing fashion!

Calvin Hui

Abstract: This chapter – 'Mao's children are wearing fashion!'[1] – is part of a wider intellectual inquiry I am engaged in that explores fashion, understood as consumer commodity and artistic production, in order to address Chinese consumer culture from the socialist to the post-socialist periods. Emphasizing the relationships between the cultural and the political-economic, the chapter focuses on how fashion, media (such as cinema, documentary, and new media) and consumer culture are complexly mediated and connected to the radical economic, political, and social transformations of China in the late 1970s and the early 1980s. It argues that the representations of fashion and consumption in contemporary Chinese cinema and feminist discourse reveal the historical contradictions of the early stage of the country's economic reforms and opening up. The first section – 'The portrait of the factory worker in her red dress' – examines the politics of consumer culture through an engagement with Qi Xingjia's film *Red Dresses Are In Fashion* (1984). The second section – 'The revisionist narrative and its discontents' engages with Chinese feminist debates about fashion, femininity, and gendered consciousness in the post-socialist period, critiquing the revisionist narrative which portrays China's modernization project as allowing a freedom of expression for women. The chapter confronts the contradictions and limitations of this argument through an examination of the changing subject–object relation between human character and fashion commodity from the socialist to post-socialist period.

Key words: fashion, cinema, consumption, class, gender, ideology, post-socialist China.

Introduction

I would like to begin this chapter by drawing attention to a photograph in the Chinese newspaper *Jingji Ribao* (*Economic Daily*) published on 3 June 1992 (see Figure 2.1) This photograph featured a female Chinese factory worker in a poetry reading competition. On the stage, against the backdrop of Chairman Mao's portrait, she recited Mao Tse-tung's poem *To the Female Soldiers* (1961).

> Five-foot rifles, flashing bravely,
> On the training ground, at break of the day,
> How remarkable the spirit of Chinese women,[2]
> They love the martial dress, not the red dress.[3]

In the poem, Mao sings praises to the revolutionary potential of Chinese women. He glorifies the military uniform that Chinese women wear and the rifles they carry. (Indeed, Mao's poetry echoes with socialist feminist slogans such as 'women can hold up half of the sky' and 'Times have changed. Men and women are the same [equal]. Whatever male comrades can do, female comrades can also do too.'[4] Yet, ironically, the woman reciting the poem onstage is wearing a floral shirt and a skirt, rather than military uniform. Standing in high-heeled shoes, her legs are slightly crossed; her pose expressing her gentility, elegance, and femininity. According to the Chinese standard in the 1980s, it is certainly visually, and probably sexually, provocative.

This photograph reveals the disjuncture between Mao's poem and the newspaper article; between Mao's portrait in the background and the female factory worker in the foreground; and between the masculinized military uniform and the skin-revealing feminine outfit. It presents the incompatibility between the representations of women and their clothes during the socialist and the post-socialist eras. It also unravels the tension between what Badiou (2011) calls the revolutionary 'event' and the politicization of the everyday, on the one hand, and the era of economic modernization and developmentalism, or in Wang Hui's (2009) words, 'de-politicization', on the other.[5]

In her essay 'Class and gender in contemporary Chinese women's literature' (2004), the Marxist and feminist theorist Dai Jinhua addresses the relationship between class, gender, and ideology in contemporary Chinese cultural productions. Perceptively, she coins the term 'invisible writings' to denote the phenomenon by which statements

Figure 2.1 The poetry reading

Source: Unknown (every effort has been made to trace the copyright owner)

on class division became invisible in Chinese society during the 1990s and occasionally relied on different methods of cultural transference. She argues that 'the topics of gender and women have become one of the important ways of doing this, highlighting and concealing the existence of class reality' (Dai Jinhua, 1999: 297).[6] Although Dai Jinhua does not explain the psychoanalytical mechanism of transference in detail, she underscores the fact that class and ideology are often embedded in the discourse of women and gender (such as those on femininity). Building on her insights, I would like to add fashion and consumption to her list. I argue that it is through the representation of fashion, gender, and consumption in Chinese cinema and feminist discourse that the changing political ideologies of the People's Republic of China (PRC) in the late 1970s and the early 1980s can be detected.

In the first section – 'The portrait of the factory worker in her red dress' – I examine the politics of consumer culture through an engagement with Qi Xingjia's film *Red Dresses Are In Fashion* (1984) – a propaganda film sponsored by the post–socialist party state to promote China's modernization. In particular, I underline the ideology surrounding how fashion and consumption are handled in the film. Rather than portraying desire, pleasure, and consumption as potentially dangerous to class struggle, nation-building, and socialist revolution (as was the case during the most intense periods of the Cultural Revolution), the red dress is presented as a sought-after commodity for the female factory workers in the post-Cultural Revolution era. Interestingly, the model factory worker is portrayed as one who desires and consumes the red dress while being a good and diligent worker, with the implication that there should be no contradiction between consumption and production.

In the second section – 'The revisionist narrative and its discontents' – I engage with Chinese feminist debates about fashion, femininity, and gendered consciousness in the post-socialist period. According to the revisionist narrative, the way in which Maoist socialism promoted sameness can be observed in the ways Chinese people dressed. The colours of proletarian uniforms – blue, green, white, and grey – were dull and monotonous. Since Chinese women had to wear the clothes of the worker, the peasant, and the military soldier, Maoism denied their natural femininity, turning them into masculine or genderless beings. However, the revisionist narrative continues, the country's modernization project allowed Chinese people to wear colourful outfits with diversified styles and to express their personalities and individualities through consumption. Chinese women were also encouraged to express their femininity and regain their consciousness as gendered beings through fashion and makeup. Here, I confront the revisionist argument by showing its contradictions and limitations. I explain that the historical reality as it pertains to clothes and gender subjectivity is more complex than the revisionists claim it to be. I also examine the changing subject-and-object relation between human character and fashion commodity from the socialist to post-socialist period, before offering some concluding remarks on the sexual politics of fashion and consumption.

The portrait of the female factory worker in her red dress

In this first part of the chapter, I examine the representation of fashion and consumption in Qi Xingjia's film *Red Dress Is In Fashion* (1984). I explain how the cinematic portrayal of the consumption of a red dress by a factory worker expresses the ideology of China's economic reforms in the late 1970s and early 1980s. The main character of the film is Tao Xinger. She is a young, beautiful, intelligent, and compassionate female worker in a garment factory in Shanghai. Through her diligence, sense of responsibility, and passion and commitment to work, she earns the title of the model worker. This can be seen from her name – *Xinger* means 'little star' – and indeed, she is the favourite of the factory supervisor. Another prominent character is A Xiang who moves from the countryside to the city to work in the factory. When A Xiang first arrives in Shanghai, she is not fashionable, but she learns to adapt to city life quickly, eventually becoming the most fashionable character in the factory. It is through Tao Xinger and A Xiang that the other female characters are introduced. All of them work in the same factory, live in the same dorm, and are good friends. Men are irrelevant in their lives.

In the beginning of the story, Tao Xinger does not show much interest in fashion. It is her habit to dress in plain colours – mostly white and sometimes dark blue. Her disinterest in fashion and consumption can also be seen in her conversation with a Japanese businessman. When asked if she prefers white shirts and blue trousers to beautiful clothes, Tao Xinger replies that her job is to make other people look prettier, not to make herself look fashionable.

Businessman   [in Japanese]

Translator   Do you like white shirts and blue trousers? Don't you like to wear good-looking clothes?

Tao Xinger	I have just finished a meeting and got off the train.
Businessman	[in Japanese]
Translator	You don't wear good-looking clothes when you are having a meeting?
Tao Xinger	No! This time, we didn't have a conference to exchange tips for fashion. Instead, we discussed how to make other people look prettier.

Tao Xinger's lack of interest in fashion is placed in contrast to A Xiang's passion for it. A Xiang comes from the countryside and her name means countryside, as in *xiangtu* (native soil or home village), or *huixiang* (going back home). In fact, her rural identity can be further confirmed by the name of her brother Tu Gen – *Tu* means 'soil' or 'earth' and *Gen* means 'root'. (In the later part of the story, Tu Gen and his wife go to Shanghai to visit A Xiang. Ashamed of her rural identity, A Xiang is thoroughly embarrassed by their visit.) Some of A Xiang's co-workers look down on her and give her the nickname – *xiangxiaren* (country bumpkin). This upsets her, and to compensate she starts to dress and act in a hyper-urban cosmopolitan way. One day, wearing a red dress, panda-eyed sunglasses, and high-heeled shoes, A Xiang boldly shows off her fashionable outfit to the other female factory workers:

Worker 1	Country bumpkin, where did you buy this dress?
A Xiang	*You're* the country bumpkin! You keep wearing the dress you borrowed from your younger sister. This dress is made from American material. You cannot get this material in China. Have you seen this before?
Worker 1	How amazing! [said with irony]
Worker 2	The country bumpkin is proud. She is wearing clothes made from American material!
A Xiang	Who calls me a country bumpkin? I am going to get very angry!

To prove that she is not a country bumpkin, A Xiang chooses to wear clothes made from foreign materials, and to further claim her urban identity she lies to her colleagues about her brother. She claims that he helps her buy fashionable outfits from Hong Kong (in fact, Xiang Gang/

Hong Kong is the other meaning of her name) and sends them to her in Shanghai. The factory workers no longer call her country bumpkin; instead, they treat her nicely, in the hope that they too can buy fashionable clothes from Hong Kong with her help.

One day, Tao Xinger discovers a red dress in A Xiang's locker and is very curious about it. Without A Xiang's permission, she takes the dress out of the locker and holds it against herself to see how she would look wearing it. The model worker loves the red dress! At that moment A Xiang enters the room looking for her dress. When she realizes that Tao Xinger is holding her red dress, she encourages her friend to try it on, commenting on how great it looks on her and offering to lend it to her:

A Xiang	Where is my red dress?
Tao Xinger	It's here!
A Xiang	Here you are. Let me see! Why don't you wear it so that I can have a look at it? [Tao Xinger tries it on.]
A Xiang	Pull this up a little bit. [A Xiang helps Tao Xinger make minor adjustments to the outfit.] Loosen your hair ... That's good. Let me see. Oh, my goodness! I am so jealous! [Tao Xinger is very embarrassed. She uses her hands to cover her face.] Let me see!
Tao Xinger	It's too revealing! It's too revealing!
A Xiang	It's like this dress has been tailor-made for you! Look at your figure. So Venice!
Tao Xinger	Venice? Venus!
A Xiang	Yes! Yes! Yes! Venus! [Then the two girls laugh.] Come! Come! Come! I can guarantee you are going to lead the fashion trend. The fashion models of the world are in trouble!
Tao Xinger	Do you think I can wear this dress?
A Xiang	Why not? I can lend it to you. Come! Turn around! Good! Tomorrow, we can go to the dress competition in the park together!
Tao Xinger	What's a dress competition? [When A Xiang first arrived in Shanghai, she had heard about a fashion trend called a 'dress competition' which intrigued her.]

Girl	A Xiang, you have been in Shanghai for more than one year. You still don't know what a dress competition is?
A Xiang	Dress competition? I have heard of it, but have never seen it before.
Girl	This is how it works. Look! A woman purposely stands beside another woman to compare dresses and see which dress is more beautiful. The more beautiful one beats the less beautiful one. This is called a dress competition.

In fact, *zhan qun*, which can crudely be translated as 'dress competition', refers to the act of presenting or showing off one's beautiful clothes in public. This was definitely a new term in China in the mid-1980s. While *qun* means 'dress' or 'outfit', the pronunciation of *zhan* can refer to three Chinese characters meaning 'exhibition', 'war', and 'cutting'. The latter is used in the film, but in fact all of the meanings of *zhan* make sense in the context of the dress competition. In the dress competition, one has to *exhibit* one's dress in public, as part of a competition or *war* in which women try to defeat one another, effectively *cutting* each other down to size. Beauty can have its violent side.

Later in the film, A Xiang and the other girls are planning to go to the park to take part the 'dress competition'. They take it very seriously and have done many things to prepare for it. The film sequence presents the labour that goes into the production of feminine beauty. First, the female factory workers are shown taking showers together. Xiao Budian sings passionately in the shower, while some girls are laughing and others are talking about fashion. They keep asking A Xiang when the fashionable clothes will be delivered from Hong Kong. While they are busy changing into their beautiful clothes Tao Xinger returns. Initially, she is not interested in the competition, but due to A Xiang's insistent persuasion, the model worker finally agrees to join them. The factory girls busy themselves putting on makeup, colouring their eyebrows and eyelashes, styling their hair, and putting on jewellery. These activities are shown in detailed close-up, emphasizing each character's individuality. The use of a shallow depth of field further enhances this effect – because the background is out of focus, the viewer's gaze is directed to how the beautiful look is achieved. Beauty is laborious is the message: the girls spend a lot of time and energy getting ready for the contest.

The film reaches its climax when the factory girls show off their fashions in the dress competition. The sequence resembles a commercial advertisement. The factory workers are ready for the catwalk. This is the moment of sisterhood: hand in hand, they walk across the park together and present themselves confidently and elegantly, attracting a great deal of attention from the viewers. Then, the model worker Tao Xinger is asked to strut her stuff on the catwalk on her own. At first, she is slightly embarrassed and reluctant, but eventually she goes ahead. As she walks down the catwalk showing off her red dress, the tempo of the music slows down dramatically and her walk is shown in slow motion. The moment she shakes her head to show off her long, smooth hair is presented in the style of a shampoo commercial. The viewer is led to focus on changes in the shape of the dress due to her movement. The red dress is shown to bring out the elegance, gentility, and femininity of the model worker, making her even more charming and attractive. Shot/reverse-shots show the viewers' reactions. From their facial expressions, it is clear that some of the female spectators are envious of Tao Xinger and her red dress. Men, on the other hand, whistle at her and a jealous girlfriend hits her boyfriend.

The female factory workers emerge as the winners of the dress competition and, living up to her name of 'Little Star', Tao Xinger becomes the star of the contest. They spend the rest of the day in the park together and are genuinely happy. While fellow factory worker Ge Jia uses her camera to take pictures, Tao Xinger lies on the grass and breathes deeply. Her facial expression suggests that she is enjoying this moment of sublime happiness to the fullest. She feels complete and fulfilled. The experience of the dress competition has helped the model worker gain the confidence to express herself through fashion and consumption. She is liberated and, no longer imprisoned by old, conservative, and moralistic values, she learns that she can be a good model worker and be feminine at the same time. The message is clear: there is no contradiction between production and consumption.

The film continues by depicting the girls, as a result of enjoying the dress competition so much, asking a fashion specialist to teach them how to dress in a fashionable way. Beauty has to be learned and acquired.

[Dressed in beautiful clothes, a woman is dancing while strutting her stuff on a catwalk.]

Girl   Who is she?

Ge Jia   She is the classmate of my sister. She is part of the fashion performance team. She can teach you how to put on makeup, how to look better than the rest, what goes

	well with what (materials and colours), as well as lots about fashion trends and working out. She is awesome. You are welcome to ask her.
Girl	Look! She has changed into another set of clothes! [. . .]
Model	Last year, the pleated skirt was in fashion. This year, it's flared skirts with large and wide plaids that are in fashion. What is going to be fashionable next is the long dress. Sports fashion will be next. Simple cuts. Light colours.
A Xiang	What kind of clothes will go well with this?
Model	How beautiful! It will go well with white or black. Now, three colours are fashionable in the international fashion circle – white, red, and black. White represents purity. Black represents propriety. Red represents passion. [The fashion class is accompanied by a comportment lesson. The fashion specialist teaches the factory girls how to pose and move in an elegant and feminine way.]
Model	3, 4. 1, 2, 3, 4. 2, 2, 3, 4. Like this! Come! Yes! You have done very well! Do this! This is pretty good. Can you see it? Yes, your hand should be like this. If we want ourselves to be pretty, elegant, and gracious, first of all, we have to raise our qualities and cultivate our cultural sensibilities. Of course, that includes doing aerobic exercises. Pay attention to your head. Come! Your arm should be higher!

In what follows, I focus on how the characterization of the model worker, the worker, and the factory supervisor expresses the changing ideologies of the PRC. Let us focus on the model worker first. At work, Tao Xinger's impressive performance has earned her the reputation of being a model worker. She also has good working relations with the other female factory workers. At home, she takes care of her parents and is a good daughter. In her spare time, she cares about those who have been left behind by society, such as the lonely old man who plays the flute on the street. (He has been abandoned by a *getihu* – private entrepreneur/shopkeeper, therefore there is a moral critique at play here, although not a sociopolitical one of the private entrepreneur.) Most importantly, the model worker Tao Xinger is interested in fashion:

Ge Jia	Our model worker is into fashion. China has hopes!
Tao Xinger	Ge Jia, you are so mean! [...]
Ge Jia	Do you dare to wear the red dress?
Tao Xinger	It's nothing! In the competition I joined, each girl was more pretty and modern than the other girl. Once you have seen something like this, you want to be Number One for the rest of your life!
Ge Jia	*Do you mean production? Or do you mean beauty contest?* [My emphasis]
Tao Xinger	*If I am allowed, I want both!* [My emphasis]
Ge Jia	Oh! You have only left Shanghai for three days, and you start to think in this way! Our Ms. Tao is liberated!
Tao Xinger	Really? [The two girls laugh.]

When Ge Jia asks Tao Xinger if she wants to choose labour (production) over participating in a beauty contest (consumption), Tao Xinger expresses that she would like to have both options. She does not see any contradiction between production and consumption.

The worker A Xiang is passionate about fashion consumption. She claims that her brother from Hong Kong can send fashionable outfits to her in Shanghai. In fact, A Xiang has been lying to the factory manager and her co-workers all along. She does not have any close relatives in Hong Kong. Instead, she has been asking the *getihu* to obtain fashionable clothes for her from Hong Kong which she then pays him for. Since the money she collects from the factory girls is not sufficient to cover the full price of the clothes, she uses her salary to pay for the remaining sum. She has to pay for other people's respect for her and in doing so lies to her boss and her colleagues.

Zhi Banzhang is the factory supervisor. From her conversations with A Xiang and Ge Jia, her attitude toward fashion and consumption is clear:

Zhi Banzhang	What's going on? [She walks toward A Xiang] You are too exposed. This is more revealing than the vests that male comrades wear.
A Xiang	If I hide it, then people can't see it!

Zhi Banzhang	If you don't want people to see it, then, don't make it so obvious. You look like a couple of foreigners. But, as long as the dresses are produced in the west, it is OK, I guess!
Ge Jia	It's made in China. Originally it was produced for the foreign market, but it was sold in the domestic market. [They both laugh.]
Zhi Banzhang	So what you are wearing is neither foreign or Chinese. One thing's for sure, though, and that is it's so tight!

On another occasion, she has a similar conversation with Tao Xinger and Ge Jia:

Zhi Banzhang	Look at this beautiful dress! Is it yours, [Tao] Xinger?
Tao Xinger	Yes, it's mine! Does it look good?
Zhi Banzhang	It's too revealing! You can wear it at home – when nobody is around!
Ge Jia	Nobody appreciates it at home!
Zhi Banzhang	You can be quiet!
Ge Jia	I am telling the truth! The only ones who love the red dress are out on the streets. Wear it at home?! You are such a conservative!

Zhi Banzhang does not have strong opinions about fashion and consumption. She neither endorses fashion and consumption explicitly nor rejects them either. She simply thinks that the fashionable clothes A Xiang, Tao Xinger, and Ge Jia wear are too revealing. In other words, she is mostly concerned with morality, rather than politics or ideology.

In *Red Dress Is In Fashion*, the attitudes of the model worker, the worker, and the factory supervisor towards fashion and consumption reflect the changes of the official ideologies in the early stage of China's modernization. The reformist factions of the Chinese government indicate that there is no simple causal relationship between fashion and consumption, on the one hand, and class, politics, and ideology, on the other. They insist that *beauty does not have a class character and clothing is not necessarily related to one's ideological well-being*. Built into their logic is the idea that it is possible for one to belong to the proletariat class and be fashionable at the same time. The new humanist subject can also be beautiful. In fact, the latter confirms the success of China's modernization project.

The revisionist narrative and its discontents

'Joining the Party and wearing dresses are two different things. However, it is strange that some people tried to make the connection between the two. In Hebei, a young woman, who had been working in the communist youth group, applied to join the Party. However, someone in her work unit commented that wearing dresses might have negative influences on others. So her application was rejected. Everyone has the desire for beauty. It is perfectly natural for a young woman to wear dresses and make herself look more appealing. The desire for beauty is an expression of the desire for modernity (civilization). How can it possibly have 'negative influences'? Whether a comrade can join the party should not be dependent on what one wears and carries, but whether one is whole-heartedly devoted to serving the people, whether one has got communist ideals and beliefs, whether one has put those values into practice. The criteria of Party membership have already been written into the constitution. How can someone in the Party judge other people by their appearances? It must be a special case. But from their perspective, the clothes of Party members must have patches, their feet must have mud, their bodies must have sweat, otherwise they would not look like Party members. However, the age when people are proud of the patches on their clothes is gone. Our society is moving forward and our values have to be updated. The old way of judging people by their appearances needs to be changed.'

(Jia Zhaoquan, 1986)

In what follows, I engage with the revisionist narrative, one of the central ideologies of China's capitalistic modernization, and address its problems and limitations. In particular, I examine contemporary Chinese feminist discussions and debates about the consumption of the red dress, as a way to unravel the historical contradictions with which the PRC was confronted in the early stages of the economic reforms and opening up. What is the revisionist narrative? How is it expressed in the feminist discourse? Let me answer this question by referring to 'A fashion comeback' – an entry in a photographic album called *China's Thirty Years* (CPA, 2009), which was published in celebration of the PRC's 30 years of reforms:

> 'The Cultural Revolution was a dark time for fashion in China. People were forced to abolish "antiquated" concepts, culture and dress, and anything associated with "the bourgeoisie". As a result, people wore neither traditional Chinese costumes nor Western-style suits, and China became renowned for its uniform dress code of blue or green "Mao suits". Those who wore jewelry or make-up faced serious consequences. The Mao suit – fashioned from sturdy blue serge – and green army uniforms were the only attire available to most of the population for decades until the end of the Cultural Revolution. Dress in China underwent a drastic change after the turbulence. In 1979, French designer Pierre Cardin staged a fashion show in Beijing, and his bold and futuristic designs excited Chinese audiences, most of whom were still wearing simple cotton-padded jackets. China's youth rediscovered the joy of dressing up as a result of Deng's open-door policy, and modern fashions began to reappear on the streets. Today, China's young are among the most fashion conscious in the world and her cities' clothes shops are jam-packed at weekends with customers eager to dress to impress.'
>
> (CPA, 2009: 65)

During the past 30 years, from socialism to post-socialism, the story of the unprecedented economic, political, social, and cultural transformations of the PRC is often told from the revisionist perspective, or what Lisa Rofel calls the 'post-socialist allegory' (1999, 2007). According to the revisionist narrative, Maoist socialism denied human nature, suppressed the natural desires of Chinese people, and created abnormal political passions in them. In contrast, the economic reforms liberated Chinese people from the communist shackles of continuous revolution, class struggle, and ideological critique, so that they could finally embrace their true humanity and express their innermost nature. Examining the rhetoric of such a discourse more closely, it is clear that the revisionist argument was often presented in terms of binary oppositions: sameness versus difference, homogeneity versus heterogeneity, and uniformity versus multiplicity. According to revisionist logic, Maoist socialism as repressive governmentality promoted sameness at the expense of difference. One example often used to strengthen the revisionist argument is the clothes Chinese people wore.

During the socialist period, Chinese people wore the clothes of the proletariat – the worker, the peasant, and the soldier. The colours of their uniform – mostly blue, green, white, and grey – were dull and monotonous. Under such political circumstances, the revisionist narrative argues, Chinese people lost their personalities and individualities and were turned into identical beings.[7] By contrast, the economic reforms and opening up policies initiated by the post–socialist party state celebrated difference and multiplicity. Such liberatory politics, according to the revisionist argument, can be observed in the fashion that Chinese people wore. The government made it clear that Chinese people's standard of living, including the clothes that they wore, had to be improved, and that the clothes offered to them should be diversified. In the post-socialist period, Chinese people were encouraged to wear colourful outfits with varied styles. They were given the choice to express their personalities and individualities through fashion and consumption.

In fact, the revisionist ideology was also widely disseminated in the 'main melody' films – the propaganda films sponsored by the Chinese government. The dismissal of revolutionary politics and ideology was expressed most clearly through the dismissal of the Mao suit. For example, in Lu Xiaoya's film, *The Girl In Red* (1984), a cinematic adaptation of Tie Ning's fiction *A Red Shirt Without Buttons*, two teenage girls – An Ran and An Jing – make fun of the obsolescence of socialist uniform in front of a shop window. Dressed in Mao suits, the two mannequins look terribly old-fashioned to them.

[An Ran and An Jing stand in front of a shop window. The mannequins are dressed in Mao suits. They look very old fashioned.]

An Ran	[To the mannequins] You poor thing. No one changes your clothes in such hot weather. [To her sister] These mannequins look as if they are suffering from jaundice!
An Jing	The wax prevents the paint from drying out![8]

Throughout the film, the Mao suit (the old) is contrasted with the red shirt (the new). The latter is similar to the red dress that Tao Xinger wears in *Red Dress Is In Fashion*. Diverging from masculinized colours, such as blue, grey, green, and black, the red dress (or the red shirt), and fashionable accessories like panda-eyed sunglasses, were symbols of femininity celebrated as symbols of modernization. This can also be observed in Bao Zhifang's film *Black Dragonfly* (1984) – another main melody film – which features a scene in which the film director Zhou Zhou, together with his wife Huang Peng (a singer) and his daughter Zhou Jing (a fashion model), tells a young and aspiring fashion designer Yang Tianping and his friend Cui Yong (an actor turned fashion model) that he is prepared to make a film about the colours of life in the aftermath of the Chinese Cultural Revolution. His assumption is that the Cultural Revolution is a dark age:

Zhou Zhou   Fashion should be rich and colourful. After the third plenum, people dare to pursue beauty [...] During those ten years of turmoil [of the Cultural Revolution], people were imprisoned in the world of blue and grey. They could not see the world of changing colours [...] Monotonous colours cannot represent our China. I [...] want to enrich the colours of life and bring beauty and life together forever![9]

This is another illustration of the revisionist narrative. The argument is familiar: repressed by the socialist regime, Chinese people's desire for beauty and colours was liberated by the forces of the post–socialist party state and global capital. Thanks to the economic reforms, Chinese people were given the opportunity to wear colourful outfits with diverse styles. They finally had the choice to express their personalities and individualities through fashion and consumption.

At this point, we need to pause and ask several questions about choice, in particular the subject and the object of choice, and the affective relation between them.[10] Indeed, why *must* we necessarily choose difference rather than sameness? Why *must* we choose individuality but not uniformity? Going further, can we choose not to choose? Is choice always free? The affective dimension of choice needs to be problematized too. Is choice liberating a desire that has been repressed, or is it simply creating new desire? If the latter is the case, is the person who does the choosing liberated or imprisoned by his or her own choice? Can choice not be oppressive to the person who does the choosing? On the surface, it seems that having the choice to express oneself is a good thing, but in some contexts choice can be anxiety provoking and freedom can be oppressive. The demand to highlight one's difference from the other person can be potentially distress causing. This point is well captured by the mainland Chinese actress Li Bingbing. In an interview, Li spoke of the embarrassing situation of *zhuangshan*. This phrase is used to describe the awkward situation in which one wears the same clothes as someone else on the same social occasion.

Li suggests that in consumer society actresses must dress differently from each other. To appropriate her observation, it is possible to say that *zhuangshan* would not so much be considered as a problem during the socialist period because, as the revisionists say, everyone dressed (or was asked to dress) in similar ways, so the coercive demand to be different from others did not exist at that time. However, during the post-socialist period, people began to be expected to dress with a unique personality. The requirement to be different, including the obligation to emphasize one's individualities through clothing, turned everyday self-presentation and identity into an arena of struggle and competition in which people have to expend energy and invest desire.

From socialism to post-socialism, from repression to liberation, the story of China's economic reforms is also couched in the language of gender. This can be seen in a CBC (Canadian) TV documentary called *China's Sexual Revolution* (2007), which offers a somewhat orientalist depiction of the gender and sexual politics of contemporary China. In the introduction of the TV documentary, the narrator announces that 'Chinese socialism' turned couples into comrades, not lovers, and cloaked men and women into the same asexual Mao suit. This is the typical revisionist story. The audience is then introduced to the perspectives offered by two diasporic Chinese/Chinese American women. The first one is Cha Jianying, the author of *China Pop* (1995); the second is Kan Yue-sai, a famous businesswoman who brought cosmetics to mainland China in the 1980s:

Cha Jianying   [During the Cultural Revolution] women were turned into men. Everyone was dressed alike, men and women. The fashion statement back then was that you can all become brothers and sisters. The only way women could show a bit of their figure was by sewing in their blue uniform so that they could have a waist line[11] [. . .] The Red Guards went on the street and cut everybody's long hair and that's a very blatant way of trying to make everyone the same.

Kan Yue-sai   They [Chinese women] dressed like men. Women dressed like men. No colour. No make-up. The hairstyle was only one kind of hairstyle. Basically no style. Nobody was wearing anything provocative. Nobody was going to prominently display their lips.

The Chinese/Chinese American Cha and Kan maintain that gender difference and fashion were denied during the socialist period. Such a revisionist viewpoint is also shared by feminist critics in mainland China. In her conversations with the British feminist critic Harriet Evans, the Chinese feminist critic Li Yinhe commented on the gender politics of socialist China:

'In China, from the 1950's to 1960's until the end of the Cultural Revolution, the atmosphere was that men and women were the same. Women had to do what men did. Women demanded gender equality and the blurring of gender boundaries. At least this is how it was promoted in the mainstream culture. For example, women had to work in the mines. Women did fieldwork on the railways. These were men's jobs in the past. This was what the media was trying to advocate during the first thirty years of the PRC. At that time, women used to cover all their female (feminine) characteristics. No women put on make-up. The clothes they wore did not show any secondary sexual characteristics. The way women dressed was the way men dressed. They tried not to highlight any gender differences. This was the tendency of the first thirty years of PRC. In the early 1980's, the beginning of the economic reforms and opening up, the display of gender differences was becoming increasingly obvious. Some women put on make-up. Some women wore clothes that exposed their bodies' secondary sexual characteristics. Some women went back home to become housewives [...] After the 1980's, Chinese women displayed a tendency of going back to their traditional gendered roles. They also displayed a tendency of emphasizing gender differences. This is how the question of sex and gender evolved in China historically.'

(Li Yinhe and Evans, 2001: 36–7)

The gender politics of the revisionist narrative can be described as follows: Maoist socialism is characterized by gender erasure or, according to some extreme and exaggerated interpretations, the eradication of sex or gender. By requiring Chinese women to wear proletarian clothes, Maoist socialism masculinized them, suppressed and denied their natural femininities, and turned them into genderless beings. The regime also emasculated and feminized Chinese men, preventing them from expressing their true masculine selves. On the contrary, the revisionist narrative continues, the economic reform policies emancipated Chinese women and recovered their lost womanhood. Chinese women were encouraged to express their natural femininities and develop their consciousness as gendered beings. They did not have to wear masculine or unisex clothing, such as the military uniform. Instead, they were encouraged to wear feminine dresses, consume fashionable clothes, and wear makeup. Indeed, wearing a sexy outfit and putting on lipstick is often seen as a form of feminist liberation to the revisionists, in a similar way to the post-feminist movements in the West. In the post-socialist period, Chinese men were also empowered to become real men and act out their raw and masculine selves. The country's capitalistic modernization is often presented as a developmentalist project of overcoming gender erasure and recovering gender difference. (Juxtaposing post-socialist Chinese feminist politics with post-structuralist and deconstructionist feminist theories, it is interesting to note that what the revisionists demanded is not the *de*-construction of gender, but the *re*-construction of it. The revisionists wanted Chinese women to have more, rather than less, gender difference and femininity.)

In the above, I show that the revisionist narrative presents itself as a progress narrative – repression in the socialist period, liberation in the post-socialist period. I also emphasize that the story of progress is embedded in gendered terms – gender sameness and gender repression in the socialist period, gender difference and gender liberation in the post-socialist period. In what follows, I will confront the revisionist argument by showing its limitations and contradictions. My objective is twofold: first, I show that the socialist period is not as repressive as the revisionists present it to be. (However, I do not claim that the socialist period is entirely non-repressive or completely liberatory). Second, I show that the post-socialist period is not as liberatory as the revisionists claim it to be. (However, I do not claim that the post-socialist period is completely repressive or non-liberatory.) My intention is to complicate and problematize the revisionist feminist argument by scrutinizing the very phrases that are most key to their argument – gender sameness, gender repression, gender difference, and gender liberation. In particular I ask: Is socialism really characterized by gender erasure (or the celebration of gender sameness)? Is the celebration of gender sameness in socialism really gender repression? Is post-socialism really characterized by the celebration of gender difference? Is the celebration of gender difference in post-socialism really gender liberation?

The answers to all these questions is 'no' and I will explain why one by one. First, the revisionist narrative argues that since Chinese women were asked to wear proletarian clothing during the socialist period, gender sameness was promoted and women's femininities were erased. Was this really the case? While the revisionists are correct to say that gender was not pronounced prominently in women's clothing, *it is historically inaccurate to say that women's femininities were completely obliterated at that time.* When we look at Chinese language sources, such as the pictures in China's Cultural Revolution Research website, Chinese men and women did dress in slightly different ways during the Cultural Revolution.[12] Moreover, when we look at non-Chinese sources, such as Michelangelo Antonioni's documentary *Chung Kuo – Cina* (1972), which chronicles the lives of Chinese living in the rural areas in the early 1970s, there were indeed signs of femininities in women's clothes. For instance, the shirts that women wore had different colours and patterns; the collars of their outer layers were wider; and their hairstyles were different too. My observation is echoed by Harriet Evans. Below is her disagreement with Li Yinhe's revisionist interpretation of the Chinese socialist experience:

'You [Li Yinhe] mentioned that men and women were the same from the 1950s to the 1960s. I cannot fully agree with you. On the surface, the ways in which men and women dressed were similar. But when you pay close attention to the photographs taken at that time, you can see that there were feminine patterns on women's clothes, and also, some women had braided hair. Women's images, including the representation of women in the official propaganda, did display signs of femininities. This is related to what I have been researching. If you look at some of the women's magazines published during the socialist period, such as *Women of China, China Youth Daily*, and the like, these publications were concerned with issues relating to sex and gender. The topics included sex education, puberty, physical development, and many other things. True, the quantity was limited, but at least they were there. Through these materials, it is clear that gender differences were indeed present [during the socialist period].'[13]

(Evans, 2006: 38)

In addition, in her book *Chinese Fashion: From Mao to Now* (2009), Juanjuan Wu points out:

'Although both men and women wore plain clothes in the same drab colours and the same square, simple cuts, minor details in women's and men's wear did exist that, to some extent, served to differentiate the sexes in Chinese eyes. For instance, to a casual observer a woman's dual-purpose jacket looked very much a like a man's Mao suit jacket, but it differed in the type and number of pockets and in the number of buttons.'

(Juanjuan Wu, 2009: 37)

Juanjuan Wu explains the difference between the Mao suit worn by men and the dual-purpose jacket worn by women. Alongside the military attire, the most fashionable clothes for men were the 'three old styles' and the 'three old colours'. The three old styles consisted of the Mao suit (formerly called the *Sun Yat-Sen* suit), the youth jacket, and the causal army jacket. The 'three old colours' referred to subdued blue, white, and grey. In addition, olive green, the colour of the military uniform, was also popular. For women, the most common outfits were the plain dual-purpose jacket and the traditional-styled jacket. Wu goes on to explain how the pockets and the buttons were different in men's and women's clothes. For men, the Mao suit had five buttons for the front closure, one button on each of the four frontal patch pocket flaps, and three buttons on each sleeve. For women, although the proletarian dual-purpose jacket resembled the Mao jacket in colour and silhouette, it had four buttons (rather than five buttons), and two rectangular flapless front patch pockets (rather than four pockets). The minor differences in their clothes do not accentuate gender, but rather indicate, like a label, either 'male' or 'female'. Wu also points out that a modest degree of fashion was permitted during the socialist period. For women, an accepted way of being fashionable was to wear the inner shirt's patterned collar on the outside of the plain jacket so that the pattern could be seen. Different styles of scarves were also considered fashionable accessories for women (Juanjuan Wu, 2009: 4). As there were still signs of femininity in women's clothes, albeit minor ones, it is not historically accurate to claim that femininities were completely erased during the socialist period.

To address the second question regarding whether, since Chinese women were asked to wear masculinized or unisex clothing, gender was repressed during the socialist period, rather than respond directly, I would like to challenge and comment on the way the revisionist narrative is posed and structured. *Rather than endorse the revisionist language like 'gender repression', 'gender erasure', and 'the murdering of gender', I suggest that it is more productive to use words such as 'gender neutrality' and 'androgyny'*[14] *to describe socialist gender politics.* Rather than simply look at the negative aspects, we can think dialectically to look at the positive aspects of 'gender neutrality' or 'androgyny'. Indeed, what did Chinese women gain and how were they empowered by gender-crossing (without being male-identified)? What kinds of new gendered possibilities were available to them when they were not expected to act and perform their femininities? What kinds of gendered options were open to them when they could act, in Xiaomei Chen's words, like 'womanly men' and 'manly women? (1999: 110). Or, to pose the question in a slightly different way, what kinds of gender options are foreclosed by the revisionist category of 'gender erasure'?

Third, according to the revisionist narrative, Chinese women were free to wear feminized clothing, such as the red dress, during the post-socialist period and it is in this way that gender difference was promoted. However, the representation of femininity in the revisionist narrative is closely linked to commercialized consumer culture. The kinds of femininities not directly associated with consumption are excluded. In other words, *the revisionist narrative's version of gender difference is limiting because it is not different enough*. To pursue this line of logic further, we can say that the revisionists deny Chinese women other ways of being feminine because they celebrate one kind of femininity (i.e., the consumerist version) at the expense of other kinds of femininities. The revisionists claim that socialist gender politics is one of gender erasure but, paradoxically, their version of post-socialist gender politics is effectively not gender difference or gender liberation, but another form of gender erasure in disguise.

To address the final question, the revisionist narrative did indeed present the opportunities to wear feminized clothes during the post-socialist period as a form of gender liberation, but to what extent is this really gender emancipation? What kinds of gender possibilities are excluded and foreclosed? Underlying the revisionist narrative is the assumption that Chinese women must necessarily dress in a feminine way in order to be considered liberated women. But why *must* they necessarily dress in a feminine way? Why must they necessarily act in a feminine way so as to be liberated? Why is it not the case that they can dress in a masculine way and be liberated? In a feminist utopia, Chinese women should be able to dress and behave in a masculine way, or in a feminine way, or both, or neither. For example, if they want, Chinese women should be allowed to dress and behave in a masculine way in the morning, in a feminine way in the afternoon, and in an androgynous way in the evening. In addition, in the feminist utopia, Chinese men should also be allowed to dress and act in a masculine or feminine manner. In other words, when the revisionists assume that Chinese women should not be asked to dress in a masculine way but, instead, they should be encouraged to dress and act in a feminine way so as to be liberated, they have really only recuperated and rehearsed the very hierarchical relationship that they were attempting to critique in the first place. Ultimately, their version of gender difference is quite oppressive (especially to those Chinese women who enjoy being and acting masculine). It shows itself to be a form of gender determinism that denies Chinese women other ways of being and acting in the world. It is therefore gender inequality. With the intention of critiquing gender erasure in the socialist period, the revisionists' version of gender difference is ultimately a form of gender erasure in disguise.[15]

I would like to continue to confront the revisionist argument by showing its limitations and contradictions. This time, my focus is on the changing subject and object relation between the human figure and the clothing commodity. In the previously mentioned TV documentary *China's Sexual Revolution* (2007) the director presents the radical changes in gender roles and sexual attitudes in China from the socialist to the post-socialist period. In one scene, a group of female Red Guards, dressed in masculinized military uniforms, march boldly in Beijing's Tiananmen Square, shouting revolutionary slogans like 'Long Live Chairman Mao!' Another scene shows a group of very feminine looking models catwalking in a fashion show. These two scenes allow us a glimpse of the changing relations between the figure of the woman and the fashion commodity, and between the subject and the object, from the socialist to the post-socialist period.

In contrast to the fashion model, a symbol of middle-class consumption, the Red Guard, a symbol of proletarian subjectivity actively engaged in socialist production and construction, is a more inclusive and democratic figure. This is explained in Harriet Evans' work. In her essay 'Fashions and feminine consumption' (2006), she underlines the politics of class and gender categories:

'The lines of differentiation in the Mao images were determined by the ideological and political tendencies of the time, and not by the social hierarchies of consumption. In the class terms of the time, they included the rural, the elderly, the uneducated, and the poor, leaving many potential spaces for a gendered and even sexual appeal across the boundaries of difference that operate in today's consumer culture. The accoutrements of fashion now displayed to appeal to women's consumer passions exclude everyday gendered identities that are not commercially valued by consumer culture. The rural, the older, the poor, and the disadvantaged are virtually absent from the images that dominate the front covers of women's magazines.'

(Evans, 2006: 179)

In comparing the representations of women and fashion in Chinese media cultures from the 1960s to the 1980s, it is clear that what characterizes women's clothing during the socialist period was the masculinized military uniform. Chinese women – including youth (*qingnian*) such as the Red Guard and the proletarian woman (*funu*) – rejected the red dress and embraced military clothing. In contrast, what typifies Chinese women's clothing from the 1980s onwards is the red dress. The fashion model and the middle-class female (*nüren*) consumer were more interested in consuming the red dress, rather than the military uniform – they consumed or, in many ways, were consumed by feminized clothing.[16] However, it is crucial to note that the way the Red Guard wore the military uniform does not equate to the way the fashion model wore the red dress. To use the language of the subject and the object to describe socialist gender politics, the Red Guard is the subject and the military uniform is the object. The Red Guard wears the military uniform and actively engages in class struggle, national liberation, and socialist revolution. *However, the subject and object relation is reversed in the post-socialist period in which fashion becomes both the object and the subject of production.* In the realm of production, fashion is manufactured in the factory and is the object of production. However, in the realm of consumption, fashion can be viewed as the subject. As a technology of commercialized consumer culture, fashion as the subject produces the fashion model as the object. The objectification of the fashion model can be observed in the way that the model does not exhibit many facial expressions when strutting her stuff on the catwalk, rather her task is to show off the fashion (which is the subject). It is in this sense that the model can be likened to a walking coat hanger. Her personality is secondary. Fashion produces, subjugates, and objectifies the model.

The revisionist narrative claims that Chinese women have been given the free choice to embrace femininity in the post-socialist context. However, if we look closely at some of the hidden social norms and cultural structures, it becomes clear that the scenario has less to do with free choice and female agency, and much more to do with how commercial advertising produces a gendered consumer subject. The advertising industry has less to do with the construction of a free and independent female subject, and more to do with the capitalistic technology of subjectification and subjugation through desire. In other words, contrary to the Red Guards who wear the military uniform, *it is the red dress that wears the models (or the middle-class women consumers). It is not that the fashion models wear the red dress, but that the fashion models (or the middle-class women consumers) are worn by the red dress.*

We could ask why the fashion model must be regarded as the object, and the fashion commodity the subject? Why does the fashion commodity wear the model? In her essay 'A chronicle of changing clothes', Eileen Chang provides a possible answer: 'The sloping of shoulders, narrow waist, and flat chest of the ideal beauty, who was to be both petite and slender, would disappear under the weight of these layers on layers of clothing. She herself would cease to exist, save as a frame on which clothing could be hung' (Chang, 2005: 66). What Chang articulates allows us to see that the fashion model, and by extension, the middle-class woman consumer, is not the subject, but the object – a hanger of clothes. Her function is to show off the clothes, to allow fashion as the subject to express itself prominently. In other words, in contrast to the Red Guards who wear the military uniform, it is the fashionable clothes that wear the fashion models (or the middle-class women consumers). The fashion models (or the middle-class women consumers) are worn by their fashion. Similarly, it is the fashionable clothes that consume the consumer, not the consumer who consumes the clothes. The consumer is consumed. She has already been chosen by the market economy to express her 'free choice', 'personality', and 'individuality'. In many ways, it is anti-freedom, anti-choice, anti-personality, and anti-individuality. The objectification and commodification of women, fashion, and the body can be further explained by the fact that sometimes women have to change their bodies (or body parts) to conform to certain social expectations and be considered beautiful. We need only think of diet, exercise, anorexia, plastic surgery, and other painful methods of beautification that bring violence to women's bodies. Wei Pengju perceptively summarizes this phenomenon: 'Fashion packages the body. The body, in return, packages fashion' (2004: 3).

In *A Primer for Daily Life* (1991), Susan Willis appropriates Fredric Jameson's theoretical innovation – the dialectic of ideology and utopian impulse in contemporary mass culture – to look at US suburban cultures. In an essay entitled 'Work(ing) out', she compares the woman who uses the machine to work with the woman who uses the machine to work out. She argues that the woman who uses the machine to work out is the subject, and the work machine is the object. In comparison, the woman who uses the machine to work out is the object and the workout machine is the subject. Willis' reasoning is thus:

'[The nautilus workout machine] gives women access to the machine but denies access to production. It requires energy and effort and negates the experience of labour. It isolates the individual from other women who work out and defines her body as an assemblage of body areas and muscle functions, each requiring a specialized machine and machine function. The nautilus machine and the woman who works out on it is the distorted 1980's equivalent of Rosie the Riveter astride the body of a battleship. As an icon in the popular imagination, the nautilus metamorphoses women's relationship to self and to labour. Nothing is produced but the body itself.'

(Willis, 1991: 73)

According to Willis, the woman who exercises by using the workout machine is the object, and the workout machine is the subject. But this is just one part of the dialectic. Willis proceeds to tell us the other part of the dialectic: '*The woman inside the nautilus machine is the object produced by the machine even while she is at the same time the producer producing herself as the product of the machine*' [my emphasis] (Willis, 1991: 75). The first clause describes how 'the woman inside the nautilus machine is the object produced by the machine.' Thus, the workout machine is the subject and the woman who uses the workout machine is the object. But what interests us here is the second clause: 'she is at the same time the producer producing herself as the product of the machine.' On the surface, the woman who uses the workout machine is the producer, or the subject. But, ultimately, the workout machine is the subject, and she is the object. The woman herself is the product of the workout machine. In other words, she is simultaneously the subject and the object but, ultimately, the object. It is for this reason that Willis argues she is 'the producer [read: the subject] producing herself [read: the object] as the product of the machine.'

In this way Willis provides an excellent analysis of the difference between the work machine (production) and the workout machine (consumption) in relation to the construction of woman's subjectivity. It is interesting to relate her observation to the discussion of the military uniform (production) in the socialist context, the red dress (consumption) in the post-socialist context, and the construction of woman's subjectivity in modern China. During the socialist period, the woman who wears the military uniform, such as the female Red Guard, is the subject and the military uniform is the object. However, appropriating Willis' insight, during the post-socialist period, '*The woman wearing the red dress is the object produced by the red dress even while she is at the same time the producer producing herself as the product of the red dress.*' The first clause is that 'the woman wearing the red dress is the object produced by the red dress' – as I have explained above, the red dress is the subject and the woman who wears the red dress is the object. But what interests us here is the second clause: 'she is at the same time the producer producing herself as the product of the red dress.' On the surface, the woman who wears the red dress is the producer, or the subject. But in fact, the red dress is the subject, and she is the object – the product of the red dress. Therefore, the woman who wears the red dress, such as the fashion model or the middle-class female consumer, is simultaneously the subject and the object but, ultimately, the object. This is why she is the producer [read: the subject] producing herself [read: the object] as the product of the red dress.

In 'Work(ing) out', Susan Willis explains the workings of the dialectic of ideology and utopian impulse in US suburban culture. She details how the glimpse of the utopian impulse is immediately arrested and contained:

'In the nineteenth century, Marx wrote against the worker's alienation. He demonstrated that in selling labor power, the worker was separated both from control over production and from the fruits of labour, the commodities and profits from their sale. The contradiction of the commodity is that it can be absolutely divorced from the worker while at the same time it is the container of the worker's alienated labor [...] In such a [capitalistic] system, the utopian impulse often finds expression in the very forms that simultaneously articulate its containment. The image of a woman producing herself on the nautilus machine and Cindy Sherman dramatically posing into her self-activated camera are both expressions of women's deep desire to deny alienation. Both articulate the desire to seize control over the production and the commodity. Both demonstrate the utopian desire to be in control, to activate the machine. And they express the highly reified desire to be absorbed into the machine's function. Both express the utopian longing to no longer see one's alienated labor in the commodity, but do so by the dystopian formula of making the self into the commodity.'

(Willis, 1991: 77)

Willis appropriates Marx's insight regarding the contradiction of the commodity to point out that the utopian impulse often finds expression in the very forms that simultaneously articulate its containment. Focusing on American popular culture, she argues that the form can be detected in the way in which women use the workout machine to exercise. This form conjures the image of how women use the work-machine to produce and labour. Applying Willis' idea to Chinese consumer culture, I suggest that the form can also be detected in the way in which women consume their fashion (e.g., the red dress), which itself is a commodity and a form of containment. Appropriating Willis' explanation, I would argue that women's consumption of fashion commodities can be interpreted as their utopian desire to deny alienation (such as alienated labor), to seize control over production and the commodity, and to be in control of their everyday lives. It also demonstrates their unconscious utopian desire to activate their collective experience of being a subject of history. However, by doing so, they make themselves the very object that they try to seize control over in the first place. The utopian impulse is immediately arrested.

Conclusion: from gender to sexuality – the sexual politics of fashion and consumption

In the above, I presented the gendered dimensions of the revisionist and socialist narratives. In particular, I engaged with socialist narratives to argue against the revisionist narratives and point out the latter's contradictions and limitations. However, both narratives are in fact inadequate, because *the category of gender can only allow us to see the historical complexity of fashion, class, and ideology (production and consumption, sameness and difference, repression and liberation) from the vantage point of the discontinuity of the socialist and post-socialist periods.* A third narrative – one that deals with sexuality in addition to gender – is needed in order to articulate the complexity of the socialist and post-socialist orders of things.

What does sexuality allow us to see that cannot be otherwise perceived by gender? In what follows, I suggest that *if we engage with the category of sexuality to examine historical materials, we can see the continuity between the socialist and post-socialist periods. More specifically: if we use the category of queerness to provide a critique of the dominant regime of hetero-normativity, we are better positioned to observe the continuity between the socialist and the post-socialist periods.* Here, by queerness, I mean alternative modes of being a sexed or sexual subject in a world that does not subscribe to hetero-normative ideologies, such as the heterosexist understanding of bourgeois marriage, nuclear family, reproduction, futurity, and so on. In other words, 'queer' in this context can mean homosexuality, but it does not necessarily have to. In the following, I focus on two dimensions of the queer critique of hetero-normativity: first, the hetero-normative male gaze, and second, heterosexuality.

Indeed, it is the hetero-normative male figure that looks at the female figure in her fashion. This gaze is gendered *and* sexualized. When we bring in the critique of the hetero-normative male gaze to the analysis, the hetero-normative male figure is the subject, whereas the woman – whether in the military uniform or the red dress – is the object. During the socialist period, Chinese women were subjected to the hetero-normative male gaze that was the socialist party state. The object produced by the male gaze was the woman as the producer and the labourer. However, Chinese women were also subjected to the hetero-normative male gaze during the post-socialist period. Their bodies – including their fashion and the way they fashioned themselves – were objectified and commodified in the market economy. This time, the subject of the male gaze was the market. The object produced by the male gaze was the female consumer wearing her fashion.

This leads to the recognition that the *hetero-normative male gaze produces contradictory sexual subjects in both the socialist and post-socialist periods*. According to the revisionist narrative, because Chinese women were asked to wear proletarian clothes, Maoist socialism denied their femininities and sexualities and turned them into genderless and sexless beings. The repressive regime de-gendered and de-sexualized Chinese women. In response to the revisionist criticism, I would like to introduce the Chinese problem of overpopulation. Indeed, how can we explain the fact that there are more than 1.3 billion people in China today? It is precisely because Chinese people had a fair amount of *reproductive* sex during the socialist period. However, it is reasonable to speculate that Chinese people also had a fair amount of non-reproductive sex (based on desire, pleasure, sensuality, and eroticism) during the socialist period. In other words, if we believe the revisionist narrative, a contradictory sexual subject – one simultaneously de-sexualized and sexualized – was produced at that time.

According to the revisionist narrative, since Chinese women had the freedom to wear colourful clothes with diversified styles and to attend to their sexual appeal during the post-socialist period, they were liberated to become gendered and sexualized subjects. It is in this sense that Chinese women were interpreted as having become sexualized, or even hyper-sexualized, subjects in the consumption-oriented economy. However, it should be noted that since the early 1980s the one-child policy mandated by the party state has rendered Chinese women de-sexualized subjects and limited their sexual expressions. Despite the presence of non-reproductive (erotic) sex, the social morality imposed on Chinese women, their fashion, and their bodies worked to limit their sexual expression. In other words, another contradictory sexual subject – one simultaneously sexualized and de-sexualized was produced during the post-socialist period. It is this contradiction of the production of Chinese women as both sexualized and de-sexualized subjects is what unifies the socialist and post-socialist periods.

In this chapter's second section, 'The revisionist narrative and its discontents', I engaged in an intersectional analysis – one involving class and gender – in order to critique the revisionist narrative. But such a strategy proves to be inadequate in dealing with the complexity of the problem concerning fashion, gender, class, and ideology (e.g., production and consumption, sameness and difference, equality and inequality). In her essay, 'Against proper objects' (1994), the feminist and queer theorist Judith Butler urges her readers to bring gender and sexuality to the same analytical horizon for social investigation and cultural critique. She asks, 'How can we fuck with gender?' To elaborate on her question: How can we fuck with gender, without fucking according to the sexual norms set up by the regime of hetero-normativity? I end this chapter therefore by suggesting that a more vigorous intersectional approach, one that involves class, gender, sex, and sexuality (and ethnicity), is indispensable if we are to deal with the convoluted nature of this problem. We have to find a way to fuck with gender, class, ideology (and ethnicity) – all of them at once. In short, a Marxist queer critique is needed to confront the revisionist progress narrative cherished by the joint venture of global capital and the post-socialist party state. It will come soon.

Notes

1. After seeing the performance of the first Chinese fashion model team in the early and mid-1980s, the Western media exclaimed 'Mao's children are wearing fashion!' The statement was quoted in several Chinese magazines and TV shows.
2. In fact, the Chinese–English translation is not entirely accurate. According to Guo Moruo (1964: 7), Chairman Mao used *zhonghua ernü* (Chinese children), not *zhonghua nüer* (Chinese girls). *Zhonghua* refers to Chinese people, including men and women. *Ernü* means boys and girls, or sons and daughters, or children. In contrast, *nüer* means girls only. The embrace of military uniform is not limited to Chinese women only, it is extended to both Chinese men and women.
3. The Chinese–English translation is obtained from Finnane (2008: 231).
4. Source: *Maozhuxi yulu* (Mao Tse-tung, 1976). N.B. 'Sameness', or more precisely, 'equality' is gendered. Mao says that 'whatever male comrades can do, female comrades can also do too.' However, he does not say 'whatever female comrades can do – caring for children,

shopping, cooking, washing, cleaning, and working fulltime – male comrades can also do too' (Honig and Hershatter, 1988: 24–5). True gender equality should entail 'whatever male comrades can do, female comrades can do too' and 'whatever female comrades can do, male comrades can do too.' Mao was aware of the oppressiveness of certain kinds of clothes and accessories on Chinese women's bodies, such as 'tall buns and long skirts', 'facial makeup', 'jewelry on their hands', and 'pierced ears and bound feet'. Mao's feminist impulse can be found in his essay 'The Women's Revolutionary Army' (14 July 1919) in which he writes 'If a woman's head and a man's head are actually the same, and there is no real difference between a woman's waist and a man's, why must women have their hair piled up in those ostentatious and awkward buns? Why must they wear those messy skirts clinched tightly at their waist? I think women are regarded as criminals to start with, and tall buns and long skirts are the instruments of torture applied to them by men. There is also their facial makeup, which is the brand of a criminal; the jewelry on their hands, which constitutes shackles; and their pierced ears and bound feet, which represent corporal punishment. Schools and families are their prisons. They dare not voice their pain, nor step out from behind closed doors. If we ask, how can they escape this suffering, my answer is, only by raising a women's revolutionary army' (Mao Tse-tung, 1919, reproduced in Schram, Ed., 1992: 353).

5. For the distinction between the event and the era see Barlow (2012) on Wang Guangmei's *qipao*. For the distinction between the event and the pseudo-event see Slavoj Zizek's critique of Alain Badiou's works. For 'de-politicization' see Wang Hui (2008, 2011).

6. The original essay was published in a book in Chinese (Dai Jinhua, 1999).

7. It is a common strategy for the revisionists to characterize the socialist period as one filled with drab and monotonous colors. This is the viewpoint offered by Gong Yan, the hostess of the Chinese TV show *Fenguan fengyu: liushi niandai jingdian jiyi: shishang*. But, in response, Yi Zhongtian provided an interesting comment. Such 'sameness,' he said, should be seen as neatness or tidiness instead!

8. The last line comes from the famous Cultural Revolution Peking model opera *Zhiquweihushan* (*Taking Tiger Mountain by Strategy*). See: *http://blog.163.com/dys566@126/blog/static/22880145200723175413 8/*

9. The third plenum refers to the Third Plenum of the Eleventh Central

Committee Congress of the Chinese Communist Party which was held in December 1979.

10. For a psychoanalytical critique of choice see Salecl (2011). For a cartoon animation about choice see Salecl (n.d.a). For her lecture on 'The paradox of choice' see Salecl (n.d.b).

11. Cha Jianying said: 'the only way women could show a bit of their figure was by sewing in their blue uniform so that they could have a waist line.' Two points can be inferred from her statement. First, Chinese women's femininities were erased during the socialist period. Second, Chinese women resisted the state-imposed masculinization of their bodies by making minor adjustments to their clothes to make themselves look more feminine. However, what Cha expressed can be used to critique her own argument. When she said that Chinese women sewed in their uniform so that they could have a waistline, she was already pointing to the presence of gender differences in women's clothes. She had contradicted herself.

12. *http://www.wengewang.org/* is the address of China's Cultural Revolution Research website.

13. Evans then proceeded to argue that such gender differences were biologically determined and hierarchical.

14. For socialist androgyny see Young (1989: 253–68).

15. We need to do some theoretical work involving sex and gender, sameness and difference, and equality and inequality. What is our feminist utopia? Our feminist utopia should be one that recognizes multiple forms of sexes (men and women) and genders (masculinities and femininities), rather than one that eradicates sex (men and women) or abolishes gender (masculinities and femininities) as such. Our feminist utopia – a world of sex and gender equality and freedom – should be a privilege-less society in which the sex of an individual (male or female), or the gender of an individual (masculinity or femininity), should be considered as inconsequential to one's struggle for sex and gender liberation. One's sex and gender should not be regarded as the determining factor of the organization of society. On the one hand, rather than simply deny sex and gender, we should oppose essentialism or biological determinism; that is, the idea that sex and gender can serve to ground and legitimize hierarchical and oppressive social norms that put the sex and gender other in disadvantageous positions. We should reject the idea that sex and gender itself can carry any political, social, and economic implications. On the other hand, we should also reject nominalism that considers the sex and gender other as abstract, idealist, and

disembodied creatures. In other words, what we should demand is not the eradication of sex and gender as such, but rather the abolition of the *determining* effect of sex and gender. When we try to approach the problem from this perspective, then what should be radically critiqued is not sex or gender (or sexual or gender difference) as such, but rather sex or gender *determinism*. What needs to be rejected is sex or gender *inequality*.

16. For the differences between *nüxing* (the category of woman in the republican era), *funü* (the category of women in the socialist era), and *nüren* (the category of women in the post-socialist era), see Barlow, (1994: 253–89; 2004). For the category of *qingnian* (youth), see Wang Zheng (2001).

3

Learning to consume Tibet

Gabriel Lafitte

Abstract: Mass tourism inscribes onto Tibet a nation-building agenda, and a self-making pedagogy, wherein tourist consumption of Tibet makes one a model of modernity, a self-made individual of high human quality, having absorbed the master narrative of Tibet's eternal friendship with Han China. Tibet is now a booming tourism destination, and 97 per cent of the 13 million tourists in Lhasa each year are Han. Tibet not long ago was viewed, from urban China, as cold, remote, poor, and backward; somewhere to go to if posted, and you couldn't afford the bribe to be sent elsewhere. For the rural poor of Sichuan, Tibet is a sojourn, a chance to get rich and remit accumulated wealth to relatives back home. Apart from a few artists, no Han Chinese were attracted to Tibet. How did this turnaround happen? How was Lhasa reimagined, as a safe comfortable family-friendly attractive destination, where urban folk can learn to individuate, to become models of modernity and discriminating consumers of the state narrative of the iconic sites of Lhasa, all of them state owned and scripted? How has the party-state engineered a popular repositioning of Tibet as a new imaginary modelled largely on recycled Shangri-La fantasies that were long popular in Western modernity? Positive representations of eternal Tibet, drenched in supersaturated colour, now abound in Chinese media, featuring timeless custom-clad Tibetans. However, as recently as 2008, official media repetitively depicted Tibetans as looting, killing, smashing, and burning any Han. How can such cognitive dissonances coexist? Mass tourism does not supplant these negative stereotypes, but instead suffuses ahistoric timeless Tibet with a nimbus of mysticism.

Key words: consumption, self-making, individuation, imaginaries, mass tourism, scenic spots, iconic sites, theme parks, master narratives, pedagogy.

Mobility is inherent to modernity. Individuals prove themselves modern by their willingness to leave ancestral land, migrate from country to city, and reinvent themselves as urban workers and citizens of the nation-state. Learning to be an urban consumer is part of this project – both individual and national – of becoming modern, of high human quality (*suzhi*), and an active participant in all that is defined as advanced. Mobility, consumption and individuation come together to constitute contemporary Chinese tourism.

In rich countries, tourism is taken for granted as an indulgent hedonic pursuit, with little social significance beyond the collective impacts on the economy and environment. But in today's China, where mass tourism and even the concept of mandated leisure time are new, a more serious agenda exists, a discourse of the citizen's responsibility to individuate, through consumption of the iconic scenic sites owned and scripted by the party-state. This is illustrated by a case study of the recent boom in Han Chinese domestic tourism to Lhasa.

In Lhasa 97 per cent of the 13 million tourists in 2013 were Chinese, coming from the affluent cities of China's coast.[1] Their numbers already make Tibet a more popular tourist destination than India, Canada, or Sweden, if China's statistics are to be believed. If one adds the numbers currently touring key scenic spots of the Tibetan Plateau such as Jiuzhaigou (*Dzitsa degu* in Tibetan), Huanglong, Kailash (*Gang Rinpoche* in Tibetan), Labrang (*Xiahe* in Chinese) and Kumbum (*Ta'er* in Chinese), the total number of non-Tibetan tourists in Tibet is already close to 20 million a year, and overwhelmingly Han.

The newly rich of China can and do travel abroad, to the US, Europe, and tropical islands. They also go to Tibet, in extraordinary numbers. Lhasa is due, in 2015, to get 15 million tourists a year, in a city that officially has a population under 300,000. That is 50 tourists for each resident. Lhasa is now fast becoming not only a mass destination for Chinese tourists, but also a luxury destination, with a much bigger footprint. Surveys show China's new rich rank Lhasa high on their list of desirable destinations. According to a Hurun Rich List report on its face-to-face interviews with 150 Chinese millionaires in 2012: 'Sanya (Hainan Island), Hong Kong and Yunnan are the top three destinations in China, while Tibet rose to 4th place from 6th place last year.'[2]

Tibet has been successfully popularized, in the minds of urban Han Chinese, as a desirable destination, populated by fiercely loyal mastiff dogs, mysterious but benevolent monks, powerful lamas, exotic medicines that prolong life and potency, plus fun and adventure for all the family. Tibet, once seen as so lacking in oxygen that each breath may be

Figure 3.1 Han tourists taking photos in Lhasa's sacred places

your last, now features in urban minds as an escape from polluted city air, according to Wong (2013). Tibet has been given a new backstory, to make it familiarly Chinese. The astounding success of the ten-volume book series *The Tibet Code* by Sichuanese author He Ma revealed a market-driven appetite for action-packed adventure stories set in Tibet, with a Chinese Tibetan hero helping rescue Buddhist treasures from their Tibetan enemies.

When the Hollywood studio DreamWorks announced in 2013 it will make a movie of *The Tibet Code*, the studio was congratulated by Han Sanping, the chairman of China Film Group Corporation, the powerful state distributor, who ascribed a broader goal to *The Tibet Code*. He hailed it as a vehicle to portray to the world 'Chinese values' and 'Chinese morality' as well as its history, culture, and landscape. Tibetans see in such phrasing a deliberate attempt to erase the distinctive Tibetan culture. But to Han Sanping, an author of China's dominant discourse, that which is Tibetan is by definition Chinese, just as Tibetan medicine is by definition part of the grand story of Chinese medicine. So a contemporary Chinese fiction of medieval Tibet, owing much to *Indiana Jones* and *The Da Vinci Code*, is in Han Sanping's words:

> 'a vehicle to portray "Chinese values" to the world as well as its history, culture and landscape. This story is about various Chinese heroes' exploration, expedition and seeking history's roots. The characters represent traditional Chinese culture and Chinese morality.'
>
> (Han Sanping quoted in Zhang Rui, 2013)

This conflation and confusion of Chinese and Tibetan narratives fits well the official policy of downplaying ethnicity as a legal right inherent to a collective nationality, reducing it to the cultural choices of individuals. The official slogan is *jiakuai jingji fazhan, danhua minzu wenti*: 'speed up economic development, downplay the national question.'

When visiting Tibet in 2012, the tens of thousands of domestic tourists arriving daily by train, and more by air, make it seem inevitable that Tibet would become a major destination. Yet this is extremely recent. According to official statistics, the first year in which more than 100,000 Chinese tourists came to central Tibet was 1992, after Tibet Party Secretary Hu Jintao's 'strike hard' campaign against Tibetan expressions of discontent, and lengthy imposition of martial law. The first year in which one million came was 2004. The railway opened in mid-2006, and in that year 2.4 million domestic tourists came. In the first full year of rail arrivals, 2007, the number of domestic tourists leapt to 3.66 million, dipped in the following year of protests and crackdowns, then in 2009 grew again to 5.44 million and in 2010 to 6.62 million.[3] According to the World Bank, this makes Tibet a more popular destination for tourists than global arrivals in Norway, Sweden, Argentina, Brazil, or India; but one that has not yet caught up with Japan, South Africa, or Egypt.[4]

In 2007 tourism to Tibet was far smaller than domestic tourism to other exotic ethnic destinations within China. According to the 2008 edition of *China's Ethnic Statistical Yearbook*, the top ethnic minority destinations for domestic tourists in 2007 were Guangxi province, Yunnan, Inner Mongolia, Guizhou, Xinjiang, and Sichuan.[5] Tibet and Qinghai were far down the list, together attracting only 3 per cent of domestic tourists to minority nationality areas. Yet by 2015 the official target is 15 million domestic tourists arriving in central Tibet annually.[6] That is about the number of tourists visiting Canada or Greece.

Growth in tourist numbers on this scale is more than the natural workings of a market economy. This explosion in arrivals is an outcome of social engineering that required of central leaders a careful plan for not only the hard infrastructure of railways, museums, palaces, and theme parks, but equal attention to the soft infrastructure of changing the image of Tibet in the minds of China's newly prosperous urban masses. Soft infrastructure also includes legislation to reschedule holidays, and a mass campaign to persuade people to spend more on leisure and consumption generally.

The state is central to this spectacular growth in Tibet as a spectacle for mass consumption. Mobility is a central target of the Chinese state's dominant discourse of modernization, as well as a key instrument in the reproduction of that discourse. Not only is mobility viewed as an aid to economic growth but it is also regarded as an important attribute of the kind of modern society that China aspires to become and, as such, is intimately linked to the goal of 'civilizing' the nation.[7]

The price of a ticket all the way from Beijing to Lhasa – over 4000 kilometres – starts at RMB 289, rising to RMB 1262 for soft sleeper class. That's US$200, or 5 cents per kilometre of pressurized heated luxury. There are hundreds of millions of Chinese who can afford this, especially if the trip is designated as a 'study tour' by one's official work unit, which picks up the tab. In mid-2012 overall passenger traffic numbers since the rail track opened were announced. The line 'has transported 52.76 million passengers since going into operation on July 1, 2006,' said Bao Chuxiong, general manager of the Qinghai–Tibet Railway Company.[8]

Three million domestic Chinese tourists to Lhasa and central Tibet in 2007, 10 million in 2012, 15 million in 2015: these official figures may be rubbery. Cadres at lower levels know their prospects for promotion depend on reporting success in achieving target numbers for what has been mooted as a 'pillar industry' of the economy of China's Tibet™ for decades.[9] The numbers may be inflated by including the substantial 'floating population' of Han and Hui Muslim Chinese who come to Tibet to make money. Not only do they go back and forth on the railway on buying trips, they return to their own provinces in the months when few tourists come, and usually return home to stay, after a few sojourning years in Tibet accumulating wealth. Neither China's census, carried out every ten years, nor other official statistics enumerate this substantial population of sojourners, who may be hidden from view by using their numbers to swell the tourism statistics. But few visitors to Lhasa have any doubt that Lhasa is engulfed in tourists, and the numbers continue to rise rapidly.

The most recent and most spectacular staging of Tibetan history and culture, specifically intended for tourist consumption, was announced in 2013 when three mass entertainment companies combined to turn the best-selling Chinese fantasy book series, *The Tibet Code*, into a movie and, they announced, a theme park. The three companies involved are a Hollywood studio and two Chinese partners with global ambitions. The partnership was put together by DreamWorks, a studio keen to earn more from the booming Chinese movie market.

This planned movie, theme park, and branded merchandise has the lot: not only fiercely loyal Tibetan dogs, swords, spears, mystery, pacey action, but even Hitler and Stalin play roles in exhibiting the universal fascination with Tibet. *Tibet Code* is preoccupied with the external artefacts of Tibetan mysticism, as power objects to be sought and fought over, much as the mysteriously powerful ritual objects of the Catholic Church feature in *The Da Vinci Code*. These sacra are at once wondrous and fearsome, long dead yet still alive, with a power to confer power or wreak harm, an ambivalence deeply felt in modern life. *The Tibet Code* does not hesitate to throw in both Joseph Stalin and Adolf Hitler, both supposedly despatching secret missions to capture that power for their evil ends, each preoccupied with Tibet as a mysterious source of power.

Lowland Chinese readers are invited to take all this as real, and conflate ninth with twenty-first century Tibet as a fixed identity. If this is now made into a movie and theme park, for the sake of DreamWorks' bottom line, all the high-tech computer-generated imagery deployed will heighten the viewer's sense that this is real. Tibet will be the playground of China's desires and fears, dungeons and dragons, wizards and spells, heroic mastiffs and evil kings, worlds of warcraft, games of thrones, rollicking adventure, romantic moments, speaking parts for Hitler and Stalin, and all of it real.

The Tibet Code first appeared in 2008 as the craze for Tibetan mastiffs peaked. This coincided with the rise of the Wenzhou model of private entrepreneurialism, and the arrival of the *laoban*, or boss (Cao Nanklai, 2011). The dogs bred by Tibet's pastoral nomads to guard tents while owners were away out on the pasture became an obsession among China's newly rich boss class. In a society based on *guanxi*, on networks of connections and exclusive loyalties, on factions of insiders clustered around powerful individuals, the mastiff embodied the ideal follower of the boss (*laoban*). The mastiff is fiercely loyal to its owner, and fiercely hostile to outsiders. Bosses paid outrageous amounts to buy mastiffs, in a bidding war to consume mastiffs and display wealth and power. The mastiff craze led to Tibet fever. The possibility that in a remote Tibetan area lives the ultimate mastiff, the purple unicorn, seems plausible.

The Tibet Code is the prime example of the 'Tibet fever' that swept China. So many books by Chinese authors are set in Tibet, past or present, giving the author licence to make improbably exaggerated plot moves seem believable. Anything can happen in Tibet. One of the latest 'Tibet fever' novels is the saucy story of a Tibetan man at the command of his Chinese lover. The Ethnic ChinaLit blogger Bruce Humes describes it: 'Chan Koonchung, the Beijing-based, HK-born author of *The Fat Years* has just launched his new, sure-to-be-controversial novel in Chinese, entitled *The Unbearable Dreamworld of Champa the Driver*. The tale is written from the point of view of a young Tibetan man who is a volunteer for an animal protection NGO and also serves as a security guard at a hotel enigmatically named after the CCP's key "maintain stability" policy, not to mention his other "identity"   as lover to a Han woman.'

Chan Koonchung's *Champa the Driver* is the new erotica, featuring the dream lover as a masculine heroic Tibetan dedicated to saving wildlife, when he is not servicing his Han mistress. This is no more odd, as a fantasy, than the rollicking plot of *The Tibet Code*, which, as translator Joel Martinsen says: 'revolves around a grand quest for the wonders of Tibet's legendary past: the treasures of a lost temple, the race of mystics who guarded it, and a massive, ferocious variety of Tibetan Mastiff, known in the historical records as the Purple Qilin.' This is China's grand new orientalist fantasy, Shangri-La reborn.

Tibet is a perfect blank canvas on which to project all of China's current anxieties, fears, hopes, and contradictions. And why not? After all, until quite recently, very few Han Chinese had been to Tibet, fewer still had had any meaningful contact with actual Tibetans, and Tibetans cannot speak up and critique what is published and filmed. [10]

Not long ago Tibet was popularly seen by Han Chinese lowlanders as unnaturally cold, so lacking in oxygen as to threaten life, a remote and barren place no one would choose to go to voluntarily. The people were known to be dirty, superstitious, stagnant, and violently ungrateful for everything China has done for them. As recently as 2008 official media endlessly repeated that Tibetans kill, loot, smash, and burn everything Chinese. Surely the 'Tibet fever' that *Tibet Daily* reporter Gao Yujie writes about has to be an improvement?

China's home-grown orientalism, like the historic orientalism of Europe towards west Asia, ascribes fixed roles and identities to its exotic objects. The Tibetans are required to play their part in a Beijing-based script. The scripted role for Tibetans is to be forever on the way to modernity, without ever reaching their goal of achieving a level of civilization equivalent to the urban Chinese who come to Lhasa as tourists. This is an unresolved tension. If Tibetans remain 'backward', 'ungrateful', and 'uncivilized', tourists will not feel welcome or even safe. If Tibetans adopt Chinese ways and language, thus improving their human quality in Chinese eyes, and becoming more civilized and employable in Chinese enterprises, they lose their exotic appeal, and will compete with politically reliable Han Chinese immigrants for hospitality industry jobs. So Tibetans must forever be in between, striving but not yet succeeding in becoming more modern, in recognizably Chinese ways. This is the paradox: Tibetans are not permitted to turn their backs on Chinese modernity, but they may not succeed either. They cannot fail but they cannot win. This internal contradiction inherent in China's mass tourism industry and overall policy towards Tibet is at the core of the unique brand China has invented: China's Tibet™. The agenda of this logo is that Tibet must be different, but not too different. It must be exotic, a mirror of otherness held to the visage of the visitor, yet also safe, familiar, domestic, with the reassurance that in China's Tibet™ all Tibetans love China, and as a destination Tibet is not only safe but even comfortable.

In these ways central authorities achieve a 'narrative uniformity that is enforced upon and over lead tourism sites [which] constitutes a form of cultural grammar by and through which the state defines travel itineraries and controls the meaning held over landscape, space, and place' (Hollinshead and Hou, 2012: 228). Cheng Yan points out that: 'the pursuit of collective and monolithic national imagery has caused a representational violence, one that is committed by the nation-state ideology operated through the organisation of tourism language' (Cheng Yan, 2010: 86).

In order to stage a daily spectacle in Lhasa, a story 14 centuries old, cherished by Tibetans and long forgotten by China, has been turned inside out. The T'ang dynasty Princess Wencheng is loved in Tibet for bringing a precious statue of Buddha to Tibet 14 centuries ago. It survives today in central Lhasa's Jokhang Temple, still blessing pilgrims who pray with great devotion. This is no longer the crux of the story, since China is at best ambivalent about Buddhism, and hostile towards Tibetan Buddhism. The central message now is of a brave young woman daring to traverse the wilds of Tibet to go as far as Lhasa, in order to spread the seeds of Chinese agriculture, civilization, and benevolence towards the backward.

The deepest irony is that, throughout, China's stance towards Tibet has taken its cues from the west. The ideas that most shaped modern Tibet were those of Karl Marx and Lewis Henry Morgan. China's embrace of Marx, to save China from humiliation by imperialism, led to compulsory class war in Tibet as well as the violent denunciation and liquidation of the educated class. China's embrace of Morgan, a largely forgotten pioneer anthropologist of American Indian tribes, is far less well known. It was Morgan who insisted that all human societies can be ranked in order of the stage of human evolutionary progress they have made. At the bottom and at the very top are communist societies of complete equality, so the path of human evolution requires ascending the ladder, from primitive communism to post-bourgeois communism. In between are slave societies, feudal societies, and capitalist societies. Anthropology, even in the 19th century, moved on from this rigid typology, which insisted that the evolutionary ladder is a law of nature. But Morgan's 'law' was woven into the communism of Stalin's Soviet Union and Mao's China, which has never repudiated it. Tibet, classified as a feudal society bedevilled by superstition and parasitical lamas, had to be liberated from itself. These were European ideas that impacted on Tibet.

Enmeshed market forces and state control combine in Tibet to rapidly make Tibet a major tourism destination. Directive state slogans, plus the wealth-creating energy of tourism enterprises, combine to impose fixed roles on the people who are the magnet for the entire tourism experience – the Tibetans. The most powerful driver of the tourist influx is the modern quest for a unique essential individual self. This quest has been embraced by the newly wealthy urban middle class of China, and Tibet is its foil. Tibet has become a polymorphous space wherein a modern civilized cosmopolitan unique identity as an advanced Chinese citizen can emerge. But this quest for a fixed identity requires that Tibetans also occupy a fixed position, opposite to the modern. Tibetans must be happy, always smiling, dancing, simple pre-modern folk, children of nature, timeless and exotic, outside of history.

Fifteen years after the 1996 Ninth Tibet Autonomous Region (TAR) Five-Year Plan announced tourism as a 'pillar industry', all is changed. Fast comfortable long-haul trains leave China's key metropolitan cities daily for Lhasa, the ticket prices heavily subsidized. Air travel, in order to compete, has become cheaper. Endless TV documentaries and soap operas of Chinese heroes selflessly serving the Tibetan masses have familiarized mass Chinese audiences with Tibet. New prosperity and the pace of city life encourage Chinese to holiday in Tibet. Tour companies, hotels, taxis, brothels, karaoke bars, and nightclubs have multiplied. Prawns and other seafood delicacies are flown in from coastal provinces daily. Lhasa is booming.

Tibet, Lhasa, the Potala, and other iconic places are, in marketing terms, long-established famous brands with a high level of recognition, but which are only now able to monetize the value inherent in their brand identity. Thus the visitors to the new upmarket hotels in Lhasa will be international tourists, who want both exotic sights and comfort. Yet most visitors to Tibet will now be Han Chinese, even in the upmarket hotels. Many of the new hotel chains investing in Lhasa specialize in business and convention travellers, and are also experienced in the construction of in-house shopping malls featuring exclusive boutique stores selling luxuries at high prices. Such facilities will appeal to Chinese enterprises, Party organs, professional organizations, trade conferences, and the new rich of China generally. What makes such venues so attractive is their combination of luxury banqueting options, luxury accommodation and leisure facilities, the latest communications technologies, boutique shops selling not only global luxury brands but also Tibetan aphrodisiacs, furs, and guaranteed cures for the ailments of age. Add in nightclubs, business centres, conference halls, and discreet meeting rooms for private business, and the mix is just right for a party-state with many ministries, bureaus, think tanks, and official leading groups, all wanting new venues to network, conduct their work reports, and conspicuously consume.

The hotel chains now building in Lhasa already have properties in China's big cities, often several, and the addition of Lhasa enables them to offer international tourists, including business travellers, a complete package, full of incentives such as introductory pricing and special rates to ensure Lhasa quickly takes its place as a profit centre. The emerging hotel economy in Tibet does more to integrate Tibet into the Chinese economy than any other private investment ever has. It further exaggerates the role of the tertiary services sector as the source of urban Tibetan employment and wealth creation. For decades, as Beijing poured money into Tibet, employment was dominated to an extraordinary extent for a poor region by administrative, logistics, freight-handling, and security personnel, all in the service industries. While primary producers – Tibet's pastoral nomads and farmers in the countryside – were neglected and attracted little finance, and secondary manufacturing industry in TAR developed slowly, tertiary employment raced ahead. The split between primary, secondary, and tertiary in the TAR is more like that of a large modern highly developed city such as Beijing or Shanghai. Now, hospitality and retail are set to boom in Lhasa as well.

But it is not only the construction of new luxury resorts and hotels, even casinos, that makes Tibet Chinese. The party-state, as we shall see, also achieves its objective by controlling the master narrative told to visitors as they stroll the iconic sites, accompanied everywhere by guides who have graduated in a master discourse taught formally in provincial and national tour-guiding academies according to a strictly governed syllabus. The message is that Tibetans and Han Chinese are friends, eternal friends, necessary friends, and indeed lovers whose destinies are entwined, ever since Kongjo (Princess) Wencheng of the Tang dynasty, married Tibetan emperor Songtsen Gampo 14 centuries ago.

The party-state may be paying a high price in capital expenditure on infrastructure – roads, airports, urban facilities, telecommunications – to make mass tourism possible; but the payoff is also big. The party-state gets to tell its version of Tibetan-ness, not only to the millions of Han Chinese visitors, but also to Tibetans. This dominant discourse, the only one allowed in the public sphere, eventually becomes absorbed, and Tibetans gradually start to believe they are lazy and backward, and in need of China's vigour and advanced approach. There is plenty of ethnographic evidence, from anthropologists such as Yeh (2007) that Tibetans do internalize this hegemonic discourse, and start to believe themselves inferior to the entrepreneurial Han. Yeh argues that 'A Gramscian analysis of contradictory consciousness is critical to understanding the trope of indolence, which is both a performative speech act and a reference to patterns of labor and time allocation. The trope is informed by contemporary state development discourse and national value-codings of "quality" under economic reform, as well as culturally, historically, and religiously constituted notions of proper work.' China's hegemony in China's Tibet^{TM}, she argues, leads to Tibetans internalizing the master narrative that positions Tibetans as indolent, and Han as industrious.

Deng Xiaoping, architect of China's conquest of Tibet, is best remembered for a pithy slogan China took to heart: 'to get rich is glorious'. To get rich is to have choices – if rich enough, infinite choices. For poor people, in a poor country in which revolutionary ideology made everyone equal, but equally poor, the prospect of choice was delicious. Choice is individual, that is its point. Choice individuates me from you. I like this, you like that. In the great democracy of relativism and consumption, we each make our choices. To have choice is to become a self, an individual, a unique person. To have choice is to become modern.

Deng's famous slogan decisively defined the end of statist domination of the economy, and opened China to the world, to enterprise and wealth creation. The command economy, in which everything is owned, allocated, and directed by the state, was officially buried by Deng's new slogan. That remains the dominant story of China's endless rise ever since Deng spoke.

If the state was yielding to an inborn innate human desire to accumulate, the last thing one might expect is that the state would have to instruct the masses how to consume. Surely the core attraction of consumer choice is that I can experiment, buying this and that, making mistakes, discovering by doing, finding what gives me the greatest satisfaction? Yet in China the ingrained Confucian statist tradition did find it necessary to establish a pedagogy of consumption, teaching the newly rich how to consume properly. Learning how to consume was part of learning how to be modern, civilized, of high human quality (*suzhi*) – it is the new form of the Confucian tradition of self-cultivation. However, the self to be cultivated is the modern self, a uniquely individual subjective self that seeks to express itself through its desires, choices and through consumption of goods and services.

Education in consumption focused on the novel concept of consumer rights. Consumers should learn to discriminate between good and bad-quality goods, to understand the responsibilities of manufacturers for their products, especially foreign companies in China, which can be held accountable by consumer campaigns. After all, in the rich countries consumers are vocal, confident they can return shoddy goods and expect a refund, or in more serious cases demand bad corporate actors be prosecuted. Mobilizing consumers would seem to be just part of the withdrawal of the state, making room for individuals to assert their rights.

But in China rights are not inborn; they are granted by the state, and what is granted can always be withdrawn. Rights extended by the state to individuals must be properly exercised in order that China, collectively as a nation-state, prospers, proves to the world it is an advanced civilization, with educated consumers ensuring product quality control. To China, this is all so obvious, it does not need stating. Consumption is patriotic, it makes money go round, it visibly raises living standards, it sets new benchmarks for others to aspire to. It is the modern alternative to the peasant mentality of saving, hiding money under the mattress as the only insurance against hardship, illness, or accident.

There has been intense pressure on China from abroad to increase consumption, elevating consumption as a solution to China's problems, a key to enduring prosperity, and an end to reliance on exports in a world of capitalist crises that destroys as well as creates demand and consumption. This global discourse, led by economists and governments, and most of all by global corporations keen to sell to Chinese consumers, considers as unnatural China's ongoing reliance on state investment to boost growth. To a remarkable extent China's GDP and growth rate are driven by massive state spending on infrastructure, with consumption being only one third of the total economy. This, the economists say, is unsustainable, unbalanced, and vulnerable to collapses in global demand for the products of the world's factory. More consumption is the answer. In any 'normal' rich country, consumption is at least two thirds of the total economy, so China has far to go. This global pressure on China to foster greater consumption has made consumption another mission of the state, built into official Five-Year Plans, almost an ideology, another benchmark of China's success.

Economists have been urging China to promote consumption for decades, and the Asian Financial Crisis of 1997, with its faltering of international demand for China's manufactured goods, saw decisive state intervention to boost domestic consumption. In 1998 tourism was declared a new key growth area of the national economy. In 1999 the state proclaimed mandatory provision by work units of three weeks of holiday time, at the lunar New Year in early spring, the national day celebrating the founding of the People's Republic in October, and the annual May Day festivities. These three 'golden weeks' of paid leave, as everyone calls them, put in place the preconditions for making China itself an object of consumption. This would seem to be a step towards making China a 'normal' modern country, since tourist mobility is so central to global modernity.

Tourism usually means individual hedonism, and a hedonic economy based on satiating individual desires, fantasies, and expectations. The individual pursuit of happiness through mobility is inherent in modernity, as is the assumption by economists that the purpose of economic activity is hedonic consumption. Individuals individuate themselves, discovering their unique identity and chosen lifestyle, experimenting with various selves by travel, sometimes to highly predictable places where fantasies of sophisticated consumption are acted out. Resorts and cruises magnetize customers with the promise that even ordinary folk can pretend to be aristocrats waited on by servants. Sometimes travel is to unpredictable places where tourists have licence to behave in ways unacceptable at home, discovering new boundaries of the self by gorging on drugs, sex, food, or other sensual pleasures. Modern tourism is about me, discovering me, being me. It is about freedom, mobility, a carefree break from the responsibilities of being a law-abiding citizen. Tourism and the state are poles apart.

Not so in China. The revolutionary era under Mao had a puritan suspicion of tourism as bourgeois, unproductive, and wasteful. Mobility was tightly restricted by the *hukou* system which designated everyone as resident of a specific rural or urban area, with limited permission to travel. When people did travel, it was en masse, in disciplined cohorts coming, for example, to be present at a mass rally in Tiananmen Square. The pre-revolutionary tradition of travel was part of the Confucian tradition of self-cultivation, by which the literati could manifest their high quality and good taste by visiting iconic scenic spots, soaking up the famous view, perhaps even taking up the calligraphic brush to pen a few poetic lines inspired by nature or an old temple.

Post-revolutionary China has reverted to the Confucian model of tourism as self-improvement and cultivation of patriotic sentiment, combined with technologies of mass transit enabling the masses to become exemplary too. Everyone could become a model tourist, improving their civilized human quality, contributing to the national level of spiritual civilization by patriotically learning 'to express the infinity of one's feelings towards the rivers and mountains of the Fatherland', to quote a 1988 tourism manual.[11] This is emotion work, a category of labour required to harmonize the self with the patriotic agenda of the state. The self must learn to become an individuated self, yet in harmony with the party-state.

Anthropologist Pal Nyiri describes the invention of modern tourism in China as somewhat like Sanskritization in India, a learning to copy the ways of the upper class, 'All of a sudden, tourism gained prominence as a lifestyle attribute of the higher-income urban population and began spreading. The state's role, both administrative and pedagogical, in engineering this change cannot be overestimated. While the crucial 1998 decision to promote tourism was justified in terms of economic development, it coincided with the appearance of the term 'leisure culture' (*xiuxian wenhua*) in the government's 'civilization campaigns' as an attribute of the 'modern and civilized citizen/bourgeois (*shimin*).' Tourism in China is understood by its managers as the consumption of bounded and controlled zones' (Nyiri, 2010: 62).

The manager of tourism is the state, at national and lower levels, since tourism is defined (and statistically monitored) as visitation to famous scenic spots, places symbolic of the Communist Party's road to power, re-enactments of historic ceremonies, and the quaint customs of ethnic groups. 'As far as the state and the tourism business are concerned, the map of China consists of a network of scenic spots ranging from imperial palaces and revolutionary memorials to nature reserves and fenced villages. The desire to travel could once again be the desire to validate one's knowledge of canonical representations. New catalogues and encyclopaedias of scenic spots expanded the list from traditional landscapes of literati travel (reconfigured as proof of a rich national culture) to landscapes symbolic of the Communist victory and the birth of New China' (Nyiri, 2010: 62–3).

> 'By the late 1980's, one could not visit or live in China without encountering an abundance of museum displays, television programs, dance extravaganzas, and theme parks displaying images of the charming and distinctive dances, clothing, dwellings, and customs of China's 55 "minority nationalities".'
>
> (Mueggler, 2002)

China's domestic tourism surge into Tibet began the year the rail line to Lhasa opened for traffic in 2006. That was the year domestic tourism took off all over China, especially for urban Chinese to visit the countryside and ethnic minority regions. Not only was there a groundswell of demand from newly rich urban dwellers, there was also a recognition in rural areas that tourism could be effective in poverty alleviation. At local, provincial, and national levels, tourism was promoted as a way of enhancing consumption, wealth accumulation, off-farm incomes, and of becoming civilized and modern. The concept of civilized tourism (*wenming luyou*) was the centrepiece of a mass campaign instructing newly rich city dwellers how to differentiate themselves behaviourally from lower-quality rural folk (Chio, 2009: 54). As Chio says, 'planners specifically invoked tourism as a viable means of promoting economic and social progress in rural areas' (Chio, 2009: 46). The official slogans of this campaign emphasized what is missing from hectic urban lives lived among strangers. They key word was *nongjiale*, which can be translated as 'joyous peasant life', or 'happy farmers' home' or 'peasant family happiness'. As Chio (2009: 47) puts it, 'The concentration on domestic tourism and tourists in 2006 effectively directed the focus of tourism onto discourses of progress through personal effort and continued central state contributions to the betterment of national unity and rural livelihoods.'

Only a few years earlier, Tibet was a hardship posting for Han Chinese, inconceivable as a tourist destination. According to the statistics of the Tibet Tourism Bureau the number of Chinese citizens coming to Tibet as tourists in 1985 was 241. By 1988 this had risen to 386, then as martial law was imposed, in official response to Tibetan unhappiness, the number in 1989 dropped to 247. However, the number of Han Chinese on official business trips to Tibet, for Tibet work forums, inspection tours, and party conferences was put at 12,000 a year and likely to rise.

The United Nations World Tourism Organization 1990 *Master Plan for the Future Development of Tourism in Tibet* – a document of hundreds of pages – scarcely mentions domestic Chinese tourism. That Tibet would become a desirable destination for domestic travellers was inconceivable. On the basis of available figures, the UN WTO forecast the future of tourism in Tibet lay with international arrivals. Tibet in 1990 was a command economy. Government hostels were built for official visitors, sparing the expense of hotels, while keeping them under surveillance. Tourism throughout China in 1990 was still an official oligopoly run by just three nationwide, state-owned travel services, CITS, CTS, and CYTS, so much so that the 1990 *Yearbook of China Tourism Statistics* numbers on international arrivals consists of three tables, enumerating the tourists received by each of these three official hosting agencies.

The UN WTO's growth strategy forecast that by 2010 Chinese domestic tourist arrivals in Tibet might rise to 3400. The actual number was more than 2000 times that. That the UN's expert consultants got it so utterly wrong is instructive. This is a failure not only of statistics and the way they are trending, but of imagination. That Tibet might be engineered to occupy a new position in the popular rich urban Han Chinese imagination was, in 1990, to Hong Kong–based consultants, unimaginable.

A major aspect of becoming a nation of consumers is turning China itself into a product for consumption. Learning to be a tourist in China has been a state-driven pedagogy in itself, with many new meanings to be taught. For a start, people had to learn to take holidays, and for long enough to reach distant places. The state was responsible for mandating sufficient holiday time to stimulate consumption, and for providing affordable high-speed mass transport by rail, to reach distant destinations within the holiday time allotted by the state. But the responsibilities of the state do not end there.

Many destinations are managed by the state, and the tourist experience in historic places is carefully staged, to ensure the right patriotic message is transmitted. This is especially true in Tibet.

While the government tried to shape domestic tourism, the drive to build it came from below, from local initiatives to grow rich, and it was only later that the state caught up. Throughout China, with one exception, domestic tourism is in the hands of local communities and local leaders, who decide what to build, what to stage, where and how to represent themselves, maximize benefits, minimize downsides, and control the tourism experience.[12] That one exception is Tibet, where the state superimposes its compulsory narrative, owns iconic scenic spots, and directs the tourist experience.

The many millions now sufficiently wealthy to have both time and money for a 'golden week' holiday need training, especially if they are to be encouraged to go to Tibet, a destination Chinese people have tended to regard with trepidation, because it seems unnaturally cold, the air thin, and very remote.

The tourism industry is developing fast, but still relies heavily on state infrastructure and state tutelage of citizens to get across the message that travel to Tibet is no longer a hazardous frontier plunge for unattached men, but is now a safely tamed destination for families. The eternal love theme of the Princess Wencheng Theme Park makes a brave Chinese young woman the central character in a romance that binds two peoples forever together, a romance that feminizes Tibet and makes Lhasa a honeymoon destination, a fast-growing category of China's domestic tourism.

Overcoming ingrained distaste for Tibet has been a major achievement, involving market forces and state exhortations to model exemplary behaviour. Now it is a manifestation of having a civilized attitude, and high human quality, if one takes the trouble to visit the key tourist sights of Tibet, all of them owned and operated by the state, ingesting the state discourse. The state has invested heavily in not only the hard infrastructure of a train capable of getting people from Beijing (or Shanghai) to Lhasa in 48 hours, but also the soft infrastructure of staging spectacles on site at key scenic spots. China has been understandably proud of the engineering achievement, building a single track south to Lhasa from the heavy industrial extraction enclave of Gormo in northern Tibet. But, in order to reach Lhasa as quickly as possible, along the almost 2000 km traverse of the Tibetan Plateau, there are only two brief stops.

Similarly, the soft infrastructure of iconic sights in Lhasa is also carefully staged, especially for the 10 million Chinese domestic visitors now arriving in Lhasa each year. This is an extraordinary accomplishment, firstly of logistics, but also of persuasion, instruction, branding, master narrative construction, as well as social and mechanical engineering.

In the 1990s, and earlier, Han Chinese were posted in Tibet, often against their own preferences, or came seeking their fortunes when peasant farming or village enterprises in their own provinces became uneconomic. Tibet was an unappealing destination, not only for cultural reasons of strangeness and difference, but for the most visceral of reasons: one might well die there of the extreme unnatural cold, or of altitude sickness in the dangerously thin air. Deeply ingrained traditional Chinese beliefs attach great importance to maintaining essential life energy in balance by avoiding extremes of heat or cold. Intense and persistently cold places are viewed as unnatural and life threatening. Those who do live in such places can only be imagined to lead brutal lives lacking choice. Who would not escape to more congenial climates if they could?

Tibet came under effective actual Chinese governance from the 1950s on. Inbuilt Chinese cultural settings made Tibet a highly masculine place for the pioneering Han, the brave and bold, the ideologically driven, the fortune hunter, and even the revolutionary martyr. They ate bitterness in order to instruct Tibetans in how to speak bitterness by denouncing landlords as class enemies to be liquidated.

In today's China, this is an ancient memory, barely believable and seldom mentioned. The embedded imaginary of Tibet was turned around, in this century, by a major campaign to reposition Tibet in Chinese minds, especially in the imaginaries of the newly rich urban Chinese who had money and time for leisure. The Tibetan Plateau became an object of curiosity and even wonder, an exotic jewel at the remotest reaches of inland China, an antithesis of everything familiar. The mountains, verdant pastures, the profuse flowering of the alpine meadows in summer became favourite topics for photographers, and for a proliferation of popular magazines that gave special emphasis to Tibet or were dedicated specifically to representing Tibet. In the twentieth century, only a few Chinese went to Tibet by choice, notably artists, writers, and film makers. One of the best known was the short story writer Ma Jian, whose 1987 *Stick Out Your Tongue* projected his alienation from communist ideology onto a Tibetan landscape which he populated with bizarre and surreal events that readers took as largely factual. Landscapes more familiar to Chinese readers would not have worked: Ma Jian's blurring of realism and hallucination, the mundane and the fantastic, required a Tibetan location.[13]

In the twenty-first century, the new representations of Tibet were lyrical, even romantic. The colours were lush, supersaturated. The landscapes were dramatic, evocative of a natural paradise that was the opposite of the urban luxury surrounding the reader. The magazines became glossier, their advertisements for luxury cars ever more upmarket. It was not only for foreign tourists that the Tibetan prefecture of Yunnan province was renamed Shangri-La; Chinese too yearned for a pure land, a Shangri-La of pristine natural purity.

This burgeoning of selective images of Tibet was largely commercial and quite profitable for magazine and documentary producers in the years before Han Chinese actually took the journey, to take their own photos modelled on the scenes they had drunk in for years. Official slogans meshed with the romantic prose of documentary voice-overs, and popular movies such as *The Touch* (2002), starring Michelle Yeoh, went even further, making Tibet the source of mystical cosmic truths.[14]

The timing of the rail line into Lhasa was perfect. It began operation in 2006, its single track giving priority to passenger traffic over the occasional freight train. The opening was accompanied by a blaze of nationalistic self-congratulation that China had triumphed in constructing, against all odds, overcoming all obstacles, the highest rail line in the world, through 'no man's land'. So it became part of patriotic red tourism to take the train, from Guangzhou, Shanghai, or Beijing, all the way to Lhasa.

How did Tibet get such a makeover, transforming it from a dangerous land for revolutionary martyrs to family holiday destination, and the fashionable location for a honeymoon? If one visits a bookstore or video outlet in any major Chinese city, there are many glossy magazines, documentaries and all ten volumes of *The Tibet Code*. Again, this is quite new. If one looks at the trilingual compendiums of all books on Tibet published in China, in Chinese, Tibetan, or English, there is not even a category for tourist guides.[15] In the bibliography covering 1949 to 1991, the only books on travel in the first three decades were war reminiscences by invading People's Liberation Army commanders, and books praising the heroism of the highway construction workers who followed. It was not until the 1980s that any publications in Chinese began listing the 'scenic spots' of Tibet. The first map for tourists to Lhasa published in China was issued in 1980, over a decade after tourist maps to Jiuzhaigou, a scenic corner of Tibet accessible from Chengdu, Sichuan's capital, were popularized. The first books in China showing enthusiasm for Tibet started in 1987 with *Yearnings for the Paradise of the Snowland* (1987).[16] In 1990 came *Tibet: Land of Mystery*, in English, aimed at an international market, a coffee table book of photos, with a text translated from Chinese. From these gradual beginnings has come the explosion of Chinese representations of Tibet as a safe comfortable yet romantic travel destination.

No longer the terrain of the intrepid and desperately poor Han Chinese, Tibet became a consumable. The magazines running lengthy colour features on Tibet grew fatter and glossier, pricier and more alluring. The Hong Kong–based *China Tourism* English language monthly long led the way, and sold binders to preserve past issues, for readers unlikely to actually travel. It was full of the rhetoric of the picturesque sublime. Dechen prefecture (later officially renamed Shangri-La) is 'a dreamland to many travellers ... Thrilling panoramas, unpolluted fresh air and the colourful traditional lifestyles of the various ethnic minorities ... This charming highland has an untold capacity to refresh one's spirit and soul ... I was intoxicated by the vivid images of the glorious landscape.'[17]

The first person singular is important to such stories, not only as proof of eyewitness, but because self-making is at the core of modernity. Tibet is a backdrop to a Chinese drama, the making of individual consuming selves. No one in China underestimates what a dramatic change this is, encouraging the swelling of desire without triggering desire for democracy, or a yearning for a voice, which could overthrow the regime. But it is a Chinese drama staged in Tibet, in which Tibetans are incidental.

The most important consumable is the photo of the Chinese tourist against a Tibetan backdrop, Tibetan architecture, a rosy-cheeked smiling Tibetan girl at one's side. The photo is for consumption back home, proof that one is modern, adventurous, cosmopolitan, civilized, and of high human quality. Chinese tourists make so much effort to take shots they do not look carefully at the objects of the lens, nor do they attempt to talk with Tibetans, who seldom have much Chinese. Cameras intrude into the most sacred of mind-purifying pilgrimage activities, such as the culmination of a pilgrimage across Tibet to reach the holiest of holies – the Jokhang Temple in Lhasa – now snapped endlessly and intrusively. In the early years of mass tourism, would-be tourists were given earnest detailed instructions on how to take the iconic photo of the iconic scenic spot from exactly the right angle. The idea was to enhance the individual self-making by the tourist, through taking the 'representative and typical' view found on postcards (Nyiri, 2006: 64–6). Today, no one needs such instructions. Everyone has subconsciously absorbed so many media images of Tibet that pointing and clicking the iconic, editing out the modern, is automatic.

Woeser, the Tibetan essayist and public intellectual, has written feelingly of this uncaring intrusion into the inner life of Buddhist pilgrims. Around the Jokhang, Tibetans viewed through the distancing mechanism of the camera close-up congregate most densely, and behave most differently from Chinese norms. If one wants to reinforce the social cohesion of being Han Chinese, by capturing Tibetan difference, there is no better place than the throng of worshippers around the Jokhang. Because the Jokhang magnetizes Tibetans, Chinese tourists in turn are attracted to the site. Since manifesting oneself as an individual, desiring and desirable, is the subtext of tourism, there is a need for a place for Han to flirt, date, hook up, and seduce each other. Where better than the epicentre – the Jokhang?

It says much about the camera that sees all and the human eye behind it that sees nothing, that the Chinese 'romance wall' came to be located right opposite the Jokhang cathedral. On witnessing this, Woeser wrote, in 2010: 'I have encountered those "Tibet Drifters" sitting at the main entrance of Jokhang Temple laughing, giggling and snuggling up to each other. Cigarettes dangle from their lips; they drink beer and sunbathe while watching Tibetans prostrating. They gaze and stare and while laughing and giggling, they also go and prostrate a few times as if it was just some kind of game, just some type of popular amusement.'[18]

In 2011, Woeser wrote:

'The so-called "Romance Wall" originally served as a place for pilgrims to offer thousands of butter lamps in small cups and as a place for those prostrating to take a rest. But after it was transformed into the "Romance Wall", it was often occupied by tourists looking for a slice of "romance" and the pilgrims had no choice but to cramp together, standing back to back when prostrating. I have seen those tourists squeezed at the bottom of the wall many times; they nestle, smoke, drink beer, laugh noisily, feed each other or lift their enormous cameras, scrupulously taking photos of the prostrating pilgrims. Some place a sign in front of their chests, writing that they are looking for a mistress or are recruiting partners etc. Some are disguised as beggars with a paper box or hat placed in front of them they shout "please, please" at the Tibetan pilgrims. Others suddenly throw themselves to the ground, imitating the prostrating of Tibetan pilgrims in a derisive way. A tourist who had visited the "Romance Wall" many times wrote online: "We sit at the bottom of the wall, smoke and laugh at these people. We don't understand their beliefs. We don't know what they are after. Afterlife?" Chinese media such as *Xinhua News*, *Tibet News Online*, *Tibet Business News* use exaggerated and embellished headlines such as "Romance Wall" in the Barkor or Lhasa's

"Romance Wall": places where it is easiest to have an encounter with beautiful women.'

(Woeser, 2011)

Media coverage made this holiest place sexy and cool, an exciting liminal space in which normal rules no longer apply, because it is in Tibet, and anything is possible. Tourists anywhere may behave badly, as if freed from the scrutiny and constraints of home, but Tibet is especially attractive as a place to lounge, sunbake, flaunt one's charms, and seek sex, because Tibet is both home and un-home; China's Tibet^{TM}, yet exotic; a domestic destination yet as different as can be imagined. Chinese money is used and the only public language is Chinese, but it's wild. Anything goes.

The habitually negative attitude of Han Chinese stationed in Tibet in the 20th century spared Tibetan women being the object of Han erotic fantasies. Han men have not chased after Tibetan women, as they do after Tai women in Xishuangbanna Jinghong. Generations of Han have been told the women of this district of Yunnan freely make themselves sexually available, which has generated sex tourism on a major scale, in contrast to Tibet, where sex workers' clients are overwhelmingly of the same ethnicity as the workers, according to a detailed survey conducted by the Australian Red Cross. Although Han men travel to Jinghong for exotic sex, they participate in a deception. Medical anthropologist Sandra Hyde writes: 'Jinghong is a city of prostitution: it provides Han Chinese male tourists with a lucrative sex tourist destination. What the male tourists come to Jinghong to consume are Tai women. However, the majority of the prostitutes are not Tai but women from Sichuan and Guizhou dressed in Tai clothing to attract Han male customers' (Hyde, 2001: 144). The customers accept this rather obvious deception, pretending to themselves that these are the exotically different women they crave. This is little different from the basic transaction between sex worker and client, in which the worker puts on a show of enjoying the sex, and the client chooses to believe the display. The staging of authenticity is not new.

China objectifies ethnic minority women, and minority ethnicities generally. 'Thus, peoples formerly marginalized as "backward" are inserted into the post-Mao national landscape – but at the price of finding their cultural resources reduced to readily manufacturable "objects" and their cultural identities to possessors of these objects, which may be sold and consumed globally' (Mueggler, 2002: 18).

China has been on a sharp learning curve. Tibet has taken a rapid transit across the sky of Chinese imaginaries. Tibet in the 1950s to 1970s was the setting for stories China told itself of the heroism of conquest, subduing both land and people. Now it is an object of desire, readily available for mass consumption. At all times, the model to be followed was Western modernity, with its concepts of desire, choice, leisure, holidays, and consumption. All of these had to be learned, and once learned then naturalized so they could fade into the background as givens no longer acknowledged as innovative breaks with the past.

Lhasa has been reconceptualized as a suite of scenic spots around which is clustered a modern city with the comforts essential to modernity and mass tourism, especially hotels, buses, heating, and the availability everywhere of extra oxygen for those fearful of altitude and thin air. The iconic buildings which make Lhasa a holy city are stranded islands, sites for staging authenticity. The empty Potala Palace, originally named for a blissful pure land Tibetans aspire to be reborn into, is as much an authentic replica as the massive tourist theme park under construction south of Lhasa, where (as previously mentioned) there are to be daily re-enactments of China, embodied by Princess Wencheng of the seventh century, civilizing the Tibetans.

Choice and consumption were the privileges of a small aristocratic elite in China. Not only did the masses have very few choices, the idea of choice was novel. But as modernity arrived, the state educated citizens, introducing new concepts, such as the holiday. For example, in the 1920s, the summer holiday – *xiaoxia* – was a novel idea; an opportunity to escape oppressive heat and humidity by holidaying in a mountain resort. 'The editor of *China Traveller* explained that Western men and women treated summer vacation as an important event and started planning for it in mid-spring' (Dong, 2006: 206). Domestic tourism required infrastructure, not only roads and hotels, but also a banking system capable of enabling tourists to access their money wherever they chose to consume. The China Travel Service, which handled all arrangements for international visitors to China in the revolutionary decades, had its origins in the 1920s in an initiative of the boss of the Shanghai Commercial and Savings Bank.

Hawaii is the explicit model Hainan follows to entice Han Chinese en masse to learn leisure consumption on subtropical beaches. What is the model for Tibet? It is not necessary to look far. Just as Chinese concepts of consumption imitate familiar Western concepts, Tibet too is being positioned as a consumable modelled on Western enthusiasms for Tibet. Today's China imitates most things foreign, and the success of domestic Han Chinese tourism in Tibet very much imitates the Western fascination with Tibet. If it were not for the Shangri-La imaginary embedded in global fantasies, it is hard to see how Tibet could have become a mass destination within China. It is the occidental fixation on Tibet as the ultimate Other that led Chinese to question their utter incuriosity about Tibet, their monochrome version of Tibet as backward, smelly, cold, poor: everything China is leaving behind, and glad to be done with.

There is a traceable product cycle of domestic destinations within China that starts with the 'discovery' of a stunningly beautiful and exotic but remote area by backpackers. Once this is written up in a *Lonely Planet* guidebook, more middle-class people from overseas, happy to pay for comfort, then also start to arrive. The cycle seems to be backpacker → middle-class Westerners → luxury resort Westerners → mass Han domestic tourists → luxury Han Chinese resort tourists. That is the conclusion of Chinese anthropologist Yujie Zhu, after doing fieldwork in Lijiang, at the foot of the Tibetan Plateau in Yunnan, a centre of Naxi culture, closely akin to the pre-Buddhist Bon civilization of Tibet (Yujie Zhu, 2012a, b).

Anthropologist Judith Farquhar says, 'Not only do travellers make paths but paths make travellers, especially in China where there is no tradition of an essential self that struggles to express itself' (Farquhar, 2002: 196). Another anthropologist Lisa Rofel, reporting on her interviews with young urban Chinese women, says: 'For the young women I met, excitement about the possibilities of a cosmopolitan future includes a search for the freedom to move through space and time that their parents did not have. One of the key ways to embody the global self is to travel across space – not, as they frame it, for the purposes of desperately seeking work or trying to move up in social status, but for the purposes of pleasure. Domestic travel for pleasure, in contrast to travel for political goals, is supposed to indicate the truly free self, reflected not in the travel location but in the sensibility embodied in the act of travelling. These women regaled me with stories about travels to the south or southwest of China' (Rofel, 2007: 128–9).

The destination matters less than the process of travelling for pleasure which, in itself, makes one modern. But the destination can attract tourists if it offers a discourse of modernity versus primitivity, light versus dark, which confirms the traveller as a truly free and modern self. This is the discourse China has created in China's Tibet[TM], in Lhasa. Individual agendas of becoming a modern individual mesh with the state agenda of being the liberators of Tibet from feudal slavery, superstition, and darkness. There is a ready audience for the official message because it dovetails with socially engineered individual needs. The Chinese lesson taught by the party-state at its key scenic spots is that the traveller is a modern essential self, and China is a modern essentialized unitary nation-state that has liberated Tibet from darkness.

Tourism is consumption in a country where economic growth is driven much more by state investment in capital expenditure than by consumption. The party-state has talked of the importance of stimulating consumption, to stimulate economic growth, since the turn of this century, but the shift has barely begun, and state-financed infrastructure construction remains the driver of the economy.

But learning to consume Tibet is about more than stimulating the economy and providing employment opportunities for Chinese speakers in Tibet. Tourism is not only a way of modernizing the economy, but of modernizing the self, creating a desiring, discerning, choosing, consuming self who experiences first hand the grand narrative told by the party-state, and becomes an advanced civilized high-quality individual by having internalized the message through going in person to the authentic replica and participating in staged authenticity.

Notes

1. Figures from 'Lhasa aims to be an international tourism draw,' *Xinhua*, 8 January 2012.
2. *The Chinese Luxury Traveller*, Hurun Report, 2012.
3. *Tibet Statistical Yearbook*, 2011, table 13-3.
4. Available from: *http://data.worldbank.org/indicator/ST.INT.ARVL* [accessed 1 June 2013].
5. *Ethnic Statistical Yearbook*, 2008, Economy Division of State Ethnic Affairs Commission, ISBN 978-7-105-10437-6/D.1733, table 15-7. The last year this yearbook was published was 2008.
6. See Johanson (2012).
7. See Oakes (1998).
8. See 'China to increase train services to Lhasa,' *Xinhua*, 1 July 2012.
9. 'China's Tibet' is a standardized phrase used incessantly in official media, signifying China's possession of Tibet. The phrase has all the attributes of a brand name, its repetitive use, quite contrary to other provinces which require no possessive prefix, suggests a concerted brand-building exercise. The author's use of the [TM] symbol makes cryptic reference to the China's Tibet brand. The brand is critiqued in Smith (2008).
10. See HRW (2013).
11. *Luyou Xiaobaike* [*Pocket Encyclopedia of Tourism*], China: Shandong Youyi Shushe.

12. See Oakes (2006), Ghimire (2001), and Xu Gang (1999).

13. An English translation was published in 2006 by Farrar, Strauss & Giroux.

14. The entire movie is downloadable at: *http://www.youtube.com/watch?v=QE8qA3XAfUQ* The climactic final ten minutes are set in Lhasa.

15. *Catalogue of Chinese Publications in Tibetan Studies 1949–1991*, Foreign Languages Press, Beijing, 1994.

16. *Yearnings for the Paradise of the Snowland: A Sichuan–Tibet Highway Travelogue*, Tibetan People's Publishing House, 1987.

17. 'The amazing Deqen Highland,' *China Tourism*, **245**, December 2000.

18. Available from: *http://highpeakspureearth.com/2010/who-is-really-safeguarding-lhasa-by-woeser/* [accessed 1 June 2013].

19. Available from: *http://highpeakspureearth.com/2011/the-media-hype-about-lhasas-romance-wall-by-woeser/* [accessed 1 June 2013].

4

Dolce & Banana, A Shanzhai Creator's Manual: production and consumption of fake in contemporary Chinese art practices

Karen Tam

Abstract: Shanzhai culture in China has permeated everyday life. Fakes and knock-offs abound in the marketplace and the global piracy trade is thriving. Chinese knock-off goods are offered for a fraction of the price of the 'original', but shanzhai produced for the local Chinese market are not just direct copies but rather products created and adapted to local needs, desires, and demands. This shanzhai creativity can be viewed as on the frontier of innovation and as a disruptive grassroots business model. Concerns about intellectual property have led to legal restrictions on creativity and copyright legislation, yet intellectual property rights (IPR) violations are allowing more Chinese consumers access to, and enjoyment of, brand products without the expense of high-end brands (Pang, 2012). This chapter looks at how shanzhai can be used as an appropriative practice in contemporary art, and as a method of resistance, subversion, and critique. Study copies and forgeries in the history of Chinese painting and calligraphy and the Canton Trade of the seventeenth and eighteenth centuries (Perdue, n.d.) can be connected to modern-day shanzhai culture, and taking a positive and constructive view to fakes and forgeries leads to a better understanding of the changes in tastes of collectors and forger-artists (Whifield, 2006). The Dafen Oil Painting Village (itself an invented village) in Shenzhen produces professional copies of existing paintings, made to order. Contemporary artists such as Michael Wolf, Christian Jankowski, Liu Ding, Leung Mee-ping, Xu Zhen, and Ai Weiwei have all at one point incorporated shanzhai discourse in their practice, and challenge the notions of authorship, production, and originality.

Key words: shanzhai, Dafen Village, forgeries, authorship, contemporary art, counterfeit culture, fake trade, consumerism, copyright, intellectual property, brands, reproductions, chinoiserie.

Introduction

From BlockBerries to Microsoft knock-offs, fake antiques to Old Master paintings, villages and even architecture, shanzhai culture in China has permeated everyday life. The term *shanzhai* literally means 'mountain stronghold' and historically referred to bandits who opposed and evaded corrupt authorities. This practice extends beyond counterfeit luxury goods – fake food scandals and counterfeit medicine scandals continue to appear in news coverage (McLaughlin, 2012). Fakes and knock-offs abound in the marketplace and the global piracy trade is thriving. Shanzhai is now even used as a branding or marketing strategy by foreign companies in the Chinese market. As Walter Benjamin writes, 'Every day the urge grows stronger to get hold of an object at very close range by way of its likeness, its reproduction' (2000: 66). The original is used as a device to sell its reproductions to the point where one wonders if we need the original anymore. But whereas Chinese knock-off goods are offered for a fraction of the price of the 'original', shanzhai goods produced for the local Chinese market are not just direct copies, but artefacts created and adapted to local needs, desires, and demands. This shanzhai creativity can be viewed as an innovative force and a disruptive grassroots business model. Concerns about intellectual property have led to legal restrictions on creativity and copyright legislation. Within this context, how have artists responded to issues of originality, mimesis, creativity, and other related concerns?

This chapter looks at how shanzhai can be used as an appropriative practice in contemporary art, and as a method of resistance, subversion, and critique. Artists like Zhao Bandhi and Xu Zhen use appropriation in their work, while addressing issues surrounding the readymade, fakes, piracy, shanzhai, art, and popular culture in China. The Dafen Oil Painting Village (itself an invented village) in Shenzhen produces professional copies of existing paintings, made to order. It is essentially a Chinese painting factory, a Warholian factory, where even copies of works by contemporary Chinese artists like Yue Minjun[1] are manufactured. Its predecessors were the Canton export art painters of the eighteenth and nineteenth centuries, like Lamqua who became extremely skilled in George Chinnery's painting style, and who produced albums and paintings for order and export. In these Chinese studios, each painter specialized in various aspects, such as bodies, clothing, trees, etc. This shanzhai copycat phenomenon is not a recent development in China nor has it been strictly one way. Since the seventeenth century, the West's fascination for all things Chinese meant a reverse trend took place in the form of Orientalism and Chinoiserie. European countries attempted to discover the secrets of producing porcelain, and created other objects in the 'Chinese taste'. This and later historical appropriations of the East by the West (e.g., Ezra Pound's poetry, Franz Kline's paintings based on his study of Chinese calligraphy) leads one to question why appropriation and imitation by a Chinese artist is seen as 'cheap' rather than serious or important.

Artists like Liu Ding worked with the idea of shanzhai in *Production* for the 2005 Guangzhou Triennial and *Take Home and Make Real the Priceless in Your Heart*, where a large quantity of unfinished paintings custom-made in a factory would be completed by visitors themselves. Liu Ding challenges the process of production, the status of artists, and the relationships with workers involved in the production of artwork. Another artist concerned with shanzhai is Leung Mee-ping whose *Made in Hong Kong* (2013) is a collection of paintings or 'tourist art' made with trade painters at Dafen Village. Questions of authorship and collaboration are brought up when we consider the production for Ai Weiwei's *Sunflower Seeds* installation, commissioned by Tate Modern for its Turbine Hall in 2012. What happens following the completion of a work? How are sunflower seeds that may have been part of the installation continually coming to market on TaoBao – the Chinese eBay? The boundary between commodity and art becomes blurred. Are these new seeds part of the artwork? Are they fakes? Are they replicas of the original seeds? Who is/are the artist(s)? If art is a product, then it will be shanzhai-ed. The original artwork is used as a device to sell its reproductions and the notion of originality, of fresh new ideas and unique inventions (which are distinguished from their reproductions), is pitted against the fake, which is associated with consumption and with the market. Shanzhai can indeed though lead the way for innovation and towards creativity.

Addressing the issue of fakes, copies, and authenticity and how they relate to the shanzhai culture of innovation and resistance in contemporary art, the first two sections of this chapter explain the historical ties between modern-day counterfeit and shanzhai cultures and the study copies and forgeries within the Canton trade of the seventeenth and eighteenth centuries, endeavouring to show how taking a positive and constructive view leads to a better understanding of the changes and tastes of collectors and forger-artists (see also Yao, 2005). The following sections look at the trade in fakes and the various forms shanzhai production takes, with an emphasis on the Dafen Oil Painting Village. The last section covers the works of contemporary artists Michael Wolf, Christian Jankowski, Liu

Ding, Leung Mee-ping, Xu Zhen, and Ai Weiwei (who have all at one point incorporated shanzhai discourse in their practice) and will look at what this means for current-day practices of consumerism in China.

Chinese paintings, calligraphies, and their forgeries

What constitutes a forgery? Are all copies, imitations, fakes, and adaptations of an original work forged? Is it the intent to deceive and to pass one's (or someone's) artwork as the work of someone else that makes something a forgery? Learning through copying and producing study copies was considered part of the tradition of Chinese painting and calligraphy, and was effectively the only means in the pre-photographic age of reproducing, circulating, and disseminating masterpieces. Reproductions of great works were treasured along with their originals and the ability to achieve a perfect semblance of an artwork was considered a gentlemanly pastime and a matter of virtuosity and pride. While, as Walter Benjamin complains, we cannot get close to the object, as tourists and visitors we derive pleasure from the novel closeness of its approximation of reality in its recreations (Dicks, 2003: 22). Works of art can be viewed as 'on-going creations' that develop from the original and change stylistically over time. Having multiple versions is standard in Chinese painting and one can expect there to be multiple versions of great works. It is only when signatures are substituted in these copies that the problem of forgery arises. By the fourth century CE when the collecting of Chinese calligraphy and painting itself became a fine art, and later when highly sought-after works by masters were in limited supply, the demand for them created a market that catered to forgeries. What perhaps differentiates well-intentioned copies from forgeries is the aim to deceive on the part of the latter, whether by the maker-forger or the dealer.

While branding manual reproductions as forgeries may preserve the authority of the original (Benjamin, 2000: 324), and collectors concerned with authenticity might reject a piece once it was identified a forgery, art historian Joan Stanley-Baker takes a more constructive view of forgeries. She calls for the identification of them, their date of manufacture, and their provenance, in order to understand connoisseurship, the ideals of collectors, and the evolution and stylistic changes of an image by a given artist or Schools over time (Stanley-Baker, 1986: 54–7). A painting, style, and a famous master's oeuvre takes on new images over the centuries as painters reinterpret past works (not necessarily by making direct imitations or copies), and as forgeries themselves are copied by later admirers and forgers. For Wen Fong too, forgeries are valuable as historical documents and in *The Problem of Forgery in Chinese Painting*, he discusses several methods of forgery (pointing out that this is not in an attempt to give what he terms a 'forger's manual'). He notes the four traditional methods of study copies as *mu* (to trace), *lin* (to copy), *fang* (to imitate), and *tsao* (to invent) (Wen Fong, 1962: 103). A tracing copy would be an exact replica of the original, while the second method would produce a freehand copy, a *fang* piece would, for example, be an imitation with elements adapted from another image, and the last method would be a creative invention and adaptation – a pastiche that incorporated elements from different pictures of a given master.

One could argue that these adaptations and interpretations are early versions of shanzhai innovations. Stanley-Baker sees the remarkable development of genuine works and of high-quality forgeries as two sides of the same creative process (1986: 56). Forgers would age paper to look ancient or use genuine ancient materials, trace or copy an artist's inscription, and acquire or reproduce the original seals of famous artists and collectors, thus making the authentication process more difficult. The tradition of painting through copying also made every Chinese painter a potential forger, and some of the greatest Chinese painters and connoisseurs were known to be master 'forgers' (e.g., Zhang Daqian). Possibly the ultimate forgery and collector's ideal collection was the treasure tower called *Baohuilou* (Pavilion of Painting Treasures) built by Zhang Taijie, a Ming dynasty dealer, who commissioned a collection of forgeries of the greatest masters in Chinese art history ranging from six dynasties to his own day, and published an accompanying catalogue.

In much the same way as current attitudes towards contemporary knock-offs, few of the traditional collectors appreciated works purely for aesthetic reasons; instead they placed worth on authorship or make and brand. Factors in the collecting and acquisition of paintings and calligraphy (and of brand name luxury goods in our times) include social and prestige values. The need for social status and the belief that masterworks are genuine has created a market for forgeries, and once a work has been uncovered as a fake what is lost is perhaps pride on the collector's part, power and authority on the connoisseur's part, and a dip in its financial value. But should monetary considerations be the ultimate ones? Should it not be the case that the historical and aesthetic values of a work be seen as important and to be appreciated, and that the forgery itself be recognized as a work of art, regardless of whether it was from the Song Dynasty, Ming Dynasty, or the twentieth century (Stanley-Baker, 1986: 62)?

Canton export paintings

Fast-forward to the eighteenth century when the Emperor Qianlong closed all trading ports except for Guangzhou, which had been a trading centre for over 1000 years. The Pearl River delta region then became the centre for China's commerce and export industry from 1700 to 1842. Known as the Canton Trade system, it was characterized by a labour-intensive process that incorporated adaptive designs and mass production, and was geared towards export (Turner, 1989: 82). Foreigners were confined to a small district called the 'Thirteen Factories' and were required by the Qing government to leave Canton (the name given by Europeans to Guangzhou) when the trading season was over. An artisanal industry developed in Canton as craftspersons and artists were commissioned to produce various artworks including porcelain, furniture, paintings, miniature carvings, and lacquerware for the European market. Chinese export art was a hybrid, combining elements of European and Chinese art, materials, and techniques (e.g., oil on canvas, perspective, chiaroscuro, reverse mirror painting). Workshops established to finish porcelain and vase painting would have had up to a hundred workers who painted the chinaware based on specific designs (portraits, scenes, coats of arms) ordered by their Western clients. Chinese export designs also produced adaptations of the wares that foreign merchants brought with them, and even imitated Western Chinoiserie designs – feeding them back for European consumption.

Lamqua (1801–1860) (also referred to as Lam Qua, Lumqua, and Lamquoi) was one of the most well-known and successful Chinese export artists who specialized in Western-style portraits and produced paintings for the Western market.[2] A forerunner of the Dafen painters, he took thousands of commissions for portraits and paintings from foreign and Chinese visitors to his studio. He was a rival of English artist George Chinnery, who came to China in 1825, and there is some debate about whether or not Lamqua studied oil painting with Chinnery – a fact the Englishman denied (Conner, 1999: 50). What is interesting for our discussion on shanzhai and the copy in art is that Lamqua became extremely skilled in Chinnery's style of portraiture and quickly absorbed and adopted characteristics of his paintings such as dramatic chiaroscuro, studied poses, and heavy modelling of fabric, to the point where it was difficult at times to distinguish their paintings from one another. The fact that European paints and canvases were readily available to Chinese artists and Chinnery was known to have used Cantonese frames did not make it any easier to do so. Lamqua's rivalry with Chinnery was well known as he could undercut Chinnery's prices and offered clients the novelty of owning a work done either in the 'English fashion' or 'China fashion' by a Chinese artist (Conner, 1999: 57–8). In fact, Lamqua's works can be categorized as those which were copies and versions of Chinnery's paintings, and those which were not copies but were very much in the style of Chinnery. In addition, the vast majority of Chinese export paintings were unsigned and carried no documentation, Lamqua's included. The rare exceptions were at the customer's request and Conner speculates that signatures were added not by the artist but by studios specializing in copying Western script (Conner, 1999: 48). The existence of several versions of portraits of Cantonese merchants lead us to question whether they were all done by Lamqua himself or by his studio artists copying the Lamqua original.

Lamqua's studio was an early precursor to the painting workshops that now abound in Shenzhen's Dafen Village. His large workshop on New China Street in the Thirteen Factories district was one of 30 in the area in the 1830s which produced export art ranging from portraits, landscapes, miniatures, and copies of existing works, on materials such as ivory, glass, rice paper, and canvas for foreign and Chinese customers (Fan, 2004; Heinrich, 2008). Studios like Lamqua's resembled those workshops of the mid-eighteenth century devoted to finishing porcelain and vase paintings, but on a smaller scale. His studio was divided into three stories with the first floor acting as a storefront with finished paintings for sale, and the eight or ten workshop painters he employed occupying the second floor, while Lamqua himself worked and painted his sitters on the top floor. Similar to a guild, his studio shared the same 'workshop culture' as other parts of the Chinese export art industry, where an apprentice would go through years of training to achieve mastery and the level of craftsmanship required. It would employ an assembly line style of working where '[a] painting might pass through several hands before it was completed. One artisan traced the outline, another drew in the figures, a third man painted the background, and so on' while 'using any techniques that fit their needs: copying, tracing, employing readymade sketches of trees, houses, boats, or animals assembled in different ways to produce a different scene' (Fan, 2004: 48). Once completed, the finished paintings were then shipped to Europe or carried home as souvenirs by Western visitors, acts which would be echoed almost 200 years later in Dafen where commissioned paintings would either be cellophaned and shipped to Europe a few weeks after orders were placed, or picked up by clients.

'Capitalism with Chinese characteristics!' – fakes and knock-offs

China has become both the largest producer and consumer of fake products. Economic reforms and the opening up of the Chinese market in the past three decades have led to accelerated economic power and growth, with some of the resultant entrepreneurial energy focused on counterfeit production. Its manufacturing and technological capabilities (and not necessarily the oft-cited cultural tradition of memorizing in education and art forgery skills), alongside its intellectual property laws have allowed counterfeit and shanzhai cultures to permeate Chinese society. Everything is now being faked in industrial quantities and exported back to the first world, masquerading as the real thing. Food, fashion, perfumes, antiques, electronic goods, cigarettes, condoms, cars, pharmaceutical drugs, books, amusement parks, and even whole villages have all been cloned. The quality of the counterfeits range widely, from poor imitations with misspelled names to replications that are so accurate that they are indistinguishable from the originals. Counterfeit markets such as Shanghai's Xianyang Market (prior to its closure and reopening as Xinyang Market) are tourist destinations and sell knock-off Gucci and Prada bags for tourists to bring back home as 'souvenirs'. Lin lists three definitions of counterfeit goods – the unauthorized use of a brand name or logo, the unauthorized production or sale of goods, and the intentional likeness of brand name merchandise (Lin, 2011: 5).

The circulation of fake goods has helped spread the luxury brand cult in Asia as such products create awareness about, and desire for, brand name goods on the part of consumers. The symbolism, social value, prestige, and status associated with owning brand products (minus their usual cost) has created a vast counterfeit market in China – especially in high-end fashion. Foreign consumers and businesses too are complicit in this fake trade, they too revel in the opportunity to pay less than the original asking price. As a form of theft, these counterfeits have at the same time added to the aura of authenticity of the brand. The associated signs and logos are more valuable than the physical product itself, and what the original brands promise is peace of mind – the certainty that they are what they claim to be.

The potential to gain huge profits is a strong incentive to produce fake products and is made possible by the fact that counterfeiters are able to avoid paying taxes, do not conform to regulations, do not shoulder the costs of research and development, and use lower-grade materials, while still benefitting from the original brand's value, and tapping into the pre-existing market for their goods (Gerth, 2010: 137). Ironically, foreign companies themselves, in their pursuit for lower labour costs, have helped propagate the fake industry. In outsourcing production to China, building countless factories and passing on all types of technology, these international companies have made it easy for unscrupulous individuals to run 'ghost shifts' in which a factory is kept running after its licensing is over, using 'cheaper materials, unofficial labour, and safety shortcuts' (Gerth, 2010: 138). This has led to health and safety risks to consumers of various fake products including Gillette razor blades, Zippo lighters, Duracell batteries (which have been known to explode), pesticides, and toxic fake pharmaceutical drugs sold nationally and worldwide. Counterfeit medicine is not limited to Viagra, but also includes those drugs used to treat various diseases and medical conditions (e.g., AIDS medication and cancer-fighting drugs), posing serious consequences and dangers to unsuspecting customers and patients.

Food too is not immune to being faked – there have been discoveries of tainted powdered milk, fake eggs,[3] alcohol, cadmium-laced rice, and illegal meat products (fox, mink, rat, and diseased or toxic meat being passed off as mutton laced with agricultural chemicals, hydrogen peroxide, and nitrate), etc. Wary consumers may opt to buy foreign products seeing them as the more expensive but reliable option, yet these are also vulnerable to mislabelling and being faked. The 'big-head baby' formula scandal in which substandard milk powder was found to be leading to severe malnutrition, and the 2008 milk scandal where the dangerous chemical melamine was found to have been added, have both further undermined consumer confidence in manufacturers and domestic brands. With the mass production of low-quality and counterfeit products widespread in China, consumers there live with an omnipresent anxiety about the uncertainty of what is real and what is fake, and an awareness that what they purchase and consume is based on what they *think* they are buying (Gerth, 2010: 133–4).

Local protectionism, reluctance on the part of the authorities, and loopholes in IPR protection in China, has made it hard to combat the counterfeit market and to enforce intellectual property laws. It is worth remembering that under Mao's communist rule, the state had sole ownership of all property. It is really only relatively recently that personal property has begun to exist in China, and intellectual property is still a new concept (Gerth, 2010: 141). As with the forgeries of Chinese paintings and calligraphies mentioned earlier and the works of Lamqua and Chinnery, sometimes even the experts and investigators find it difficult to distinguish between the real and the fake. For example, in one case, a real Louis Vuitton store in Hangzhou was shut down by government officials due to missing tags.

However, while consumers are never sure what they purchase is what they are getting and have to be wary of the potential health and safety risks of certain fake products, there are positive aspects to shanzhai culture. If interpreted as a resistance through theft, poaching, appropriation, subversion of technology, policies, and trade, shanzhai piracy can be seen as a benefit for less well-off Chinese consumers who would not otherwise have access to consume the 'authentic' products. It may be seen as an act of resistance to imperialism in the market and, in the case of video piracy, the domination of Hollywood imports. Appropriation is also a way of critiquing and subverting the original purpose of brands and their products. This said, of course not all who make and consume counterfeit goods are rebelling or resisting transnational corporate entities and/or the state.

Shanzhai spirit – creativity and innovation

Through counterfeiting, mimicry, and appropriation shanzhai culture operates as a survival tactic – an economic tool for resistance to the abuse of corporate and governmental power; a form of grassroots activism (Lin, 2011: 58). Whereas the production of fakes and knock-offs is intended to defraud and deceive, shanzhai culture is upfront about its imitation and its fakery. This 'underground' economy not only generates huge revenues but leads to innovative products and creations in the Chinese market.

When the Communist Party took over in 1949, many entrepreneurs fled to Hong Kong to start new businesses and shanzhai was the term used in the late 1940s and 1950s to refer to local imitations of their products (Lin, 2011: 3). Shanzhai work units were composed of three to five workers of the same family who made unauthorized goods to sell, and the term eventually encompassed homemade and counterfeit products too.

Shanzhai now refers to anything unofficial and unregulated and its products reflect and meet the tastes and needs of their consumers. They may be imitations of famous brands offered at lower prices and sometimes with more features. For example, Shanzhai cell phones or copy cell phones are functional imitations of popular foreign brands manufactured in China. Yet because they are locally made, they can offer mash-up features such as models with seven speakers for Chinese farmers to leave on the perimeters of their fields and still hear them, or with LED lights which can be used as a flashlight. As migrant workers prefer cheap cell phones to the expensive brand name ones, shanzhai creators make huge profits as they do not have to submit to standard product testing or pay taxes, advertising costs, or research and development costs. Despite this, Lin notes that 'in some cases, the shanzhai version was found not inferior to the real one' (2011: 18).

Production of shanzhai products runs parallel to the booming export industries and factories in the Pearl River delta region, especially in cities like Shenzhen and Dongguan, and has expanded to include shanzhai cars and consumer electronics like digital cameras and flat screen televisions. Shanzhai workshops or copycat studios proliferate, developing not just cell phones but also software applications and pseudo-iPads using reverse engineering as a method of counterfeiting. By going beyond simple copying of brand name models, the shanzhai industry is answering local needs and desires through the innovation and design of genuinely new models.

Among the benefits of shanzhai culture are the creative possibilities found in such innovation, and the decrease in price of products such as cell phones which has made otherwise unattainable luxury products more accessible and affordable to a growing consumer base of lower-income customers. Many such products are sold openly, with ads suggesting that buying Chinese products is patriotic since the consumer will be enjoying what the brands have to offer without providing profits to foreign companies (Gerth, 2010: 153). The shanzhai phenomenon has gained a level of social acceptance counterfeits do not enjoy. It is seen as a grassroots culture whose outputs are creative appropriations that enable the democratization of technology, and whose producers are grassroots entrepreneurs who take advantage of technology and loopholes in IPR laws to create their own brands and innovate from the originals.

Interestingly, the pirate goods themselves are not immune from being shanzhai-ed – there are even fakes of successful shanzhai brands. Furthermore, in another twist of shanzhai culture, Droog Lab, the experimental arm of the Dutch design collective Studio Droog, plays with the notion of the copy with their project, *The New Original* – a collection of 26 works of copies of Chinese objects in Guangzhou, all produced in Shenzhen, with the intent of copying China's mode of operation. The Droog project suggests and demonstrates that the processes of copying and imitation are more than mere replication, where small adaptations are made to the originals, and can be seen as 'a real driver in innovation' (Studio Droog, n.d.). Pieces included modifications on classic Chinese teapots and vases, and a miniature Chinese restaurant set inside a fishtank, thus inverting reality.

This opens up many questions. When is copying products from other manufacturers illegal and when is it innovation? Are copies of paintings still artwork forgeries if they are whole creations or significant alterations of existing artworks? Are those who make them forgers, copyists, appropriators? In his much cited essay, 'The work of art in the age of mechanical reproduction', Walter Benjamin recognizes that although a work of art has always been reproducible, from imitations and replicas of manmade artefacts to copies of original works by masters, the aura of a work of art is associated with its originality and uniqueness and the decay of aura occurs with the advent of modern reproductive technologies and the reproducibility of a work of art through mechanical means (Benjamin, 2000: 323). In order for the concept of authenticity to exist, one needs that of the original. Yet perhaps in an age of simulated reality with an infinite number of reproductions (technical and electronic), the copy itself should be considered legitimate and an authentic work of art, despite the knowledge that it is a copy. The original work of art (or product in our discussion here) may be used to sell its reproductions, but the copies themselves continuously add to the aura and authenticity of their original. Ironically, shanzhai products detract monetary value from brands but at the same time preserve and add to their 'aura', 'authenticity', and value. If we follow Stanley-Baker's call to appreciate forgeries as works in their own right and as documentation of the evolution of images and works of art, and apply it to shanzhai culture in order to see the evolution of products and product designs, we can begin to understand how small innovations and DIY hacks can lead to an exciting new culture based on a new model of 'created in China'.

The Chinese government's attitude towards shanzhai is ambivalent, Lin citing one official defining it as theft and a violation of IP rights, while others see it as an opportunity to innovate (Lin, 2011: 23). Culture and creativity can be part of what Michael Keane terms China's 'great new leap forward' and the desire and process to move from a 'made in China' model (a label which many consumers connect with cheap knock-offs) to a 'created in China' model would engender just such creativity and innovation over time (Keane, 2006: 286). Using a definition of creativity that privileges utility over aesthetics, he looks at how it can contribute to the economic development and export success of China (Keane, 2006: 286). Outsourcing production is usually associated with manufacturing, but does occur in the creative industries (e.g., Chinese animation and painting 'factories'). The low cost of its location, resources, and labour gives China its edge, but limits creativity and innovation as only labour is required in the outsourcing. What Keane sees as a basic problem with such production and its accompanying model of 'designed in the West, made in China' is that 'China gains little from the intellectual property generated' as well as any associated value (Keane, 2006: 291). The costs of supporting research and development, creating incubating centres (for Chinese success), financing, producing, and distributing original content are high, whereas copying and imitating requires minimal reproduction costs. Keane believes that for China to compete in the global cultural economy and to become known for high-value production, structural changes are needed including 'a combination of market correction, appropriate intellectual property models and policy liberalization over time' (Keane, 2006: 291).

'Never meant to copy – only want to surpass': shanzhai architecture and villages

Entire villages, neighbourhoods, and towns in Europe have been replicated in China, down to the smallest detail. There are copycat iconic buildings such as the Sydney Opera House, the Eiffel Tower, and many replicas of Washington's White House across Chinese cities. In some instances, entire communities have been recreated, like the British village of Thames Town near Shanghai. In 2012, the village of Hallstatt in Austria, a UNESCO World Heritage Site was replicated in Huizou city, Guangdong province. Chinese architects had secretly photographed and mapped extensively the Austrian homes and structures to create a simulacrum based on imagery software that transformed the photos they took into a 3D model (Platt, 2012). Created by the China Minmetals Corporation, the Chinese Hallstatt looks exactly like its alpine original, complete with a church clock tower, chalets, a lakeside location, exact replicas of statues, and even the sound of cowbells. Its buildings are intended to be sold to investors, but the replica village is also open to the public as a tourist attraction. While some residents of the Austrian Hallstatt were initially surprised and outraged to find that their town has been cloned, the mayor Alexander Scheutz eventually realized the economic benefits of signing up for a cultural exchange with their Chinese twin, a move which provided a means of cultural promotion and tourism (Wainwright, 2013).

Perhaps the most ambitious replica project so far is that of New York's Manhattan in Yujiapu, previously a fifteenth century fishing village near the city of Tianjin (CNN, 2011; Kinder, 2011). Scheduled for completion in 2019, it is promoted as the 'largest single financial centre in the world' and will measure 3.86 million square metres. London-based architect Zaha Hadid has designed several projects in China and is well respected there. Her Beijing building complex, Wangjing SOHO, is being pirated in Chongqing and has had to compete with its copycat in order to finish construction first.[4] While China's intellectual property laws include protection for architectural works, one lawyer predicted that the most the court could do is to order the defendant to pay compensation as opposed to ruling that their building be torn down. Hadid's own philosophical view on the use of her work is one that sees the exciting potential of the clones, providing that the results of the copy contained some innovation (Platt, 2012). Chongqing Meiquan, the Chinese developer of Meiquan 22nd Century, the knockoff Hadid building, incorporated the controversy into their marketing material launching an advertising slogan: 'Never meant to copy – only want to surpass.'

The art of shanzhai – Dafen Oil Painting Village

What differentiates shanzhai products and paintings from forgeries is that, particularly in the case of works in the Western canon, the buyer or collector is not under the impression that they are the genuine article. Dafen Oil Painting Village, named so in order to distinguish it from 'national painting' or the traditional Chinese painting genre, is located on the outskirts of Shenzhen. It is home to over 8000 artists, artisan-painters, and apprentices who knock out thousands of copies of photographs or paintings of Western masterpieces daily for export back to the West, often in multiple identical versions. Its main industry is the mass production and exporting of these art commodities, which go through a quality control system – an aspect not usually connected with art. As with Lamqua and his contemporaries, the painters in Dafen work in any painting tradition and style, whether Western or Chinese, creating copies of such classics as Van Gogh, Dali, Da Vinci, Rembrandt, and Warhol. A single painting can have 200,000 versions, all hand-painted.

The annual sales of Dafen Village reached 343 million RMB in 2006 and surpassed 500 million RMB in 2010. Human labour as 'mechanical reproduction', however, becomes de-valued in Dafen and sits in stark contrast to the high cultural value of the original paintings – the masterpieces (Wong, 2008: 33).

In *Original Copies*, Philip Tinari looks at Dafen Village and refutes the mainstream media narration of Dafen as just a 'painting sweatshop' and 'a hotbed of forgeries and knockoffs,' finding that as with shanzhai cell phones the Dafen painters do not necessarily make copycat reproductions, as they 'undertake subtle skilled forms of adaptation and innovation' (Tinari, 2010: 297–9), reminiscent of the painter-forgers centuries ago. Internet sales that make the Dafen business model possible can be viewed as an updated version of the workshop culture of the Canton Trade. Unlike the stereotypical images of the anonymous Chinese worker toiling away and pirating all sorts of objects for export, production in Dafen is less of a factory system than one of commissions coming in through various social networks. Working as a cottage industry, in much the same way as pre-industrial artisans, Dafen Village and its workshops are reminiscent of Fan Fa-Ti's description of a typical Canton Trade studio. Dafen is 'a dense warren of alleyways and six and seven storey concrete buildings containing nothing but apartments and workshops dedicated to oil painting', and where 'in less than one quarter of a square mile, some seven hundred galleries and five thousand artists convert oils and canvas into oils on canvas, realizing commissions from all around the world' (Tinari, 2010: 298). Echoing Lamqua's workshop, sample paintings ranging from portraits of world leaders to copies of canonical works, kitsch images of poker-playing dogs, and imitations of works by contemporary Chinese painters like Wang Guangyi and Yue Mingjun are hung salon-style in Dafen's open storefront workshops. Made-to-order images, generic landscapes, and uploaded digital photos turned into 'art' can be painted in any style the customer desires. Unlike 'traditional' paintings, the artworks made in Dafen are regulated by quality control with those that accurately resemble their models approved, and those that do not meet the standard revised or destroyed (Spalding, 2006, 2010: 9). Art materials (e.g., pigments and supports) are classified according to quality, and prices are determined by the painting's level of difficulty. Adapted works rather than straight copying of a known master are priced higher, and at the high end sold under the name of the person who painted them. Once completed, the paintings are cellophaned, rolled up, and couriered to their destination, all within a few weeks of the commission.

In an attempt to regulate Dafen and to promote it as a 'viable economic cultural industry', the district government set about upgrading the village in 1998, putting up plaques recounting its creation myth, which involved a Hong Kong painter who had arrived in 1989, rented buildings, and hired art students and artists to create and reproduce oil paintings for export (Tinari, 2010: 302). Dafen Village was declared a National Model Creative Industry Base in 2006. Dafen Oil Paintings has become a cultural brand both in China and abroad, with some studio owners setting up retail businesses in Shanghai and Beijing to sell 'authentic' Dafen paintings. Delegations of officials from other municipalities and provinces regularly tour the village to study it in the hopes of creating their own Dafens and replicating its success.

A Management Office was established in 2006 to settle and coordinate IPR disputes and enforcements as issues of copyright infringement and intellectual property theft commonly occur in connection with 'painting villages' such as Dafen. In 2005 Canadian artist Robert Genn led an international campaign against Arch-world.cn (now shut down), a Chinese website which was pirating, lifting, and capturing thousands of high-resolution images of paintings by artists, and claiming to 'represent' more than 2800 artists (see *Vancouver Sun*, 2005). Duplicated on demand in China and sold for as little as $15, it was not clear whether these were photographic copies, giclée prints, or handmade paintings. Genn estimated that about 800 Canadian artists were victims of Arch-World.cn's activities, and initially when the Canadian government and Chinese embassy in Ottawa failed to help, he encouraged his subscribers to email 'cease and desist' messages to the Chinese company. At first the Chinese firm took down all images requested as well as those by all living artists, but they reappeared not too long afterwards.

The new artist-clients

Contemporary artists both from China and the West have used Dafen Village as the source and subject of their work, as well as a go-to factory from which they can place orders for readymade paintings, similar to the workshops of the Canton Trade two hundred years prior. Art historian Winnie Won Yin Wong notes that in Dafen, 'painting for artists who sign their names on the canvases after delivery has been common practice for nearly twenty years. In some respects, conceptual artists are simply new clients with new sales tactics' (Wong, 2008: 37).

While media responses to Dafen may stereotype the village and its workers as anonymous mindless workers, artistic responses to Dafen may equally be problematic for reasons of exploitation and authorship. In what follows I will briefly discuss the work of contemporary artists Michael Wolf, Christian Jankowski, Liu Ding, Leung Mee-ping, Xu Zhen, and Ai Weiwei who have all engaged with Dafen in one way or another.

Photographer Michael Wolf's 2006 series of photographs of Dafen Village depicts individuals each holding a painting which presumably they specialize in copying. What strikes the viewer immediately is that, unlike the typical Dafen paintings of generic scenes or canonic Western masterpieces, these paintings are contemporary works of art, or rather, they are copies of works by artists such as Francis Bacon, On Kawara, and Ed Ruscha, instead of being the mass hand-painted Van Gogh reproductions. Each photograph is titled by a number followed by the name of the artist copied and the price of the reproduction, yet, as Wong notes, Wolf 'pointedly stops at naming the copyist portrayed', denying them any sort of authorship (Wong, 2008: 36). When Wong attempted to follow up and requested contact information for the individuals in the photographs from Wolf, he replied that he had lost all contact with the painters but confirmed that some were the painters themselves and others were gallery workers.

After reading about Dafen Village in the newspaper, artist Christian Jankowski developed his *China Painters* (2007) series, where he showed photos of a new art museum under construction in Dafen to 17 painters and commissioned them to create paintings they would like to see hung on the museum walls. These ranged from replica Old Masters to family snapshots and socialist-realist propaganda, some quite innovative and imaginative, including a Daliesque work. Each painting is signed on the back by the Dafen painter, yet comes with a certificate authenticating them as the work of Jankowski. This brings to the discussion issues of authorship, value, and the relationship between artist and commodity. One of the painters who participated in Jankowski's project, Yin Xunzhi, surprised Jankowski and his team as he apparently painted reproductions of contemporary works in his studio. Yet, when Winnie Wong met with Yin to interview him about the Jankowski project, she recognized him and his friends as those participants in Michael Wolf's photographs. It turned out that most of the paintings in Wolf's images were painted by Yin himself as commercial orders for a client (Wolf) who would come to Dafen Village to collect the works (his readymades) and organize the photo shoots. So rather than a straightforward photographic documentary, Wolf had planned and staged his images. Despite addressing discourses of appropriation, authorship, and commodities in this work, when exhibited, all signs of the production process and the participating 'shadow artist' have been erased, and Yin Xunzhi denied authorship. As Wong argues, through appropriation and ownership, authorship is transferred (2008: 42).

In his work, Beijing-based artist Liu Ding questions the value associated with and accorded to artworks. Addressing notions of originality and authorship, *Products, Part I* (2005) from his *Samples from the Transition* series, was a commission for the Second Guangzhou Triennial where he invited 13 professional artists from the 'painting factory' in Dafen Oil Painting Village to produce paintings in the space of four hours (18 November 2005 from 3 to 7 PM). Performing their task on a pyramid of platforms (a reference to the hierarchies in art), the workers (who were paid their usual factory wages) demonstrated their assembly line process, moving from canvas to canvas. One artist painted only a tree, another a stork, etc. until 40 nearly identical landscapes were completed, displayed, and kept on view during the remainder of the exhibition. By having the process of production, the labour, and the workers visible and on view, the paintings' status as commodities is revealed (Spalding, 2010: 9) and leaves the viewer to question how and why the Dafen paintings differ from the rest of the paintings in the Triennial. Tinari's critique of Liu's *Products* finds it problematic since the workers are put on display for audience consumption 'like so many sideshow performers, possessing neither voice nor agency' and Liu was in danger of exploitation even though his piece was an attempt to address it (Tinari, 2010: 299).

Liu Ding's work on the artwork's value and status as a commodity continues in his 2008 *Liu Ding's Store – Take Home and Create Whatever Is the Priceless Image in Your Heart* piece at Bristol's Arnolfini. He commissioned artists from Dafen to recreate a floating visual motif – a sunset, a waterfall, a tree, a mountain – against a white background where everything else appears to have been erased. Liu then signed the works and sold them each for £100, with the invitation that the collector-buyer could either take the painting home to complete the artwork or hold onto it as an investment in the hopes that it would appreciate in value. This introduces the issue of authorship: if the collector-buyer finishes the work, does the work come to completion with their participation or would it be considered defacement, and consequently bring down the value of the work? The collector-buyer is torn between the desire for profit and the desire to paint in and express the 'priceless image' in their heart. Through the methods of production, display, artist signature, and pricing Liu transforms the act of mass production into one of artistic production. The buyer is integral in this commentary on commodity culture, adding and taking away authorship and value through the purchase of the commodity and their own investment.

Hong Kong–based artist Leung Mee-ping had an apprenticeship with a commercial painter in Dafen Village in 2007. Helped by her fellow painter-apprentices she produced *Made in Hong Kong*, an installation of duplicate paintings designed by Leung but based on mainland Chinese tourist impressions of Hong Kong. A reflection on the creative industry and a re-interpretation of trade paintings, her Hong Kong–themed series included images of Mickey Mouse, Bruce Lee, Jackie Chan, scenes of Victoria Harbour, film stills, etc. The work took on a performance aspect as, unlike Wolf, Jankowski, and Liu, Leung inserted herself into the production process. This is shown in an accompanying video entitled *Made in Shenzhen* showing her training process as a Dafen trade painter. Leung sold the paintings in pairs based on the understanding that the single painting is an original work of art, while the pair operate as knock-offs.

While the term 'shanzhai' is typically used to describe knock-offs and copies of consumer goods, in a discussion on Xu Zhen's provocative exhibition, *Impossible Is Nothing*, held at Beijing's Long March Canteen in 2008, fellow Chinese artist and curator Gu Zhenqing uses the term in the context of authenticity and falsification. Xu Zhen's performance installations – *Decoration* (2008) an aircraft inside the art gallery with digital screens in an adjacent space showing what appears to be two astronauts working inside the spaceship, and *The Starving of Sudan* (2008) which re-enacted the scene from Kevin Carter's Pulitzer Prize-winning photograph of an emaciated African child and a vulture – are referred to as 'a shanzhai station and a shanzhai African landscape' in terms of their presentation (Wong, 2009: 50).

Addressing issues of authenticity, power, and cultural authority, Ai Weiwei employs two strategies in his conceptual work – multiplying and reproduction. In 2010, his large-scale installation *Sunflower Seeds* covered the floor of London's Tate Modern Turbine Hall (Kleutghen, 2010). Composed of 100 million handmade porcelain sunflower seeds, handcrafted and painted in Jingdezhen (China's centre for porcelain and ceramic making), by 1600 local (mostly female) artisans who worked on the project for two and a half years, it was a project that spoke not just of labour and time, but also of the power of the collective versus the individual – a metaphor for Chinese society.

Weighing over 150 metric tons, the sheer volume of these multiple objects created a sense of fragility and weightlessness, yet a dramatic immensity. When it opened, visitors eagerly interacted with the piece, rolling around the 'beach' of seeds, building piles of them, and scooping up seeds in their hands. Within two days of its opening *Sunflower Seeds* was roped off as the ceramic dust created by the friction caused by peoples' footsteps rubbing the unglazed porcelain was deemed to be a health risk. Disturbingly, no questions were raised on the health risked faced by the workers during the production process, although Ai has stated that Jingdezhen workers were given a wage and that the sunflower seed project provided a new source of income and allowed local communities to use traditional techniques and skills. In this case, while the concept and design are Ai Weiwei's, the seeds were fabricated by hand (rather than being manufactured by machines) – by the labour of the nameless female artisans of Jingdezhen. The sheer scale of the installation emphasizes China's booming population and the power of the collective. *Sunflower Seeds* provides a good example of how, in the production of an art object, participants hired as workers fall into two models. The first model is what Zheng Bo refers to as *gongren* – workers who function as manual labour; the second is *gongmin* – participants engaged as citizens. Workers who participated and produced the objects for Ai's installation arguably fall into the first model as they 'had no access to the discursive sphere where the meaning of the work was generated through public discussions' (Bo, 2012: 119–20).

Not too long after the exhibition opened, a single seed, said to be from *Sunflower Seeds* (presumably pilfered), was sold on eBay for £28 and more seeds were found offered for sale. Shortly after the Tate Modern exhibition, in February 2011, 100 kilograms of the seeds were auctioned at Sotheby's in London for $559,384, and in May 2012 a ton of seeds fetched $782,000 at Sotheby's in New York (see Kennady, 2011; *International Business*, 2012). During a question-and-answer session of the *Shanzhai: Originals and Fakes* discussion at the Hayward Gallery, a member of the audience shared an amusing anecdote about their discovery of these seeds on Taobao (the Chinese E-Bay). It begged the question, could the sellers be the same artisans who worked on Ai's piece and who saw the potential for profit, subversion, rebellion, and reclaiming of authorship? When does a contemporary artwork such as *Sunflower Seeds* stop being a work? A listing on Taobao had a price of 1.50 RMB for a single sunflower seed, describing it as handmade in Jindezhen. Would this be considered a knock-off or fake version of Ai's *Sunflower Seeds* because the project had ended? Is it still an artwork since it was made by the same artisans who had produced his installation? The Taobao ad apparently ended with the warning that the porcelain seeds 'are not to be allowed within reach of children or the elderly, since they can easily be mistaken for foodstuff.' In a new development and repurposing of Ai's piece, the London-based curatorial partnership, Day + Gluckman, launched an appeal in February 2013 to anyone with porcelain sunflower seeds from Ai Weiwei's exhibition at Tate Modern to 'fess up' and lend the seeds to them for their exhibition, *Couriers of Taste: History, Cultures, Collecting and Consumerism* at Danson House in Bexleyheath, UK (BHT, 2013). The show explored themes of international trade, global consumerism, authorship, and value. Can the 'stealing' of the seeds still be considered theft if Ai's intention had always been for the seeds to be taken? Is it still his work? At Danson House each group of seeds was kept together and labelled according to where they came from, so becoming a map of the routes the seeds have taken since the Tate exhibition. Both Tate Modern and the Lisson Gallery (which represents Ai) are 'quite comfortable' with the curators' project (Milliard, 2013).

Ai Weiwei brings up the debate on authenticity, cultural authority, and value systems in many of his other works, leading the viewer to question what is real and what is fake. His 1995 iconic gesture, *Dropping a Han Dynasty Urn*, documented in three black-and-white photographs, claims to use an antique urn, yet causes us to wonder whether the urn was really from the Han Dynasty. How can we verify its authenticity when all we have are photographs? Were the *White Wash* vessels dipped in industrial paint really 4000 years old? Did he actually smash Kangxi period bowls in *Breaking of Two Blue and White Dragon Bowls*? One reading of these gestures and use of 'antiques' is as an act of smashing the representations of traditional Chinese art and culture thereby questioning authority and the value of these objects – a value based on rarity and the authority of specialists and experts. Ai hires the most skilled artisans in Jingdezhen (the site of the former imperial kilns) in Jianxi province to produce porcelain to the same standard of highly prized antique ones. There is no collaboration or input from the workers, who are simply silent labourers fulfilling a client's wishes. For one project, he had them create replicas of eighteenth century blue-and-white porcelains made during the Qing Dynasty. Yet, in the light of this knowledge and the fact that Ai Weiwei was once an antiques dealer, connoisseur, and collector of antiques, one questions the interpretation that these were gestures of rebellion. Ai himself as an antiques dealer would have been confronted with questions of authenticity, and has incorporated these debates into his art practice. Therefore, these works can only be seen as rebellious if one believes that what Ai is smashing are the authentic objects. Could these supposed antique objects be simply replicas? If we consider Ai's blue-and-white porcelain works to be fakes, does it change our perception of his art and of the object itself and would these objects be deemed less valuable? This is the same question as emerged in the earlier section on forgeries in Chinese painting. In this case, Ai's replicas invoke Duchamp's concept of the readymade, where the copy attains the same value as the original even as a mass-produced object.

Danielle Shang cites Ai Weiwei speaking in 2000 about his porcelain-based work and the issue of authenticity:

'What is real and what is fake or a reproduction? My porcelain works are the highest quality blue-and-white porcelain. Here is something packed with historical and cultural meaning. The works I've commissioned were of imperial guan standards, reproductions of the finest blue-and-white porcelain of the Kangxi, Qianlong and Yongzheng periods, which in turn represented the apex of China's porcelain tradition. During this period, there was nothing more prized. Porcelain production, collection and connoisseurship had reached their pinnacle, the peak of their cultural authority. Today, using the best artisans in Jingdezhen, we can reproduce this quality. If they were real in a modern context, let us say exhibited in a contemporary art exhibit, does their original value continue to exist? If it exists, then what is the significance of its existence? If they are fake, then how do they differ from authentic period pieces when they are exact replicas with no recognizable differences? If there is no recognizable difference between this piece and an authentic period piece then what does this do to the value of the original period piece, or for that matter, the modern replica ... ?

(Ai quoted in Shang, 2012: 43)

Conclusion

The antique market is rife with fakes, and even provenance can be doctored. China's enthusiasm for collecting its own past has led to the creation of the *World Collections* television program on Beijing Television which focuses on antique porcelains. Collectors are asked to bring in their antiques for appraisal and, if unmasked as counterfeit, the host smashes the fake with his *hubao chui*, or 'treasure-protecting hammer'. Museum and auction house specialists are part of the cultural authority validation authenticity system, and rely on their ability to distinguish (or not) the fake from the genuine. Throughout art history, artists around the world have made forgeries or copies of earlier works of art either for financial gain, deceitful motives, or to learn techniques and methods. The original artwork may be used as a device to sell its reproductions – its fakes. Michael Taussig questions how much of a copy a copy has to be in order to have an effect on what it is a copy of and, if the copy extracts power from the original leading to the image becoming more powerful than what it is an image of, do we even need the original (Taussig, 1993)?

What are the implications of this for artists and contemporary art, and do we as the audience (or as artists) care if something is or is not 'authentic' anymore? Are contemporary art projects such as Zhan Wang's *Artificial Rocks* and Cai Guoqiang's restaging of the *Rent Collection Courtyard* at the 48th Venice Biennale fake? Where do they fit in with a long tradition of copying earlier artworks? The acts of copying or making fakes and copies, adopting the language of fakes, blurring what is real and what is fiction are, for the artists, comments on the unstable status of the 'original' and 'authentic', on the expanding definitions of authorship, as well as on consumerism and commodity culture.

While counterfeits and shanzhai culture violate IPR and can be seen as acts of theft, they also allow greater numbers of Chinese consumers access to, and enjoyment of, brand products without the expense associated with the genuine articles. The grassroots culture of shanzhai, its localization, and the fact that sometimes shanzhai products outperform the originals allows for a certain level of social acceptance of the violation of intellectual property rights (Gerth, 2010: 54). Yet the mentality of consumers in China towards fakes today is also sometimes cautious, as unscrupulous makers of fakes have made it easy to mass-produce and flood the market with commodities that pose health and safety risks for the consumer.

Regardless, there is no doubt that shanzhai is shaping the landscape of consumerism in China and questioning notions of originality and creativity. Shanzhai producers put their own twists and innovations on 'real' or 'authentic' luxury brand products to suit local needs and demands. The question remains as to whether they are asserting their own agency or engaging in cultural hijacking. If we relate Meredith Abarca's discussion on Mexican food and authenticity to shanzhai culture, acts of cultural hijacking do not occur when someone else's productions get modified or altered since those always belong to the original creator, but rather when the hijackers claim authenticity and authorship (Abarca, 2006: 4). What these alterations and 'tinkerings' offer is the possibility for cross-cultural dialogues and the foundations for a successful and exciting culture of creativity and innovation.

'Truth becomes fiction when the fiction's true. Real becomes not-real when the unreal is real.'

Cao Xueqin, *Dream of the Red Chamber/The Story of the Stone*
(1973: 130)

Notes

1. Available from: *http://www.oilpainting.dafenyouhua.net/shop_list/99/1.html* [accessed 17 April 2013].
2. Lamqua was also one of the first Chinese painters to be exhibited internationally, including at the École Turgot in France, London's Royal Academy of Fine Arts, and the Boston Athenaeum. There are records of Lamqua in European and American travel books, invoices, letters, exhibition lists, and signatures, yet his Chinese name has not been established with certainty. What is known or supposed about Lamqua is based on Western sources.
3. One of the more disturbing segments in the UK's Channel 4 documentary *Fake Trade* shown in 2008 was the production of fake eggs, a process demonstrated by an inspector using a mixture of toxic ingredients (gelatin, benzoic acid, alum, etc.). The yolk is created by adding a yellow colouring powder to a liquid which was then poured into a mould and mixed with 'magic water' containing calcium chloride. The white of the egg was then shaped with a mould, and the shell formed from paraffin wax and an unidentified white liquid. The fake egg costs half of a real one, especially since there is no need to keep live chickens. There are even three-day courses in the production of artificial eggs. The fake egg can be cooked, fried, or steamed, and although bubbles form on the white of the egg, those who have tasted it say it tastes very much like the real thing. It contains no nutrients andaccording to scientists will cause dementia if ingested in the long-term (see also Kaiman, 2013).
4. Hadid's SOHO complex is scheduled for completion in 2014.

5

Thriving medical consumerism in the margin of the state: a case study of medical pluralism in Southwest China

Qingyan Ma

Abstract: As post-socialist China continues its economic reform and transition to market economy, increasingly different kinds of commodities are available. Medical service, although a special kind of commodity, has been no exception to this general trend since 1979. By focusing on medical consumerism and the individual's agency in choosing medical services, I present how the individual in Weixi Lisu Autonomous County in Yunnan Province, the southwest corner of China, actively engages in market reform and healthcare reform by taking on, reconfiguring, or resisting state public health discourse. Through examining how medical pluralism, as constituted by biomedicine, local herbal medicine, traditional Chinese medicine, and witchcraft, is contextualized in the market economy in this region, I argue that there is a significant change in medical pluralism following the transition into a market economy and the expansion of neoliberal globalization, which in turn impacts upon local people's view of ethnic identity and their relationship with the state. By locating my research of medical consumerism in the southwest borderland, the so-called 'margin of the state', I am particularly interested in exploring the penetration of market, capitalism, neoliberalism, and globalization as is manifested in local people's choice of medical care. This is simultaneously and inescapably intertwined with the state's agenda of development and modernization of healthcare and the ethnic minority areas at large. In addition, I argue in this chapter that top-down market reform and development from the state has unintended consequences for the individual at the local level. This chapter will contribute to our understanding of medicine, modernity, and consumption in contemporary China.

Key words: consumption, development, globalization, medical pluralism, medicine, modernity.

The problem

During the time I was collecting ethnographic data in a village in Southwest China in 2011, I was shocked by the scene of patients lining up outside the village clinic to receive intravenous (IV) drips. Regardless of age, gender, and the distance to the clinic, everyone who made the journey along the unpaved road to this clinic primarily asked for one thing: an IV drip. This scene was repeated everyday during my stay in the village and I was told by the local villagers that it had been the same ever since the opening of the clinic in 1992. Such a scene led me to ask one simple question: Why are people so attracted to IV drips? An IV drip, taking the form of glass bottles or plastic bags filled with liquid, hypodermic needles, and plastic tubes epitomizes the treatment of biomedicine in the eyes of the local villagers. So the underlying questions that can be raised are: Why does biomedicine, as represented by IV drips, despite its pharmacology and biotechnology, become seen by local peasants as a miracle cure? How is medical pluralism – as constituted by biomedicine, known as Western medicine (WM) in China, traditional Chinese medicine (TCM), and local herbal medicine and witchcraft[1] in the multi-ethnic locale in Southwest China – played out in post-socialist rural China and what are the implications of the changing medical pluralism seen in the market economy?

The context for these questions is the changing conditions under which people make medical choices. In line with post-socialist China's transition into a market economy is the availability of increasingly more kinds of commodities on the market. Medical services, although being a special kind of commodity, have been no exception to this general trend since 1979. In this chapter, I examine the relationship between medical consumerism and medical pluralism, as constituted by biomedicine, local herbal medicine, TCM, and witchcraft in Southwest China's Weixi Lisu Autonomous County. By locating my research into medical consumerism in the southwest borderland, the so-called 'margin of the state' (Das and Poole, 2004), I am particularly interested in exploring the penetration of market, capitalism, neoliberalism, and globalization as manifested in local people's choice of medical care. This is simultaneously and inescapably intertwined with the state's agenda of economic development and modernization of healthcare in ethnic minority areas. In addition, I argue in this chapter that top-down market reform and development from the state has had unintended consequences for the individual at the local level. By focusing on medical consumerism and the individual's agency in choosing medical services (Lupton, 1997), I present how the individual, through the physical and discursive playing out of their medical choice between biomedicine and other medical practices, actively engages in market reform and healthcare reform by taking on, reconfiguring, or resisting state policies in post-socialist China. Thus, I will further shed light on the changing relationship between the individual and the state in the current neoliberal globalization we are all involved in.

The theories

This chapter is concerned with the theories of medical pluralism, consumption, biopower, modernity, and development. According to Arthur Kleinman (1997), medicine can serve as a social idiom, which means it can be used to redefine and negotiate social identities. Similarly, in her ethnography about the medical system in the highlands in Bolivia, Libbet Crandon-Malamud (1993) argues that when medical pluralism exists, through the primary resource of medicine, people have access to secondary resources, the principal one being social mobility. Therefore, medical choice is based not on medical efficacy but on political concerns. In the case study of medical pluralism in Lijiang Basin among the Naxi in Southwest China, Sydney White (2001: 172) suggests that 'medical pluralism, in its essence, is how relationships of power and meaning are played out between diverse therapeutic practices in a given context' and is integrally linked to the politics of cultural identities. In my study of medical pluralism in Weixi, I further situate local people's medical choice in the changing social, political, and economic context in post-socialist China. In particular, I argue that there is a significant change in medical pluralism following the transition into a market economy and the expansion of neoliberal globalization, which in turn impacts local people's individual agency and their relationship with the state.

One consequence of the development of a market economy in post-socialist China is the transition towards a consumer society (Gillette, 2000; Yan, 2000; Zhu, 2010). Zukin and Smith-Maguire (2004: 189) argues that 'historically, these changes depend not only on the development of markets for the exchange of goods but also on the weakening of state, religious, or other normative controls over material means of expression and the rise of new, independent rationalities.' Among these changes, medicine stands out as a specific case. Previous research of the consumerism of medical services mostly focused on Western societies with a long-standing history of free market capitalism (Lupton, 1997), or medical tourism in developing countries. For example, in the case of Australia, Lupton concludes that one approach to study medical consumerism is to see how to empower patients so they can have more rights and capacity for autonomy over their medical decisions so as to achieve the best possible outcome for them. The other approach is to look at how medical services maximize their competitiveness in the market economy so that the medical professionals can survive in a free market (Lupton, 1997).

The significance of people manoeuvering among distinctive medical practices in post-socialist China echoes Zukin's argument that there is an established market (although this may not be perfect), in which patients can choose between all kinds of medical practices. However, this lessening of state control does not necessarily mean that the state has been weakened. My fieldwork data show that biomedicine ends up being the predominant medical practice both for the medical professionals and for laypeople when they search for a cure, although biomedicine and other aforementioned therapeutic practices are not mutually exclusive. Instead, they are overlapping or integrating with each other. Under market conditions, medicine is also presented as a commodity, whereas biomedicine has achieved its dominant status over other medical practice, which becomes a manifestation of people's fetishism for biomedicine in a context that has plural medical practices. In their study of modernization and herbal medical knowledge in a Caribbean village in Dominica, Quinlan and Quinlan (2007) suggest that modernization – like an increase in consumer items – may have little effect on traditional herbal knowledge; however, people's medical choice is not solely based on their knowledge of medicine. The fetishization of biomedicine saw it become a commodity whose value has far exceeded its original efficacy. Timothy Burke (1996: 5), borrowing from Marx, suggests that 'fetishism is more than (but includes) the meanings invested in goods; it is also the accumulated power of commodities to actually constitute, organize, and relate to people, institutions and discourses, to contain within themselves the forms of consciousness through which capitalism manufactures its subjects.'

With this in mind we have to ask what the value of biomedicine is vis-à-vis other medical practices, given that the nature of commodity is something produced that has value and can be exchanged (Marx, 1977). Marx argues that an object can acquire value only by appearing to embody, or represent, some quality beyond itself. He further stated that it can never be just 'a thing' but always appears, like a character on stage, as something representing something further (Marx, 1977: 76–7). So what does biomedicine and other medical practices represent in the post-socialist market economy? On the one hand, biomedicine, as supported by modern science and experiments, in the official discourse in China, symbolizes civilized advanced scientific medical practice, whereas other therapies, including TCM, local herbal medicine, and witchcraft, are considered otherwise. The science supremacy discourse is in line with the Marxist evolutionary theory that the Communist Party of China (CCP) adopted, which is also underlying the state pursuit for modernity. On the other hand, producing and promulgating scientific knowledge through various channels is the essential mechanism of biopower. The state, through increasing its medical authority, strengthens the national authority to govern its population (Foucault, 1991, 1994). Such a hidden and subtle operation of the state provides an important perspective on the way in which governmentality works (Boyer, 2003). Giorgio Agamben (1998) also proposes that the way sovereignty works is by governing the 'bare life' of its citizens. Nikolas Rose and Carlos Novas (2005) elaborate the concept of 'biological citizenship' to describe citizenship projects originating from government authorities that aim at incorporating individuals into the formation of the nation state by emphasizing their biological existence. While 'strategies for making up biological citizens "from above" tend to represent science itself as unproblematic … these vectors "from below" pluralize biological and biomedical truth, introduce doubt and controversy' (Rose and Novas, 2005: 446–7). The top-down permeation of scientific knowledge to back up biomedicine is an important part of the state public health strategy that China has employed.

By the same token, the commodification of medicine in the market economy is an inevitable consequence of market reform in post-socialist China, which on the other hand coincides with the state pursuit for modernity and its development agenda. As James Ferguson (1994) points out, the intentionality of development planning is always important and often produces unintended outcomes. It is these unintended consequences of development and local individual articulations of modernity that matter to anthropological inquiry. By laying out the theories, I am going to present the individual role for medical consumerism in post-socialist China.

The setting

The case study I present here was part of research I conducted in Weixi Lisu Autonomous County in Yunnan Province, located in the southwest corner of China. From the perspective of political geography, this region is located far from the political center of China and shares borders with other nation states, such as Myanmar (Burma) and India. High mountains, deep gorges, and rushing rivers in the region create additional difficulty in transportation and communication between the locale and the outside world. In terms of the nation state, Southwest China is characterized by versatile ethnicity. In my research in Weixi, the largest ethnic group was Lisu, then Naxi, Tibetans, and Han. Most of these groups are engaged in agricultural production. All of these characteristics of Southwest China, as manifested by its location and ethnicity, conform to what Das and Poole (2004) calls 'the margin of the state', which is peripheral not only in terms of the spatial model, but also marginal in the Han-centered Chinese state. From the historical perspective, James Scott (2010) uses the term 'zomia' (originally coined by Willem van Schendel of the University of Amsterdam to describe the huge massif of mainland Southeast Asia) to portray the people living in the mountains of the Southwest as anarchists attempting to flee from the Han Chinese state governance and the influence of Han-centered civilization. While I appreciate both Das's and Scott's efforts to focus on the previously understudied region, I would like to follow the more recent trend in the scholarly work of Southwest China that argues for the 'de-centering of China' – that is elevating the study of Southwest China above and beyond the sino-centric concept of China by centralizing the region as the radiant nexus where people, commodities, religions, modes of governance, concepts of modernity, and development projects flow in and out (Huang and Liu, 2012). By doing so, it is possible to better capture the nuances of state governance in rapid globalization, and thus better answer Das's question as to 'how the practices and politics of life in the margin shapes the political, regulatory, and disciplinary practices that constitute the state?' (Das and Poole, 2004: 4).

In addition to its 'margin of the state' location with the majority of the population as non-Han ethnic groups, Southwest China has always been the target for various development projects that follow the central Han Chinese state's 'civilizing' agenda (Harrell, 1995) as well as the Marxian narratives of unilineal social evolution adopted by the Communist Party. The essential goal of these development projects is to modernize the region, although being 'modern' itself is a complicated term. Developing a public health system has always been important among these projects. The changing public health system in rural China, which is nonetheless rooted in the social, political, and economic context of a given historical moment, has great influence over local residents' medical choice.

Since 1978, the economic reforms that transformed the Maoist-planned economy into the post-Mao market economy under the governance of a centralized state have constituted a process referred to as 'socialism with Chinese characteristics' (Greenhalgh and Winckler, 2005). As part of economic reform, the dismantling of communes in rural areas and the subsequent implementation of the household responsibility system placed the family at the core of production again.[2] The household responsibility system in the post-Mao era does not only 'liberate the productivity'[3] of the peasants, as the family regained their agency to decide what crop to plant and when and how to plant the crop all by themselves, it also means the family is left vulnerable to fluctuations in the gain or loss made by the crop. Therefore, when a certain family member is sick and cannot engage in field farm work, the burden of the work will fall to other family members. Despite the workload, financial burden is another big concern. In the field of public health, the dismantling of communes also led to a loss of support for cooperative medicine and for barefoot doctors (farmers who received minimal medical training in the Maoist period; White, 1998). The transition to the post-socialist market economy resulted in most rural peasants being excluded from post-decollectivization healthcare. In the following decades, rural peasants in China were more or less left to their own devices to pay for healthcare, while urban residents were still guaranteed a certain form of insurance due to the complicated distinction between the rural and the urban under the rule of the Communist Party (Potter and Potter, 1990). In many ways, China took a more neoliberal stance on health policy.

After three decades of 'economic reform' China has become an emerging global power, but its areas of rural poor present the opposite image of this picture. The outbreak of SARS in 2003 especially challenged the country's fragile public health infrastructure in rural areas (Kleinman and Watson, 2005). In the aftermath of the SARS epidemic and the countrywide public health crisis that ensued, the 16th National Congress of the Communist Party of China proposed a strategy called 'New Cooperative Medicine' (NCM), basically a revitalization of cooperative medicine established under collectivization during the Maoist period. NCM exemplifies the Hu Jintao administration's effort to 'construct a harmonious society' aiming at providing basic healthcare for rural peasants (Zhang and Liu, 2007). In the following years, NCM was gradually expanded from trial areas to the entire countryside, including Weixi County, where it was introduced in 2006. In order to participate in NCM, each peasant must pay 10 yuan[4] a year for which he or she is given a certificate of participation in the program. The certificate must then be brought to the clinic or hospital, in order for the patient to receive a designated percentage of reimbursement from the state. Through the NCM initiative each person is eligible for healthcare benefits totaling up to 15,000 yuan per year.

NCM is a state-subsidized healthcare program that can provide basic healthcare for rural peasants. In contrast to cooperative medicine supported by communes in the Maoist period, NCM is operated in the market economy and under the influence of globalization. This means patients are already fully aware of the wide range of medications available. In the meantime, in addition to the state subsidy, patients have to pay a considerable amount of cash out of their own pocket. The contextual difference between NCM and cooperative medicine, and the absence of state-supported healthcare for nearly three decades, greatly influences the choices that rural peasants make when seeking medical treatment.

From Maoist cooperative medicine and barefoot doctors to NCM in the post-Mao era, the presence of biomedicine has always been evident, together with traditional Chinese medicine (TCM) and local herbal medicine, which constitute the primary resources of medical care available to local residents. In Maoist cooperative medicine, the state emphasized the role of TCM and local herbal medicine, which were more affordable and available to rural residents and which had played an important role in the healing process of rural peasants. However, the real change in the relationship among the different medical practices took place after economic reform. After 30 years of economic reform, local rural residents were used to having to find and pay for the healthcare they could afford. In other words, they were on their own when it came to taking care of their health. As most local peasants had limited financial resources, their choice was if it was minor you waited for your body to heal itself. If it was major you were waiting to die.[5] So with the advent of NCM and the knowledge that a large portion of the medical expense was then covered by the state, patients gained more freedom to choose between medical services. It is within such a context that the medical consumerism of rural peasants stands out as a dramatic phenomenon in Weixi. In the following section, I will present a close portrait of the changing medical pluralism in rural China and its relationship with the rise of consumerism.

The medicines

The ethnographic data for this chapter were gathered from my frequent visits to Weixi Lisu Autonomous County from 2007 to 2011. Throughout these periods, my primary methodology was archival research, multi-sited participant observation, household survey, and interviews. Based on the data I collected, I categorize four major therapeutic practices that are coexisting in the current context in Weixi – local herbal medicine, TCM, witchcraft, and biomedicine. My field research indicates that local people have their own idea or, to be more specific, a 'folk' conception about health, sickness, medication, and treatment. Based on this 'folk' conception, local people hierarchize different therapeutic practices.[6] In what follows, I will describe how local people manoeuver among these medical practices so as to achieve the best efficacy possible in the post-socialist market economy.

Herbal medicine

Herbal medicine has the longest history in Weixi compared with other therapeutic practices. As a mountainous region covered by natural forest, Weixi has very rich resources for herbal medicine and most of the herbs can be picked directly from the land. Local people dry some of the herbs under the sun or above their fireplaces; others are used fresh. Usually people boil the herbs in water and drink it just as one would tea. They use some herbs as a substitute for first-aid plasters for external traumas or as plaster to set bone injuries.

In the Maoist period, under cooperative medicine, there was an emphasis on the use of local herbal medicine in the countryside, so as to solve the shortage of biomedicine and to lower the cost. The village doctor, Zheng He, who I met in Dacun,[7] was one of the barefoot doctors trained in the Maoist period to recognize different herbs and know how to use herbal medicine. Zheng continues to serve as the village doctor today, and still provides herbal medicine for patients without additional charge.

However, through my interviews I found that, in the memory of some of the elderly local villagers of Dacun, using herbal medicine in the Maoist period was due to being 'too poor and too backward to afford any kind of biomedicine', which was why they were waiting to die, if their illness was major. I am not able to know how these people would comment on herbal medicine in the Maoist period, but certainly their comments today have already been influenced by what they feel about the current status of herbal medicine vis-à-vis biomedicine.

One of my interviewees was Haiying Yu, a 36-year-old female who had married when she was 22 and had two sons aged 14 and 12. She was a frequent visitor to Doctor Zheng's village clinic in Dacun. Haiying claimed that she had been sick for nine years, but she did not know exactly what her sickness was or what had caused it. She felt pain all over her body, which kept her from engaging in any farm work or heavy lifting. For the past nine years, she had been seeking medical care everywhere from the regional hospital in northwest Yunnan, to the prefecture hospital in Deqing Tibetan Prefecture, to the county hospital in Weixi and the township clinic. Haiying said she received biomedical treatment, in particular IV drips, in all of these hospitals, but they didn't work. She still felt pain. She said that each time she visited these hospitals she could not finish the treatment due to her insufficient personal finances. So every time she came back from these hospitals, she had to continue to go to Zheng's clinic to receive more IVs. Because of her sickness, her family had fallen deeply into debt. When I asked her whether she took herbal medicine, she said she never stopped taking herbal medicine, although it was not effective. 'I have to take IV drips. It is the only thing that can cure my sickness. If I had more money, I would be cured now.' In other words, although Haiying took herbal medicine everyday at almost no cost compared with the IV drips she received from time to time, she did not consider herbal medicine as a potential cure for her sickness. Almost every person I interviewed in Dacun said they would rather take biomedicine, in particular penicillin, for flu, cough, fever, or any other unpleasant disease.

Another interviewee was Jiaxing, a 58-year-old retired worker from the Diqing Tibetan Prefecture Power Company, and the son of a well-known herbal medicine doctor, Shaobin, in Dacun. Jiaxing said he did not trust herbal medicine and he would never take any of it, although his father was the herbal medicine doctor people turned to in the neighbourhood. Herbal medicine is usually passed down from father to eldest son, but Jiaxing distrust of herbal medicine meant he did not learn herbal medicine from his father despite being the eldest son of Shaobin. Therefore, when Shaobin can no longer ply his trade, herbal medicine will likely discontinue in the area.

Despite the general consensus that herbal medicine is less effective than biomedicine, most people in Weixi still take herbal medicine. From my investigation in both the village of Dacun and the county seat of Weixi, I witnessed how herbal medicine has been an integral part of local people's lives. In the 42 households I surveyed in Dacun, every one had a history of using herbal medicine. In Zheng's words, 'everyone in Dacun knows herbs to some extent.' In particular, the villagers I interviewed often mentioned there were four herbal medicine doctors in Dacun and they were each well known for their specialties. Shaobin, at age 80, was one of the doctors well known for treating internal sickness, such as stomach ache. Wubin, a male of age 67, was the most famous doctor due to his treatment of bone injuries like fractures. Wubin was a barefoot doctor in the cooperative medicine period, so although being proficient in herbal medicine, he also knew biomedicine. Throughout my time in Dacun, I heard many cases about Wubin's miracle treatment of breaks and fractures. He even treated Zheng's husband once, who fell off the tractor and broke his leg. Based on his diagnosis of patients' bone injuries, Wubin would prepare different herbs to wrap the injury or fracture. He always gathered them himself from the mountain. When I asked him how much he would charge patients for his treatment, he smiled and said he would never name a price, and that people gave him whatever they wanted to give. 'Sometimes, they give me cash; sometimes, they give me food, firewood, or even mushrooms they found in the mountain. I don't like the word "pay". I don't do this for money. I just want to help,' Wubin said. What is clear, however, is that Wubin has gained great respect and fame in the village – most people agree that herbal medicine is more efficacious at treating bone injuries than biomedicine.

When it comes to the county seat of Weixi, people's knowledge of herbs is still extensive. During my fieldwork in Weixi Mothers' and Children's Hospital, Dr. Yang, who worked in the hospital, frequently invited me to her home. Her two-storey single family house had a vegetable patch, in which she also planted some herbs. When I first went there, she pointed at each kind of herb and told me its name and function. She said she would pick different kinds of herbs directly from the vegetable patch and make tea with them. On one occasion when I said I had a sore throat, Dr. Yang picked a few dandelion leaves and mixed them with dried yellow chrysanthemum to make herb tea for me. I asked her how she knew the herbs. 'Just common sense. Everyone knows it,' she said.

Traditional Chinese medicine (TCM)

TCM shares many similarities with herbal medicine, the most evident is that almost the same herbs are used. But the outstanding difference between the two is that the medical theory behind TCM has a systematic basis from etiology, diagnosis, prescription, and evaluation of efficacies (Farquhar, 1994), whereas herbal medicine involves household-based herbal remedies (*dan fang yao*) (White, 1993) that lack a systematic theoretical basis. The four herbal medicine doctors in Dacun like to be addressed as such (*cao yao yi sheng*), and none of them would call themselves doctors of TCM, including Zheng. Zheng told me she did not know much about TCM. She knew the quality of herbs and the application of the herb for certain symptoms, but that was all. Zheng suggests another difference between TCM and herbal medicine is that you can purchase TCM in the drugstore, but you have to look for the herbs yourself in the mountains if using herbal medicine. I travelled to all seven townships in Weixi and did not find a TCM clinic in any of them. Only in the county seat of Weixi is there one. There is also a TCM Department in the Weixi County Hospital, but this mainly serves urban residents. As a result, TCM is not a popular therapeutic option for the local villagers. However, TCM does provide a theoretical backup for herbal medicine. In Wubin's home, he showed me a very old booklet, titled *Pictures of Plants Used for Lijiang Herbal Medicine (Lijiang Caoyao Tuji)*, which was written during the Cultural Revolution by a group of local herbal medicine doctors in Lijiang and published by Lijiang Cultural Revolution Committee. The book includes pictures of local herbs along with a description of their use in TCM. The book is undoubtedly a legacy of the Cultural Revolution and Mao's call to promote TCM within the cooperative medicine system. It is also additional proof of the relationship between TCM and local herbal medicine.

Witchcraft

Witchcraft can be considered little more than geomancy in Weixi. While remaining mysterious to some extent, it has been revitalized in the post-socialist era after being subdued during the Maoist period. The term 'witchcraft' has a broad meaning in different contexts. I choose to translate the original Chinese term *wu shu*, as articulated by local residents, as 'witchcraft' because it is the closest literal translation. The particular form of witchcraft used in Weixi has its roots in the different religions popular in this region, including Tibetan Buddhism, Naxi Dongba, Daoism, and local folk beliefs.[8] Local people refer to witchcraft practitioners as herbal medicine doctors. The difference between witchcraft practitioners and herbal medicine doctors lies in the former using witchcraft to diagnose the symptom and give advice not limited to herbs. Both those seeking witchcraft to treat their symptoms and the practitioners of witchcraft say somewhat tongue in cheek they are 'doing a bit of black magic'. Any form of witchcraft in the Maoist period was forbidden and represented in the official discourse as superstitious, backward, outdated, harmful, and a stumbling block to the development of science. This Maoist legacy of naming the practice of witchcraft as superstition continues today. On the one hand, people are reluctant to talk about witchcraft with strangers. For example, when I first arrived at Dacun, I asked people about witchcraft, and they denied any existence of it immediately. Zheng's son, Guang, told me: 'we don't have witchcraft anymore. It is superstitious and backward. We are better off now. We don't need that.' Other people said 'we haven't heard witchcraft mentioned for a long time. It is outdated. We all believe in science right now.' On the other hand, when people get used to you, they begin to talk about witchcraft, although they still prefer to use the word 'superstition' to describe the activity.

The next time I stayed in Dacun there was no mention of witchcraft. I began to believe there no longer was any. That is, until one week before I was due to depart, when my primary interviewee Chumu, who is Guang's wife and Zheng's daughter-in-law, asked me whether I was interested in going to look for medication for her son, adding that this medication would involve some witchcraft. I said yes. The next day, along with her husband, we went to another village situated on the other side of the mountain from Dacun to look for a particular witchcraft practitioner. He was actually a fortune teller, the son of an old herbal medicine doctor who inherited the ability of fortune telling from his grandfather. The fortune teller began by igniting three pieces of incense. Then he asked Chumu to throw five dice onto a piece of old yellow hardboard paper and enquired about her son's Chinese zodiac. The location of the dice on the paper enabled the fortune teller to tell Chumu the reason for her son's sickness. Before going to see the fortune teller, Chumu told me that she thought her nine-year-old son was not in good health – he had frequent diarrhoea and a cough. Even though her son's grandmother, Zheng, was the best doctor in the neighbourhood, Chumu still thought her son had not recovered fully. So she decided to see this fortune teller. After 'doing a bit of black magic', the fortune teller asked Chumu whether there was any tree in her garden that was dying. Chumu said yes. Then the fortune teller told her that was the reason of her son's sickness and instructed her to water the tree three times a day for three days. The fortune teller went on to say that he had herbal medicine for Chumu's son too. 'Superstition and herbs combined together can cure your son. Just one of them won't work,' the fortune teller told Chumu. Before departing, Chumu gave him 200 yuan. The fortune teller refused to take the money at first but, as Chumu insisted, he finally accepted it. On our way back to Dacun, Chumu told me how great this fortune teller was. She had been to see him before, and he had cured her long-term sickness. He was the best-known fortune teller in the neighbourhood. Because there were few fortune tellers as good as him, she was willing to travel a long distance and pay him a large amount of money. (The money Chumu gave to the fortune teller accounted for almost one thirtieth of their annual household income.) Chumu's belief in the fortune teller is shared by others – but most people do not seek this avenue to treat their symptoms. For example, Haiying, who was a frequent visitor to Zheng's clinic and who had been to many hospitals, said she would never choose witchcraft to treat herself. What she really believed in was biomedicine.

Biomedicine

Biomedicine, often referred to by local people as Western medicine, is extremely popular. Local people often say that biomedicine, particularly that involving antibiotics and getting hooked up to IV drips, is a quicker way to relieve pain, recover faster, and save money as a result of enabling them to return to work as soon as possible. Although they have to pay for biomedicine, in contrast to herbal medicine which is generally free, the shorter recovery time actually lessens the financial burden on the family and requires fewer family members to share the workload. Biomedicine is the rational choice for people acting as free agents in the market economy.

When I stayed in Dacun, I spent many fieldwork hours in Zheng's village clinic and caught the flu. Two days later, Chumu also caught the flu virus, probably from me. We both had sore throats and felt drowsy. Chumu suggested we both go to Zheng, her mother-in-law, and ask her for some IV drips. 'Penicillin is what we need,' said Chumu. I said I had had the flu before, but it would take more than a week to recover no matter what medication you took. She did not listen to me. She went to ask Zheng to give her IVs. On the first day, Zheng hooked her up to a penicillin IV drip. Zheng also suggested I do so. I said I often had the flu, but I did not need to get hooked up to a drip as I preferred to take tablets or pills. Antibiotics were not always necessary. Zheng and Chumu were surprised by my reaction. They responded: 'we have never heard of anyone with the flu refusing antibiotics.' Although Chumu and I recovered more or less at the same time, she thought she did not suffer as much as me, because she had hooked up to an IV and had taken antibiotics. However, during the time Chumu was suffering from the flu she was drinking many kinds of boiled herbal tea, which was part of her daily routine. She thought the herbs in the tea helped her recover, but would not cure her. This experience with the flu reminds me of my first conversation with Zheng when I had just arrived at Dacun – after being shocked by the line of patients waiting for IV drips outside her clinic:

On our way to Zheng's house from her clinic, I asked her how many patients she would treat each day. 'Almost 15 or 16 on average,' said Zheng, 'and they are all looking for IV drips, all kinds of IV drips. Were it not for IV drips, they wouldn't bother to come to the clinic. It is inconvenient for them to leave home and travel to the clinic. So when they come, they definitely expect IV drips.' 'Is IV really necessary to treat their symptoms?' I asked. 'No, not always. But once they come here, they just expect it,' Zheng said.

(Excerpt from field note on 23 May 2011)

Zhichai He, a 58-year-old male, was another frequent visitor to Zheng's clinic. He was well known in the village as an alcoholic. He declined to be interviewed by me when I first met him waiting for an IV drip at the clinic, insisting that I needed to buy him a bottle of beer. He said 'without a bottle of drink, I cannot find the words.' After I had bought him beer from the grocery store next to the clinic, he started to talk. Zhichai said he was also preparing herbal medicine at home while sitting at Zheng's clinic waiting for IV drips. After getting hooked up to the IV drip, he would later go home to take the herbal medicine. 'Herbs alone cannot cure my sickness, whereas my sickness can be cured by getting hooked up to IV drips. But when the two are combined I recover sooner,' said Zhichai. I asked him whether he knew what kind of medicine was in the IV drip. He said no and he did not care. He said he would come to the clinic for IV even when he had a hangover or lack of appetite. Even when he was not sick, he would still sometimes come to the clinic to ask Zheng to give him what he called 'energy' IV.[9] After taking it, Zhichai said he felt refreshed and comfortable. Since the introduction of NCM by the state, Zhichai considered the cost of visiting the clinic to be reasonable.

In addition to antibiotics and IV drips an important role in people's recovery is played by the placebo effect. The disposable hypodermic needles, plastic tubes and bottles filled with liquid that accompany IV drips on their own are known to provide patients with a huge placebo effect. Of greater concern is the fact that patients choose to ignore or simply do not know the degree of drug resistance built up by frequent use of antibiotics and IV drips. As laypeople, they have no professional knowledge of what is inside the bottle or how efficacious it is, but they are fascinated by the equipment compared with that involved in herbal medicine. Doctors, on the other hand, have to conform to patients' requests for IV drips, and sometimes, antibiotics in order to survive in the market economy.

The actual act of hooking up to and taking IV drips usually lasts for one to two hours, sometimes longer, a lengthy procedure compared with taking pills or tablets. So taking IV drips actually gives the patients a break from their daily lives. As Haiying put it, sitting in Zheng's clinic taking IV represented a moment of leisure in her busy daily life. The clinic gave people a temporary break from their routine life. By the same token, queueing outside the clinic for hours to take IV drips was a chance for villagers to socialize. By going to Zheng's clinic everyday when I stayed in Dacun, I got to know most of the residents and they got to know me before I went to their homes.

Concluding observations

Clearly, most local residents take more than one medicine at the same time. When considering the different practices and treatments adopted by Haiying, Chumu, and Zhichai and the many other people I met in Weixi, they all had their own opinions about how to achieve the best results from the different treatments available, paramount among which was the tendency to overuse IV drips and antibiotics. Under the changing governmentality of post-socialist China, the individual in China is inevitably involved in the current processes of neoliberal globalization, regardless of their ethnic identity or where they live. Therefore, they have to be responsible for their own health. The presence of other therapeutic forms and their roles shows that local people actively engage in the market economy as well as the state discourse about modern health by their own dynamic mix and match of different kinds of medical practices.

However, the hegemonic notion of science has been internalized in people's consumption of and attitude towards biomedicine. In one sense, people are now free to choose biomedicine as their treatment but, in another sense, their predominant choice of biomedicine is a manifestation of the biopower the state enforces. My case study shows biomedicine is at the intersection of macro state biopower and micro individual consuming power. Through the consumption of biomedicine, people not only get healthy and strong bodies expected by the state, but they also maintain responsible PRC citizenship regardless of their ethnic identity. Therefore, the triumph of biomedicine in the ethnic minority borderland is in congruence with the state's nation-building agenda in the form of a market economy.

Moreover, as consumption itself is the process that reflects the opportunities and constraints of modernity (Zukin and Smith-Maguire, 2004), and the penetration of biomedicine in daily lives is also part of modernity, people's embracing of biomedicine – despite being combined with other medical practices in the current context – becomes a way for them to articulate a local version of modernity through medical consumerism. If each local version of modernity is what Timothy Mitchell (2000) argues as staged so as to be arranged to produce the unified global history of modernity, biomedicine is certainly staged as symbols of modernity. In particular, as the most evident and most accessible form of biomedicine in the local village, IV drips can be visualized and experienced by most local residents first hand. Thus, local people's obsession with IV drips is another way of expressing their yearning for modern life and involvement in globalization. Moreover, the fact that local herbal medicine is by and large free makes it less valuable and thus less effective in the eyes of local residents. I will end this chapter with a quote from Haiying, whose articulation of biomedicine and money can properly illustrate an unintended consequence of the development of modern public health and consumption in the margin of the state:

'I sold anything valuable at home for cash for my treatment. But my sickness is still here. I still have pain. My sickness is not cured. It has never been completely cured. For nine years, I've been to seek intravenous (IV) drips once I had saved some money. After I spent all the money, I had to come back. I've never had enough money to completely cure my sickness, although I have been seeking treatment continuously for nine years. Had I been rich enough, I would have been cured by now.'

(Taken from interview with Haiying in 2011)

Notes

1. I use the term 'witchcraft' here because it is the closest literal translation of its Mandarin form *wu shu* as presented by local people. However, the particular form of witchcraft popular in this area is much closer to geomancy, which I described in detail on p. 118.
2. In the Maoist period, the family was only part of the commune. Therefore, family was not the basic unit for agricultural production (Potter and Potter, 1990).

3. 'Liberate the productivity' or *Jie fang sheng chan li* in Mandarin is a quote from Deng Xiaoping.
4. In 2010, 10 yuan was equal to US$1.4.
5. I heard this many times from local people while doing fieldwork in the villages in Weixi.
6. It is not my intention in this chapter to discuss the 'folk' concept of health in Weixi. What I want to present here is how people articulate their medical choice in a changing historical context – not the local pathology of sickness and disease.
7. Dacun was my primary fieldwork site at the village level. It is located in the east of Weixi. There are 42 households in Dacun. The residents include ethnic Lisu, Naxi, and a few Tibetan.
8. As mentioned in the third section of this chapter ('The setting'), there are a number of ethnic groups present in Weixi, such as Lisu, Naxi, Tibetan, and Han. Each has its unique religious beliefs. As a result, witchcraft practised by people in Weixi is at the intersection of different religions. No attempt has been made here to look at witchcraft in detail, to do so would require another study. In this chapter, my primary concern is with its therapeutic function and how it compares with other therapeutic practices.
9. Zheng later told me the 'energy' IV was little more than IV with glucose and saline.

6

Frugalists, anti-consumers, and prosumers: Chinese philosophical perspectives on consumerism

Geir Sigurðsson

Abstract: This chapter is a survey of classical Chinese philosophical views of consumption. It mainly focusses on Confucianism, but includes brief treatments of Mohism and Daoism as well. It begins by reviewing earlier discussions of Confucianism and capitalism, which were initiated by Max Weber in his well-known comparative analysis of the Protestant Ethic and the religions of Asia. While Weber concluded that Confucianism was unlikely to stimulate the formation of the kind of industrial capitalism that came to the fore in Europe, some later thinkers sought to contradict his thesis by arguing that Confucianism was a seminal factor in the speedy modernization process of East Asian economies in the twentieth century. As this chapter will show, however, these views have been motivated by suspect intentions and are therefore questionable. The discussion will then move to the classical Confucian and some neo-Confucian texts in order to extract the general Confucian views on consumption, revealing an unmistakable and consistent tendency to consider material wealth and all that it entails as subordinate to virtue and morality. An even stronger aversion to consumption is expressed by Mohist and Daoist thinkers. The conclusion is that Chinese philosophy is overall more likely to discourage than to stimulate consumption, which may possibly be a factor in the low domestic consumption in contemporary China.

Key words: capitalism, Chinese philosophy, Confucianism, consumption, Daoism, Mohism, propriety.

Introduction

Consuming is a matter of life and death. This has applied at all times and will apply to all human beings as long as the species remains in existence.

A large proportion of human life has always been spent on the aim of prolonging it by securing necessary consumables. But during the last half century or so, new and more urgent dimensions of consumption have been emerging, prompting novel exploration and disposition. Unequal distribution of goods has always characterized human life on planet earth, but the extent of this inequality has never been as extreme in the world as it is today. Farmers, fishermen, hunters, and other producers of goods from nature have always had to take some level of sustainability into account and ensure that these goods will not be entirely depleted at one time in order that they will be available at later times as well. But the present world is facing serious and even total depletion of certain vital natural goods, not primarily because of its already massive and rapidly increasing human population, but because of overconsumption in its most prosperous parts.

While certainly conditioned by circumstances, human consumption has always tended to move beyond the absolute necessities of basic nutrition, clothing, and shelter to more supplementary goods providing comfort, entertainment, or beautification. But a real consumerist society, one in which people consciously organize their lives around the acquisition and merchandising of goods that are not needed for mere subsistence, is essentially a modern phenomenon. Largely a global desideratum, this particular mode of life and value orientation is intensifying in both scope and degree, motivated by the current system of global capitalism, which consistently demands higher levels of domestic consumption in order to boost the image and marketability of each society by means of higher scores on the GDP index. As a human activity, consumerism may very well be the most important 'driver' of global environmental change, accounting for 'a gradual but accelerating switch from a nature-dominated to a human-dominated global environmental system' (Palsson et al., 2013: 3). From this point of view, while consuming is certainly a matter of life and death, consumerism may turn out to be a matter of mere death. It is therefore of the utmost importance to understand ordinary people's cultural attitudes to consumption, identify ways of thinking that will seek to keep it within limits, and, if feasible, endorse their adoption or at least try to learn from them.

The unprecedented speed and scale of economic development taking place in China during the last few decades has transformed the entire country into a producer society and its more affluent parts into consumer societies. The differences between the two, as Baumann (2005: 26) observes, is 'one of emphasis, but that shift of emphasis does make an enormous difference to virtually every aspect of society, culture

Figure 6.1 The co-existence of the spiritual and the consumerist in Shanghai

and individual life.' The prosperity enjoyed by the regions around the east coast is now comparable with a number of the world's developed countries. This is all the more dramatic considering that only a few decades ago supplementary consumer goods were not only scarce but most people, even in the cities, would not be able to afford them. Today, the Chinese population, or at least a large part of it, is rapidly entering the global club of consumers.

But economic development has not only changed Chinese society with regard to markets, production, and consumption, though these may constitute the most conspicuous aspects on the surface. While the door of the Open Door Policy was perhaps never fully open, significant cultural changes have also taken place in China, changes that may in fact be closely associated with the emergence of the Chinese consumer society. Maoist China vehemently opposed traditional Chinese philosophical and religious traditions as they were considered the main culprits for China's stagnation in the late Qing dynasty. Since Confucianism was the official state ideology in China during the last two dynasties, this applied in particular to values, practices, and institutions associated with Confucianism, while Daoism, Buddhism, and other religious and philosophical schools were also seriously undermined through prohibition and the stigma of 'reactionary tendencies'. The onslaught during the Cultural Revolution against the 'four olds' (*si jiu*), moreover, made it even life-threatening to reveal any attachment to items, practices, and values that could be termed 'traditional', while Confucius himself was denounced along with Lin Biao in a special campaign in 1973–76. In the wake of the Open Door Policy, however, traditional values and ways of thinking have been enjoying a slow comeback. The reasons for this resurgence are complex and can only be briefly addressed in this chapter.

It is first of all vital to acknowledge that despite Party efforts, traditional Chinese philosophy and religion were never completely eradicated from Chinese society, let alone from the Chinese 'mind'. Religious practices continued in secrecy throughout the country, though mostly in rural areas, and classical Chinese philosophy was still both clandestinely and openly studied, admittedly often in order to demonstrate its reactionary and malevolent nature. Some practices firmly embedded within Chinese philosophy and religion, however, such as Chinese medicine, were officially sanctioned. Moreover, and perhaps more ironically, Mao's modifications of Marxist theory can hardly be made sense of without taking into account Mao's own understanding and interpretation of classical Chinese philosophy, not least Confucianism. In this sense, Maoism is itself significantly inspired, even influenced, by traditional Chinese thinking.

Second, the 'new era' in China has witnessed a serious decline in adherence to Marxism and Maoism among the general population. As argued by a number of scholars, this has led to the emergence of a 'moral vacuum' in China calling for new spiritual resources in people's everyday living (Bell, 2008; Fan, 2010). While this state of affairs has certainly brought about an increase in the number of Christian converts, the resurgence of Chinese popular religion, Confucianism, Daoism, and Buddhism is all the more dramatic. This goes hand in hand with people's general interest in traditional Chinese design, symbolism, and rituals that has become increasingly noteworthy in the Chinese consumer market.

Third, and related to this, it may very well be the case that the 'spiritual void' felt by many Chinese citizens is itself largely produced by the shocking impact of consumerism and a money-oriented society that have contributed to a depersonalization of social and familial relations in the modernizing Chinese society. While there has been a growing belief in recent decades that Confucianism has served as a positive cultural factor for the rise of capitalism in East Asia, Croll (2006a: 37) has suggested, on the contrary, that in China 'it is the everyday commodification of personal relations which has encouraged the rehabilitation or rise of Confucianism, rather than vice-versa' and 'it was consumption or the profusion and increasingly exclusive interest in goods and money that led to a simultaneous nostalgia for Confucian and, by implication, socialist ways of relating.'

The purpose of this chapter is not to explore or evaluate whether or to what extent traditional philosophy and religion are enjoying a comeback in contemporary China, although its composition certainly takes for granted that this is in fact taking place. Rather, in the following, I shall attempt to extract Chinese views of human consumption from the classical philosophical corpus. To be sure, during most of the long history of Chinese philosophy contemporary problems related to consumption had not yet materialized and were therefore not regarded as such. But Chinese thinkers still had something to say about consumption, though they had other factors and consequences in mind.

The rise of the 'hundred schools of thought' during the spring and autumn period in ancient China was a response to a disintegrating society in the midst of escalating warfare. While these schools were not specifically countering consumerist behaviour, some of the dominant values and motivations of this period against which they turned could be seen as being aligned with consumerism. Egotism, greed, and wealth-seeking were commonly perceived by the proponents of these schools as the main underlying factors that were ripping society apart, leading to attacks on neighbouring states and continuous attempts to encroach upon their inhabitants, possessions, and lands. In their different ways of confronting this sad state of affairs, clear attitudes to consumption can be detected and are sometimes explicitly stated. In the following, I shall attempt to seek out these attitudes in some seminal Chinese philosophical schools, namely Confucianism, Daoism, and Mohism.

Of these, it is indisputable that Confucianism has been the most influential school of thought in the history of the Chinese people. During the Chinese Empire, which was in place with some interruptions for two millennia, Confucianism was certainly not the only source for the imperial ideology, but it was clearly the most significant. For this reason, the main emphasis here will be on Confucianism. The school of Mo Di (c. 480–390 BCE), or Mohism, strongly criticized Confucianism during the ancient period, but dissolved as a separate school around the time of the first Chinese Empire, the Qin, in 221 BCE. Nevertheless, it can be reasonably assumed that Mohism had some impact on Confucianism as it developed during the Qin and Han dynasties, and since Mohism is also particularly interesting with regard to the topic of consumption, I have decided to include a short discussion of the school. Daoism, still very much alive and kicking in China, as well as having heavily influenced East Asian Buddhist schools, cannot be left out of the discussion. While the Daoist philosophy was probably not suitable as an official political ideology in China, it was always present behind the scenes, so to speak, and one can reasonably assume that it was a quite influential factor on the culture and attitudes of the 'common people'. Mohism and Daoism will be discussed together in a separate section, but the first two sections will be dedicated to Confucianism.

Are Confucians 'capitalist-roaders'?

Consumerism is inseparable from modern capitalism. Capitalism thrives on consumerism, as its dynamism stands in a direct relationship with the intensity of demand and the ability to supply. The Confucian attitude to consumption and consumerism is therefore perhaps best approached by reviewing briefly the abundant discussion of Confucianism and capitalism that has already taken place. As mentioned above, Confucius was targeted along with Lin Biao in a campaign during the latter half of the Cultural Revolution. Lin Biao, it was said, 'used the doctrines of Confucius and Mencius as a reactionary ideological weapon in his plot to usurp Party leadership, seize state power and restore capitalism in China' (Publisher's Note, 1974). Whether or not justifiable, the Confucian philosophers were seen back then by the radical wing of the CCP as 'capitalist-roaders'. The teachings of Confucius and Mencius were regarded as constituting an ideological system of the exploiting classes and they themselves were seen as representatives of the moribund 'slave-owning class' (Chao Chung-fan, 1974).

This was not the first time Confucianism was discussed along with capitalism, nor was it to be the last. Max Weber, in his influential study of religion and capitalism, had argued that Confucianism was unlikely to contribute to the development of the kind of systematic rationalized capitalism that was emerging in Europe and North America in his time (Weber, 1988). This is not because Confucianism implemented policies that were downright inhibitive of commercial activities. To be sure, Confucians had a generally negative view of the commercial class, which was probably a reflection mainly of Legalist views (Hansen, 2000) but was still explicitly held by seminal Confucians such as Xunzi (third century BCE), as we shall see. Nevertheless, Confucian scholar-officials produced favourable economic policies during the imperial period in China. But there were other reasons for Confucianism's failure to contribute to a rationalized capitalist system. I shall limit myself to only two on this occasion. The first adheres to the rise of industrial producer capitalism and, therefore, to Weber's thesis, while the second has to do with the contemporary type of consumer capitalism that has increasingly characterized Western societies since the mid-twentieth century.

Admittedly, there are limits to Weber's analysis of Confucianism and Daoism, as it is largely based on questionable second-hand sinological sources. Furthermore, Weber himself, though undeniably an intellectual giant, never had the opportunity to conduct research in China nor did he ever learn Chinese. Nevertheless, his insights into the confluence of ideology and external circumstances on subjective attitudes leading to certain ways of life (*Lebensführung*) are keen, often compelling, and should at least not be dismissed off hand. Weber makes a clear distinction between economic policies and economic attitude, and while the Confucian scholar-officials presented many favourable policies, the Confucian culture did not, according to Weber, produce any comparable kind of economic attitude to the one engendered by Protestant Christianity. Despite its strict ethical system, Confucianism did not lead to a methodically rigorous bourgeois way of life. Compared with Puritan Protestantism, the Confucians experienced no ethical tension between this and another world that compelled the individual to systematize his or her life from an inward motivation in such a way that a rationalized homogenization of all values came to the fore. Instead of a drive to rule, dominate, and transform the world, there was a much stronger tendency to adapt to the world as it is, thus to transform *oneself* (Weber, 1988). In this sense, China produced no comparable process of rationalization that was eventually to take over virtually all aspects of life in the form of a domineering economic system. Commercial activities were quite 'loose', adapted to the situation each time, and did not lead to rationalized bureaucracy, bookkeeping, law, and regulations. It is in this sense that Weber's thesis ought to be understood: Confucianism could very well have stimulating effects on some kind of capitalist-friendly practice, but not the historically and culturally particular kind that was to emerge in the West.

Modernization theory owes much to Weber's writings, despite not having taken into account his – admittedly oblique – critique of modern values, and their fragmentation as a result of disenchantment, followed by their homogenization in rationalized capitalist activity. We see this, for instance, in the now weakened but still to some extent ongoing discussion of Asian values and their role in modernizing East Asian countries such as South Korea, Taiwan, Hong Kong, and last but not least Singapore.

The coinage of 'Confucian Capitalism' involves an effort to identify particular Confucian traits that are supposedly instrumental in the fast economic progress in these four societies, now also including China. In this discussion, the 'Confucian values' of discipline, collectivism, and social humanism became the key explanation of Chinese entrepreneurial behaviour, and references to Chinese business practices in the formulation of the 'bamboo network', 'guanxi capitalism', or 'diaspora capitalism' became widely used in business circles (Yao, 2002). There was a clear desire to 'disprove' Weber's thesis and demonstrate that a Confucian culture was actually no less capable than the Protestant Ethic of developing a modernized kind of capitalism.

The political scientist Mark T. Berger referred in 1996 to 'values and virtues in East Asia that are strikingly similar to those (Protestant) qualities that are perceived to have underpinned the rise of the West in an earlier era' (Yao, 2002: 6). A Confucian work ethic, a Confucian kind of family-based loyalty, a Confucian sense of duty, and a Confucian kind of thrift – all these were now celebrated as quasi-Protestant qualities that serve as excellent conditions for a successful and modernized capitalist society. A closer look at the deeper motivations and the political backgrounds for generating such ideas, however, reveals that the case may be largely overstated.

The first explicit link made between Confucianism and the economic growth of East Asian societies is commonly held to have been made by Herman Kahn in *World Economic Development: 1979 and Beyond*. The book is written in a decade of severe economic problems in the West, including the oil crisis, trade deficits, and rising inflation, while the economies of Japan, Hong Kong, Taiwan, and South Korea were able to overcome rising oil prices and the general economic crisis in the world, enjoying far higher growth rates than the United States and Western European countries. Kahn suggests that we may have to accept that 'societies based on the Confucian ethic may in many ways be superior to the West in the pursuit of industrialization, affluence and modernization' (Kahn, 1979: 121). He states that the key contributing factor for the rapid growth in these countries is Confucian cultural values of 'dedicated, motivated, responsible and educated individuals and enhanced sense of commitment, organizational identity, and loyalty to various institutions' (Kahn, 1979: 128). While not exactly a neoliberal, Kahn believed that there were no limits to the progress that capitalism (and technology) could produce, and he felt that too many people in the United States were too critical of capitalism and its social influences. He called these critics the 'Anti-Growth Triads'. Hence his motivation for writing about the East Asian economies in this fashion was in fact a kind of scare tactics to boost support for capitalist practices in the US, as he feared the Confucian societies might challenge the legitimacy of Western, in particular American, hegemony. For instance, he writes:

> 'It is likely ... that members of Neo-Confucian cultures will get a sense of superiority, whether cultural, racial, or nationalistic. ... Japanese society, South Korean society, and to a lesser extent other neo-Confucian minorities around the world may become arrogant and self-satisfied in ways that would be unpleasant if not dangerous. Some Confucian societies have a long history of cultural arrogance, self-confidence and self-respect. ... We noted in our travels in these neo-Confucian societies they have begun to accept their 'cultural superiority' with great ease. Indeed, many want to carry it a bit further than we feel is either useful or justifiable.'
>
> (Kahn, 1979: 125)

Whatever the validity of Kahn's thesis may be, his notion of the Confucian economic ethic began spreading, eventually reaching the very civilizations to which it was meant to apply. Some of them were even to become its most enthusiastic proponents.

The major take-off of the Confucian capitalist thesis took place in Singapore in the 1980s and 1990s, after the Singapore government introduced Confucianism in the school curriculum in 1982. What ensued is sometimes called the 'Singapore challenge', a major philosophical, sociological, and even economical discussion about Asian, notably Confucian, values as the ideal platform for social and economic (i.e., capitalist) modernization. A central figure in this process was the respected Harvard scholar of Confucianism, Tu Weiming, who was doubtless brought to Singapore to confirm the stimulating characteristics of Singaporean Confucianism for its capitalist modernity. In the writings produced in this process, however, Tu is most cautious when making comparisons between the Confucian and Protestant Ethic in light of Max Weber's thesis. It must be admitted that he also largely ignores Weber's critical attitude to modern capitalism, and for the most part interprets Weber's thesis of the Protestant Ethic as a positive and creative transformation, though he mentions in passing that 'the Protestant ethic that has contributed to the rise of capitalism in the West has led to all kinds of problems such as excessive individualism and excessive rights-consciousness' (Tu, 1984: 86). However, Tu Weiming is unwilling to subscribe to the thesis that 'there is a narrowly specified causal relationship between the Confucian ethic and economic success' (Tu, 1984: 88) and would later go on to state that 'the method of finding the functional equivalent of the Protestant ethic in the "modernized" or "vulgarized" Confucian ethic is too facile, simple-minded, and mechanistic to merit serious attention' (Tu, 1996: 3). He further says:

> 'The question in what sense has the Confucian ethic contributed to the economic dynamics of industrial East Asia seems less interesting than a much more profound subject of investigation: How does the Confucian tradition, in belief, attitude, and practice, continue to impede, facilitate, and guide the modern transformation in East Asia, and, in the process, how is it being rejected, revitalized, and fundamentally restructured?'
>
> (Tu, 1996: 6)

The government-sponsored Confucian programme in Singapore clearly desired to take the issue much further than this and demonstrate Confucianism's suitability as a cultural basis for a modernized capitalist society. But it should be by now rather obvious that this campaign was first and foremost ideologically driven rather than genuinely searching for understanding of the extent to which Confucian characteristics could have a positive influence on a functional capitalist society. It appears, in fact, that the People's Action Party under Lee Kuan Yew's leadership was seeking to create a convenient ideology of authoritarian Confucianism in order to secure its place in power. It is, for instance, interesting that in the 1970s and into the mid-1980s, the Singapore leadership praised and encouraged 'rugged individualism' until it suddenly began endorsing its exact opposite, namely a Confucian kind of collectivism, duty, and self-sacrifice (Englehart, 2000).

Another potential difficulty with Singapore is that its claim to being a 'Confucian culture' may be somewhat questionable. Most of its current inhabitants of Chinese descent are Hokkien Chinese whose ancestors were imported by the British Empire as plantation workers in the nineteenth century. To what extent is it reasonable to assume that they brought along a strong Confucian tradition? Admittedly, this issue opens a can of worms, as the same question could most certainly be asked about the Chinese population at large. While Confucian-influenced values may be a part of Chinese culture, they do not tell the whole story and, as sinologist Benjamin

Schwartz has noted, 'there are distinct anti-Confucian trends in Chinese thought. Confucian and Chinese are distinct categories' (Tu et al, 1992: 5).

Can Confucians be consumer-capitalists? Can consumer-capitalists be Confucian?

If it is unclear whether Confucian traits are likely to have a stimulating effect on industrial producer capitalism, it seems far less compelling when considering our modern consumer capitalist system, for Confucians would in most circumstances be reluctant consumers and generally rather frugal. Interestingly, however, they would not see anything wrong as such with material wealth as it simply provides conditions for good living. At first glance, this may seem contradictory, but, as will become clear, a closer look at Confucian teachings reveals that it is not. Ruiping Fan observes the following with regard to material wealth:

> 'Material rewards are accepted as generally good, so that there is a pragmatist affirmation and openness to various means (such as central planning, the market, or both) as the source of monetary wealth, which is in turn a source of family and individual well-being. Confucians are this-worldly in pursuing a good life and human flourishing. They work for their families within a non-Puritanical acceptance of material success in this world in which material wealth is taken as, *ceteris paribus*, good and not grounds for moral suspicion. Wealth is desirable and should be pursued, as long as one does not pursue it by violating morality.'
>
> (Fan, 2010: 233)

Wealth, however, is not an acceptable goal in its own right, as Confucius himself states rather clearly in *Analects* (7.12): 'If wealth were an acceptable goal, even though I would have to serve as a groom holding a whip in the marketplace, I would gladly do it. But if it is not an acceptable goal, I will follow my own devices' (*Analects*, 1998).[1] On another occasion, where Confucius is engaged in conversation with one of his disciples, he expresses his approval of the dictum 'Poor but enjoying the way; rich but loving ritual propriety' (1.15). This view comes through more clearly in the following statement: 'Wealth and honour are what people want, but if they are the consequence of deviating from the way, I would have no part in them. Poverty and disgrace are what people deplore, but if they are the consequence of staying on the way, I would not avoid them' (4.5). Wealth is thus first and foremost an expedient tool for improving one's moral development. Other things being equal, it is to be preferred to poverty, but only insofar as it will not corrupt the individual in question. After all, Confucius has nothing against making a nice profit:

Zigong	We have an exquisite piece of jade here – should we box it up and put away for safekeeping, or should we try to get a good price and sell it off?
The Master	'Sell it! By all means, sell it! I am just waiting for the right price!' (9.3)

Greed, egotism, and extravagance, however, are all deplored. When fishing, Confucius himself avoided excess by using a line, not a net (7.27). Frugality is presented as a commendable virtue, while miserliness is not. Nevertheless, frugality leading to miserliness is better than extravagance leading to immodesty (7.36). An exemplary person (*junzi*) is often contrasted with a petty person (*xiao ren*) whose actions are motivated by narrow egotistic interests of personal gain instead of a sense of fairness or the desire to advance public welfare (4.11; 4.16). Exemplary persons, on the other hand, come to the assistance of those in need, but do not increase the wealth of those who are already wealthy (6.4; 11.17). 'I have heard,' Confucius says, 'that the ruler of the state or the head of a household: Does not worry that his people are poor, But that wealth is inequitably distributed ... For if the wealth is equitably distributed, there is no poverty' (16.1). The assumption is that there are sufficient resources for everyone to live decently, and that scarcity is caused by individual greed of those in power. When the despot King Xuan of Qi confides in Mencius that he is fond of both money and sex, Mencius reassures him that such fondness is perfectly acceptable as long as it is shared with the people (1B.5) (see *Mencius*, 1970). 'The accumulation of wealth' as it says in the 'Great Learning' (*Da Xue*)[2] chapter of the ancient *Book of Rites* (*Li Chi*), 'is the way to scatter the people, and the distribution of wealth is the way to collect the people' (*Li Chi*, 1967 (Da xue §26)).

For Confucians, it is everyday life that matters, both as a source of wisdom and as an object to be improved or at least constantly harmonized in the ceaseless reconfiguration of people, animals, things, and overall circumstances in which we find ourselves. One's most mundane actions, responses, and habits are indicative of one's personal development. They are exercises. As a matter of fact, the good life is a matter of continuous exercise. And life, at least the good life, is always a *social* kind of living. Since everyday life requires constant and regular consumption of things, how we consume is an integral part of the exercise of life. What and how we eat, how we dress, what sort of things we acquire, and how we acquire them are all indispensable in the process of our personal cultivation. It is here that *li*, the customs of self and interpersonal behaviour come into the picture. While often translated as 'rituals' or 'ceremonies', *li* also entails informal actions or gestures of etiquette, decorum, and courtesy which are thoughtful, but in the case of the most advanced individuals also spontaneous, responses to unique circumstances arising in reciprocal relations between two or more persons. They are not necessarily pre-ordained, though in the course of history many precisely laid-down rituals, ceremonies, and rules of etiquette have been formed and consolidated under the authority of tradition. But tradition according to Confucianism is not a fixed entity and must adapt itself, however resistantly, to the continuous changes taking place in the physical and cultural environment, and this applies as well to even the most seemingly anchored kinds of *li*.

The Confucian emphasis on *li* is immediately relevant to the question of consumption, for acts on this basis would constitute the only instances in which potentially immoderate expenditures could be seen as justifiable. Respect and deference toward others as well as toward the natural forces (energies in the world and in our bodies as Confucians believed) are often displayed through lavish gifts, delicious food, exquisite clothing, and other costly means. This was duly noted and criticized by Mo Di as we shall see in the next section. The *Book of Rites* contains many intricate descriptions of what things, food items, clothing, etc. are required for certain rituals, sacrifices, and ceremonies: 'Whatever heaven produces, whatever earth develops in its growth; – all were then exhibited in the greatest abundance,' as the book says about sacrifices (*Li Chi*, 1967 (Ji tong §4)[3]). In some cases, these can seem excessive. Those of us who have been guests in China, or, for that matter, in any of the other East Asian countries, have had the often unconscionable experience of being served delicacies during a single meal in more quantities than the diners could possibly have devoured in several days, and felt the embarrassment of receiving presents vastly disproportionate to the ones we brought along ourselves. These are instances of traditional customs that are originally Confucian, of 'appropriate' ways to receive and treat honoured guests, especially those 'from distant quarters', as Confucius himself indicates in the very first analect attributed to him. 'Propriety', it says in the *Book of Rites*, 'is seen in humbling one's self and giving honour to others.' It therefore comes as no surprise that relative to Western countries, a large proportion of luxury items are bought as gifts in contemporary China: 'Gifts for government officials, gifts for lovers, gifts for clients' (Rabkin, 2012). Now as before, however, there is an unquestionable emphasis on reciprocity:

> 'In the highest antiquity they [sages] prized (simply conferring) good; in the time next to this, giving and repaying the thing attended to. And what the rules of propriety value is that reciprocity. If I give a gift and nothing comes in return, that is contrary to propriety; if the thing comes to me, and I give nothing in return, that also is contrary to propriety.'
>
> (*Li Chi*, 1967 (Qu li §6)[4])

Certainly, it is expected that gifts will be reciprocated in one way or another. Perhaps this aspect has been overly formalized throughout the ages in Chinese culture so that a presenter of a gift will now expect some concrete favours in return. But gifts are still to a large extent a sign of good will and sincere intentions, and, from a Confucian point of view, they ought not to revolve merely around the display of external goods. The section on sacrifices quoted above from the *Book of Rites* continues: 'Everything was there from without, and internally there was the utmost effort of the will: – such was the spirit in sacrificing' (*Li Chi*, 1967 (Ji tong §4)).

As Chapter 10 in the *Analects* reveals, Confucius himself placed considerable emphasis on proper attire depending on circumstances (e.g., 10.6) and seems even to have been some kind of gourmand, as he 'would not eat food that was improperly prepared, or that was lacking the appropriate condiments and sauces' (10.8). But he would never be immoderate, nor eat more than his fill (10.8), and be quite willing to make changes to certain formal rituals should they traditionally require items that had become expensive (9.3). 'In observing ritual propriety,' in any case, 'it is better to be modest than extravagant' (3.4). Some occasions, moreover, may in fact call for more modesty in terms of diet or clothing, such as periods of purification during which 'he would invariably wear a spirit coat made of plain cloth' and 'invariably simplify his diet' (10.7) and 'in the presence of someone in mourning' when he 'would not eat his usual portions' (7.9).

Li are traditionally formed guidelines as to how we should act in our particular roles, relations, and circumstances. Their gradual adoption is a learning process that should teach us how to act reciprocally, respectfully, and responsibly toward others. While certainly entailing cultivation of one's person, such learning is not aim directed in a simple sense as the relations and all that they engender are changing with time along with all those involved. Thus, the configuration of these relations as informed by *li* is in a continuous process of re-evaluation. Roger T. Ames speaks of *li* as 'achieved propriety in one's roles and relations,' thus emphasizing that *li* are first and foremost enacted in the dynamic context of social relations, beginning in the family (Ames, 2011: 109). While there is certainly a blurry frame within which my enactment of *li* is expected to take place in each of my roles, I nevertheless have considerable scope to creatively personalize that enactment in each case (cf. Ames, 2011). The description of Confucius's own comportment betrays both the extensive scope of *li* according to his embodiment of these customs in real life and his creative personalization of them. As noted in the *Analects* (1998: 52), *li* applies to a way of life carefully choreographed down to appropriate facial expressions and physical gestures, a world in which a life is a performance requiring enormous attention to detail. Importantly, this *li*-constituted performance begins from the insight that personal refinement is only possible through the discipline provided by formalized roles and behaviors.

Li, then, are both the means and end of life as a work of art in constant progress. As discipline and training they constitute the means, and as the end, perhaps, they are exemplified by the life of Confucius himself as recorded in the *Analects*. His behaviour, however, is not presented as laying down universal rules to be imitated. It is, on the contrary, highly personalized as manifesting the particular character traits of Confucius himself, and therefore a mode of action ultimately inimitable by others but certainly inspirational to them. Every action enjoys its particularity as an action performed by that particular person in that particular circumstance and her particular phase of life (Sigurðsson, 2012).

Hence the level of consumption is in all cases dependent on, and thus secondary to, the appropriate action as guided by *li*: 'Virtue is the root; wealth is the branches', as the *Book of Rites* states quite clearly (*Li Chi*, 1967 (Da xue §26)). The point, in other words, is not material goods and their acquisition and consumption, but propriety. Excessive attention to such things is at the same time a distraction from what truly matters. Paying attention to detail is important, but losing oneself in detail is no good either. Thus priding oneself for being frugal is at best missing the point and at worst hypocrisy. Confucius reprimands those who have 'set their purposes on walking the way' but 'are ashamed of rude clothing and coarse food' (4.9). But when he remarked that his disciple Zilu felt no shame for 'wearing a shabby old gown while standing next to someone wearing fox and badger,' and then quoted the ancient *Book of Songs* (*Shijing*): 'Not jealous, not greedy, How could he be but good?', Zilu 'kept repeating the lines over and over again,' upon which Confucius says to him: 'How can this remark deserve to be treasured so?' (9.27). In this instance, Zilu gets lost in detail, apparently in the belief that not being ashamed of shabby clothes is a sufficient condition for being considered an exemplary person. He fixes his eyes on superficial appearance and loses sight of the heart of the matter. For the ancient Confucians, then, extravagance and excess are, as a general rule, undesirable. This, however, does not exclude the possibility that such behaviour could be acceptable in some very unusual circumstances. But one can assume that such circumstances would be rare.

During the centuries of China's disunity after the collapse of the Eastern Han in 220 and until its reunification in the Sui and Tang dynasties around the turn of the seventh century, Confucianism declined as a major ideological force in Chinese society, while Daoism and Buddhism became more prominent. Although the resurgence of Confucianism from the Song dynasty onwards in the tenth century was explicitly directed against both Daoist and Buddhist philosophical ideas, it was nevertheless significantly influenced by both of them. While not specifically discussed in this chapter, we can still note that the Buddhist programme for attaining spiritual salvation makes it generally antagonistic to materialism and excessive consumption. Adhering to the Mahayana school of thought, the Chinese Buddhist schools took the 'middle ground' and were generally not prone to asceticism, but they nevertheless warned against greed, overindulgence, and attachment to material things as major sources of suffering, dissatisfaction, or disquiet (Chinese *ku*, Sanskrit *dukkha*). Most of them further affirmed the Madhyamika teaching of the 'emptiness' of things and thus the ultimately illusory state of the phenomenal world (Thompson, 1996). Such and often strikingly similar views, while not based on the same premises, were shared by Daoists, as we shall see in the next section. Thus, the Neo-Confucianism that was to be formed through the influence of both Buddism and Daoism was even more guarded than its ancient forerunner against being spoiled by desires of a material kind.

Suffice it to take a few examples to illustrate this point. The Neo-Confucian thinkers underline much more so than the ancient Confucians the importance of calming desires. Zhou Dunyi (1017–73) speaks, in a Confucian-Buddhist manner, of modern music that 'arouses desires and increases bitterness without end' and criticizes rulers for having 'indulged their material desires without restraint' (Chan, 1963: 472). He further promotes the aim of 'having no desire', which, as Chan (1963) notes, was never before advocated by Confucians. However, in a manner similar to earlier Confucians, Zhou Dunyi also takes material wealth and riches as being 'secondary' to the real wealth of a moral kind of life:

'The noble person takes agreement with the Way as honour, and personal peace as wealth. Therefore he is always at peace, with nothing lacking. He regards ceremonial carriages and caps as small change; he regards gold and jade as dust. The weight [of his riches] cannot be exceeded.'

(Quoted in Chan, 1963: 472–3)

This quote is intriguingly similar to Weber's reference to the English Puritan church leader and theologist Richard Baxter's (1615–91) metaphorical remark that 'the care for external goods should only lie on the shoulders of the saint like a light cloak, which can be thrown aside at any moment' (Weber, 1930: 181). For Weber, fate decreed that the cloak should become an 'iron cage' or rather a 'shell as hard as steel', which would be a more suitable translation of the German original *stahlhartes Gehäuse* (Baehr, 2001). In other words, Weber believed that rationalized capitalism had narrowed down our valuations in such a way that considerations of monetary gain had overridden all other possibilities. Both Baxter and Zhou Dunyi, while not being opposed to material gain as such, seem to think that it is of little or no significance compared with moral issues, and can be easily brushed aside if it finds itself in conflict with moral values. The question is whether this has turned out to be the case in the development of these civilizations.

Anti-consumers and prosumers: Mohists and Daoists

As indicated in the last section, Mo Di and his followers chided Confucians for carrying out exorbitant funeral ceremonies. They also condemned their musical performances for being wasteful. Both criticisms are based upon the Mohists' generally rather austere philosophical outlook and the most logically clear example found in ancient China of a criterion for assessing the value of actions. The criterion is utilitarian, based upon the estimated benefits (li)[5] and/or harm (hai) of the action for society. Mo Di and his followers may have belonged to a class of craftsmen as their writings often make use of metaphors associated with the various crafts. They are also highly pragmatic in their outlook, while their pragmatism narrows itself down to immediate usefulness, vigorously opposing any kind of 'useless' ornamentation and decoration:

> 'What is the purpose of clothes? It is to protect us from the cold of winter and the heat of summer. The proper way to make clothes is such that they keep one warm in winter and cool in summer and that is all. Whatever does not contribute to these ends should be eliminated. What is the purpose of houses? It is to protect us from the wind and cold of winter, the heat and rain of summer, and to keep out robbers and thieves. Once these ends are secured that is all. Whatever does not contribute to these ends should be eliminated.'
>
> (*Mozi*, 2001: 78)

Had the Mohists not assumed the existence of a personalized and just divinity represented by *tian* or 'heaven', it would in fact be tempting to regard them as radical socialists. In any case, they seem to have been members of the unprivileged class, expressing their contempt of luxury and idleness, and adopting the soteriological stance of expecting *tian* to bring fortunes to the virtuous and misfortunes to those who encroach upon the innocent and weak.

Mo Di's criticism of the Confucian insistence upon decent funeral practices and musical performances must be seen in light of the fact that the period in which he lived was one of great social crisis and peril. Fierce warfare between the various states on the Great Plains of China broke out after 475 BCE and was to last until China was unified under one emperor two and a half centuries later. Hence death was frequent and so were funerals. One may reasonably assume that the Mohists found it impractical in such circumstances to carry out expensive funerals and lengthy mourning periods to the same degree as during times of peace. Similarly, they found the insistence on taxing the people in order to finance musical performances untimely while 'those who are hungry are unable to get food, those who are cold are unable to obtain clothing, and those who toil are not afforded a chance to rest' (*Mozi*, 2001: 106). Mo Di continues:

> 'These are the three greatest hardships upon the people. But what if we play the great bells, strike up the drums, sound the zithers, blow the pipes, and dance with shields and battle axes? Will this enable the people to procure food and clothing? I believe that such performances will not

produce such results. But let us set aside such concerns for the moment. For now great states attack lesser states and great families assault lesser families, the strong rob the weak, the many do violence to the few, the clever deceive the simple, those of noble rank act arrogantly toward those of humble rank, and rebels and bandits flourish and cannot be stopped. But what if we play the great bells, strike up the drums, sound the zithers, blow the pipes, and dance with shields and battle axes? Will this bring order to the chaos that presently reigns in the world? I believe that such performances will not produce such results.'

(*Mozi*, 2001: 106)

Considering the state of affairs in his time, these arguments seem rather compelling, and appear merely to say that in times when financial resources are limited, it is reasonable that people's basic welfare should be prioritized. Quite similar arguments were, for instance, made in Iceland after the economic collapse in 2008 when people debated whether the construction of the half-erected concert hall Harpa in Reykjavik ought to be continued or not (Helgason, 2011).

Nevertheless, Mo Di goes pretty far in his overall condemnation of music, which he claims is downright harmful. He says, for instance, that should 'men of rank and the gentlemen of the world really want to promote what is beneficial to the world and eliminate what is harmful to it, then they will prohibit and put an end to this thing called music' (*Mozi*, 2001: 110). Combined with the Mohist insistence upon consuming only the immediately useful, their contempt for embellishment, and their rigorous work ethic that, for example, criticizes mourning periods for 'prohibiting people from pursuing their vocations for an extended period of time' (*Mozi*, 2001: 83) appear in many ways as a Chinese version of the Puritanical Protestants. After all, music and entertainment was prohibited for a long period in many Protestant countries, including Iceland. Helgason (2011: 86) reminds us of the fact that for centuries 'Iceland was a country without music. There were no musical instruments; dancing was banned by the church ... There was very little fun to be had.'

Confucians, on the other hand, regard 'spiritual' elements of human living, such as ceremonies and musical performances, as indispensable for both individual development and social solidarity. In their view, expenses for such activities are therefore not only defensible but necessary in order to maintain and enhance a civilized society. It is difficult to assess the extent to which Mohism managed to have a lasting impact upon Chinese culture but, given that it contains a motivating force for a capitalist system in a manner similar to the Puritan Ethic, then the source of that force is much more likely to be found in the 'Mohist Ethic' than with the Confucians.

I shall now finally turn to the other anti-consumerist school of thought in China, namely Daoism. The Daoist philosophy is no less antagonistic to consumerism than Mohism but for different and more intricate reasons. Consumerism is a phenomenon that thrives on social valuations, fashion, status, images, affirmation by and comparison with others in order to establish an identity: 'The roads to self-identity, to a place in society, to life lived in a form recognizable as that of meaningful living, all require daily visits to the market place' (Baumann, 2005: 26). But the 'conspicuous consumer' who endeavours to indicate to others how accomplished he is in life through, say, expensive paraphernalia, goes against everything for which the Daoists stand. They are social sceptics, suspicious of popular trends and customs, and seek to minimize their influence on desires and artificial needs. As with the other schools of thought arising in ancient China, Daoism is a response to belligerent behaviour and the craving for wealth and power that prompts it. Daoists go right to the source of the problem, wishing to eliminate or at least significantly reduce the desires themselves, and thus to realize a calm and peaceful community where desires are few and feeble. In *Yuan Dao* (a section from the philosophical anthology *Huainanzi*, dating back to the second century BCE), the human predicament of being aroused by external things is described in vivid detail:

A man is quiescent when born –
This is his Heaven-endowed nature.
He moves when aroused –
This is the stirring of that nature.
The human spirit responds when things come on the scene –
This is the movement of the intellect.
When the intellect comes into contact with things,
Feelings of attraction and aversion are produced.
Where these feelings of attraction and aversion have taken shape,
And the intellect has been enticed from the outside,
One is unable to return to himself,
And the Heavenly principles in him are destroyed

(*Yuan Dao*, 1998, §5 p. 73)

The object is therefore to reduce desires to a minimum, and this is precisely what good rulers should do for their subjects, as the core Daoist text, the *Tao Te Ching*, recommends:

'Not to honour men of worth will keep the people from contention; not to value goods that are hard to come by will keep them from theft; not to display what is desirable will keep them from being unsettled of mind. Therefore in governing the people, the sage empties their minds but fills their bellies, weakens their wills but strengthens their bones. He always keeps them innocent of knowledge and free from desire, and ensures that the clever never dare to act.'

(Tao Te Ching, 1989; §3)

Though not sharing the Buddhist metaphysical framework of *samsara* and transmigration through the law of *karma*, the Daoists argue in much the same way as the Buddhists that aroused desires lead to a vicious circle of endless dissatisfaction and envy that leads to silly and in some cases even violent behaviour. One therefore loses sight of the good life when hurling oneself into the race for consumer items that turn out to be ultimately worthless:

The five colours make man's eye blind;
The five notes make his ears deaf;
The five tastes injure his palate;
Riding and hunting
Make his mind go wild with excitement;
Goods hard to come by
Serve to hinder his progress

(Tao Te Ching, 1989; §12)

One may surmise, then, that Daoists would disapprove, to put it mildly, of the advertising industry and its efforts to create, as British-born Chinese academic D.C. Lau observes, 'new desires for objects [that] no one would have missed if they had not been invented' (*Tao Te Ching*, 1989: xxix). Wang Keping, a commentator on the *Daodejing*, is also quite explicit on this point:

'The development of material civilization is prone to foster and reinforce people's desires for possessions. A close observation of modern advertising bears this out. It thus reduces people to the plight

145

of being passive consumers or slaves of commodities. A considerable proportion of human anxiety, frustration, and depression, which together comprise psycho-cultural problems, can be perceived as a consequence of the commercial display of desirable things. If by any chance all the mass media ceased to display such things, I assume that tension, either in a social or psychological sense, may well be relaxed to a great extent.'

(Wang Keping, 2011: 91).

And yet another commentator, Hans-Georg Moeller, argues in like manner:

'Obviously [Daoists] did not envision a capitalist market economy with its culture of creating demand and desires through advertising and a public ideal of ever-increasing prosperity. The early Daoists, it seems, were not interested in 'heating up' the economy by stimulating the acquiring of goods and possessions. Consumption was meant to be rather basic.'

(Moeller, 2006: 91)

Confucians and Mohists may have been sceptical of wealth and riches, recommending, as in the case of the Confucian thinker Xunzi, that the state 'keep statistical records to reduce the number of merchants and traders' for the sake of preventing farmers and craftsmen from abandoning their vocations in pursuit of greater profits (*Xunzi*, 1990, vol. 2: 123). But they certainly favoured the idea of facilitating economic growth as it would attract people to the state and thus increase its population. Daoist thinkers, on the contrary, were opposed to having a large state and therefore also against 'economic expansion and interstate commerce, both of which increase the desire for material goods and trigger an unremitting cycle of acquisition and exchange' (Behuniak, in press). The ideal Daoist state has a small population who 'find relish in their food, and beauty in their clothes, will be happy in the way they live and be content in their abode' (Tao Te Ching, 1989, §80).

Daoists may be described in a way as prosumers. They envisage a life in which we adapt to our immediate surroundings and simply consume what we ourselves produce. In a global capitalist world, such a vision is probably not realistic. The reigning policy in the last Chinese dynasty, the Qing, was much in line with this Daoist vision, expressing scarce interest in exotic things and global economic exchange. In the Opium Wars of the nineteenth century, however, this policy was violently crushed by the neo-colonial, industrial, and capitalist powers of the globalizing world. Present predicaments may in fact compel us to adopt a comparable vision that prompts us to focus first and foremost on the social and natural circumstances in which we live on a day-to-day basis. Their preservation and cultivation are most likely what will turn out to be decisive for the future of mankind.

Concluding reflections

What stands out in this overview of Chinese philosophical thinking is a decisive tendency to moderate consumption. Surely this is not surprising. After all, philosophical and religious thinkers or schools that promote immoderate behaviour are few in number. In all civilizations and at all times, they have sought to restrain the human inclination to accumulate material things and inspire people to broaden the horizon and embrace other values believed to be more beneficial to a stable, secure, and morally desirable society. Even Epicurus, despite the misleading association of his name with a devotion to sensual and material pleasures, endorsed simplicity in life in order to achieve a state of *ataraxia*, meaning tranquillity of the soul or freedom from disturbance.

A notable exception from this, however, is neoliberalism, a modern economic theory that in recent times has taken on quasi-religious characteristics in the political arena. While hardly adopted anywhere in an undiluted form, it is clearly a very influential ideology in the world economy, pushing for increased domestic and international consumption in order to stimulate global economic growth.

Contemporary China is sometimes held to be under strong neoliberal influences (e.g., Klein, 2007), and the twelfth Five Year Plan launched in 2011 envisages the expansion of domestic demand as a major driving force of the economy (BCCC/CBBC, 2011). Domestic consumption in China as a proportion of national GDP remains low, only 34 per cent compared with 60 per cent in Japan, 64 per cent in the United Kingdom and a huge 72 per cent in the United States (WB, 2013). Needless to say, these figures only tell a part of the story, and one would have to take a number of additional factors into consideration, such as population size, household income, and the magnitude of exported products, in order to draw conclusions from them about people's disposition to consume. In China, moreover, the lack of a functional social security system is held to be a major motivation for the Chinese people's high savings rate. This said, one cannot help wondering why the savings rate is so low and consumption so high in the United States, where the social security system is also quite deficient. Politics provides only a part of the explanation.

How do societies become consumerist? If Weber's analysis of the Protestant work ethic as a cultural stimulus for rationalized capitalism and the establishment of a producer society is correct, the question remains how that culture, whose rigorous frugality was an essential condition for playing such a role, was transformed into a consumerist culture. Perhaps such a transformation consists precisely in undermining culture, in weakening the habits and traditions that constitute it. After all, traditional behaviour, as Weber himself observed (1972), borders on the incomprehensible and irrational when considered from the point of view of the instrumental rational model propelling modern capitalism. A consumerist has a hard time understanding why or indeed *how* one would not like to, say, acquire and possess the latest trend in some merchandise or buy oneself a larger abode. Cultural habits and traditions are in this way antithetical to consumerism. In a consumerist society, as Baumann (2005: 25) has pointed out, habits are indeed continually, daily, at the first opportunity thrown aside, never given the chance to solidify into the iron bars of a cage. Ideally, nothing should be embraced by a consumer firmly, nothing should command a commitment for ever, no needs should ever be seen as satisfied, no desires considered ultimate.

It may be convenient for the 'training' of Chinese consumers that ever since the May Fourth Movement, and especially during the Mao Tse-tung era, there has been an ongoing effort in China to undermine traditional Chinese culture. Socialism has at least this much in common with neoliberalism; both regard traditional values and thinking as obstacles to their social models and therefore aim at their elimination. The prominent American neoliberal Samuel Huntington (2000: xv) is quite explicit in this regard when he advocates in a foreword to a book endorsing the political change of cultures to take as much as possible from Protestant Anglo-American culture: 'how can cultural obstacles to economic and political development be removed or changed so as to facilitate progress?' The final aim may be different, but Huntington's approach nonetheless echoes Mao Tse-tung's remark that 'reactionary culture ... must be swept away. Unless it is swept away, no new culture of any kind can be built up. The new culture and the reactionary culture are locked in a struggle in which one must die so that the other may live' (Mao Tse-tung, 1954: 141).

Thus, ironically, the fierce Maoist anti-traditionalism in the twentieth century may actually have facilitated the penetration of Chinese consumerism in the twenty-first. In the absence of stable social values, the need for positive self-identity, the wish to portray oneself to others as successful, may have brought a certain tendency to conspicuous consumption on the scene. The demand for brand and luxury products in China has been noted with anticipated excitement by market researchers, who estimate that China is fast becoming the world's largest market for luxury products (e.g., Kotler and Armstrong, 2010). So far, however, it is hard to tell whether this is an ongoing and spreading trend in Chinese society, or whether it should be understood in a more restricted manner as a rather typical *nouveau riche* response to instant wealth. The extent to which consumerism is able to dominate everyday life and values in China still remains to be seen.

We cannot establish beyond any doubt whether cultural factors have a decisive moderating impact on current Chinese consumption practices. But what is fully clear is that the most important and influential philosophical schools in China throughout the ages are in full agreement, though they may differ in degree, that one should be circumspect in one's consumption. At least in this regard, I believe, these schools are still fully relevant today as normative social forces, not only to the Chinese or East Asians, but to the entire world. They may be obstacles to the neoliberal understanding of 'progress', but certainly not to life on earth in the future.

Notes

1. Quotations from the *Confucian Analects* are taken from the translation by R.T. Ames and H. Rosemont Jr. (*Analects*, 1998). Throughout the chapter, I shall merely refer to the respective section in parentheses. For the convenience of the reader, all sources originally in Chinese are taken from available English translations.
2. *Da Xue* ('Great learning') is a chapter in *Li Chi: The Book of Rites*.
3. Ji tong ('A summary account of sacrifices') is a chapter in *Li Chi: The Book of Rites*.
4. Qu li ('Summary of the rules of propriety Parts 1 & 2') is a chapter in *Li Chi: The Book of Rites*.
5. The meaning of this character *li* is 'benefit' or 'profit' and has merely phonetic but no semantic relations to the Confucian *li* of propriety.

7

'To live is to serve the people': the spirit of model soldier Lei Feng in postmodernity

Andreas Steen

Abstract: Since Mao Tse-tung initiated the campaign 'Learn from Lei Feng' in 1963, the young soldier has become China's most famous model hero, whose virtues are still officially promoted. After 50 years, however, his image and 'spirit' are criticized as 'floating' between politics and morality, nostalgia, education, and commerce. This chapter explores the fate of 'Lei Feng' since the early 1990s by looking into the interaction between promotional strategies and audience/consumer response. Strategies to officially popularize the hero, corruption scandals, and widespread information about cases of moral decline inspire debates about the 'Lei Feng spirit', its absence as well as its need. It is argued that the original 'spirit' may still find support, yet the majority of young people seem to reduce it to the more international notion of simply 'helping others'. In this context, officially promoted tools such as computer games and films struggle to survive in China's competitive cultural market. Irony and entertainment promote the message – the popularity of Lei Feng as a revolutionary myth and icon boosts sales of memorabilia, souvenirs, hats, and shoes, though probably without much effect on spreading his virtues.

Key words: Mao Tse-tung, CCP, propaganda, reform policy, Lei Feng, campaign, consumerism.

Introduction

'... We should conduct more public activities to promote cultural and ethical progress, encourage volunteer service, and carry out regular activities to learn from paragons of virtue such as Lei Feng and publicize their exemplary deeds. . . .'

(Hu Jintao, President of the PRC, 2003–13,
Report at the 18th Party Congress, November 2012)

'China has had hundreds of these somewhat fake role models. . . . They don't work because they don't represent the right values. Lei Feng is a good guy but he doesn't have critical thinking skills, doesn't reflect on things and only follows marching orders.'

(Li Chengpeng, sports reporter and novelist
with a huge *weibo* network, 2013)

'We promote the Lei Feng Spirit because Lei Feng is an "ordinary" hero. His "heroics" were done in his daily life, and we can do the same if we wish. His spirit isn't about communism or socialism nothing ideological but about the basic human nature. If everyone could follow Lei Feng's path, the community will become much healthier.'

(Xing Huaqi, compiler of *The Selected Works of Lei Feng*)

'Rather than saying we need this man who died over 50 years ago, we need his spirit to trust and help each other.'

(Li Zhi, 20, university student, Beijing)[1]

On 5 March 1963, Mao Tse-tung initiated the campaign 'Learn from Comrade Lei Feng' (*Xiang Lei Feng tongzhi xuexi*). Lei Feng (1940–62) was 'Chairman Mao's good soldier' (*Mao zhuxi de hao zhanshi*), an ordinary soldier in the People's Liberation Army (PLA) who had died young due to an accident. As a model hero, he became famous for constantly reading the four volumes of the *Collected Works of Mao Tse-tung*, which were to him like food and weapons – the source and root of his spirit to always serve the country and support the revolution like a never-rusting little screw in an engine. The 'spirit of a screw' (*luosi jingshen*) emphasized virtues such as loyalty, patriotism, and uncritical acceptance of orders, which on propaganda portraits tended to be combined with Lei's character of a friendly, modest, selfless, and helpful young man. His joy of doing good deeds for the people, summarized in his famous phrase 'to put the limited life into the unlimited service for the people,' was another highly promoted virtue in later campaigns.

毛主席的好战士——雷锋

Half a century after the initial campaign, Lei Feng still returns on 5 March, officially celebrated as Lei Feng Day, and the Chinese Communist Party (CCP) continues to strongly promote his ideals of leading a frugal and obedient lifestyle, with an emphasis on CCP loyalty, patriotism, and the joy of 'helping the people' (*wei renmin fuwu*). People were all too familiar with the quote of the new secretary of the CCP and future president of the People's Republic of China, Xi Jinping, when he said in his speech to the nation in November 2013, 'The time of one's life is limited, but it is limitless for one to wholeheartedly serve the people' (Yu, 2013).

Lei Feng and his 'spirit' appear to be strongly debated topics in China's public sphere, especially around 5 March. Official policy promotes the spirit in a highly positive way, highlighting countless examples of Lei Feng–style activities. Critics and numerous polls evaluate popular acceptance of the spirit and are also quoted, though much less than in foreign newspapers, which sometimes seem to be all too eager to see China's superhero collapse. When looking at the pace of China's reform policy, the effects of globalization, individualization, and the commercialization of people's everyday lives, one may very well argue that the image and meaning of a Maoist model soldier and his virtues are outdated today. And while many Chinese do think exactly this, news revealing bribery, corruption, and nepotism, as well as laments about a general decline of morality, incite people to engage in discussions about these virtues. Above all 'Lei Feng' has been drawn into the waves of postmodern arbitrariness or possibilities, thereby leaving the strict frame of party propaganda, and entering the world of (revolutionary) commercial popular culture, which is open to all kinds of readings and applications.

At present, and embedded in a wave of popular propaganda art from the revolutionary period (Mittler, 2008), Lei Feng has the same kind of presence as would a formerly successful pop star – that of someone who has been promoted since his early death and whose image is now 'floating' between politics and morality, nostalgia, education, and commerce. Thanks to several decades of poster propaganda, his likeness is famous in all parts of China. His diary has been reprinted several times in different versions, as new information and photographs are released. His biography and 'spirit' are well known, as they have been promoted in newspapers and books (both for children and for adults), in schools and universities, at conferences, in documentary and promotional films, in museums, exhibitions, cartoons, computer games, and on numerous homepages. In addition, numerous songs refer to him and his 'spirit', schools and buildings are named after him, and awards designed to honor selfless commitment are given the motif 'modern Lei Feng'. Finally, a whole industry is concerned with producing images, cups, hats, T-shirts, bags, lighters, posters, shoes, and other merchandise. In other words, 'Lei Feng' is not only propaganda designed for mass education, but also an icon, a spirit, and a brand. Since the Internet age began, Zhang Zhong (2012) remarks, the Lei Feng Brand (*Lei Feng pinpai*) has become more and more popular. As John Fiske argues, political campaigns and content old and new, provide 'the raw materials, the primary sources', for a creative productive process around the legacy and the image of 'Lei Feng' (Fiske, 2010: 112).

In 2012 and 2013, the CCP launched the biggest Lei Feng campaign for 20 years, designed to promote his virtues and to commemorate the 50th anniversary of both Lei Feng's death and the campaign. As a matter of fact, today 'learning from Lei Feng' is promoted as a recipe for the cure of almost all social, political, moral, and educational ills, for high-level cadres as much as for intellectuals, white and blue-collar workers, and pupils in school. This chapter explores the conflict between Lei Feng's official promotion, his ongoing popularity, and predictions about his demise. I will not go into the details of the early campaigns in the Maoist and revolutionary period, but begin with the early 1990s, when Lei Feng had lost much of his previous propaganda value.[2] By then, after 30 years of organized Lei Feng experience, from childhood to adulthood, in various campaigns, and on Lei Feng Day, the model soldier was 'not the preserve of one segment of Chinese society but part of the common community of experiences' (Reed, 1991: 8).

In the following decades of the postrevolutionary and postmodern era Lei Feng's image changed from a frugal soldier and Mao enthusiast, to a reformer, and finally to that of an almost hip youngster. Yet three basic characteristics remained untouched – constant focus on what is best for the CCP and China, selflessness, and joy in helping others. These values are still accepted if not admired among certain audiences. Younger generations, nevertheless, are selective and may agree to Lei Feng's moral virtues, but criticize and even ridicule his ongoing connection with politics in times of intensified communication networks and daily information about governmental corruption. Today, Lei Feng is regarded as a positive but naive character. Discussions about his heritage and meaning fill China's media, and it would be no exaggeration to say that 'Lei Feng' is at the center of a general debate about power and morality, which obviously helps to increase his commercial value.

'The Lei Feng spirit will always exist!'

Chinese postmodernity developed during the early 1990s, against the background of globalization and new capitalist and commercial freedom. Deng Xiaoping's 'southern journey' of 1992 is usually seen as the starting point, because it opened and legitimized a new era of market economy and consumption. This combination, according to Dirlik and Xudong Zhang (2000: 10), was also meant to distract people from political questions and prevent the repetition of social action such as that of 1989. In other words, Chinese postmodernity, insofar as it promotes a culture of mass consumption, is closely linked to governmental strategies. This is also the reason postmodernity in China is often understood as the postrevolutionary and postsocialist period (Dirlik and Xudong Zhang, 2000: 4–5). According to Sheldon Hsiao-peng Lu, contemporary China 'consists of the superimposition of multiple temporalities; the premodern, the modern, and the postmodern coexist in the same space and at the same moment. . . . Spatial coextension, rather than temporal succession, defines non-Western postmodernity. Hybridity, unevenness, non-synchronicity, and pastiche are the main features of Chinese postmodern culture' (Lu, 2001: 13).

China's entry into postmodernity, generally understood as an 'era of indifference' (Zima, 1997: 26), coincided with a new educational policy that was implemented after the Tiananmen protests in 1989. The 'Patriotic Education Campaign' was officially launched in 1992 and was aimed at reforming history education. Officials felt that the young generation had to be re-introduced to the CCP's victory over imperialism that had put an end to the century of humiliation – both of which legitimize the Communist government. Two years later, the CCP laid out its wider objectives, namely 'to boost the nation's spirit, enhance cohesion, foster national self-esteem and pride, consolidate and develop a patriotic united front to the broadest extent possible, and direct and rally the masses' patriotic passions to the great cause of building socialism with Chinese characteristics' (Wang, 2012: 99).

Until then, promotion of the Lei Feng spirit had seen many ups and downs, due to being undermined by the realities of the reform process. Already in 1988, Schell (1988: 293) observed: 'The practical problem was that fewer and fewer Chinese wanted to be screws, much less parts of a machine.' Now, following the dismissal of workers from state-owned factories, news about corruption, violence, and economic insecurity, people began to ask 'Lei Feng, where are you?' (Reed, 1998; Han Xu, 2012). Propaganda officials were convinced of the Lei Feng spirit and launched a large campaign after the Tiananmen protests had been forcefully suppressed in June 1989. In November, the PLA Culture Publishing House published a selection of texts from the diary (*Lei Feng riji xuan*), the fourth edition of which was published in 1990. In his introduction Yang Baibing stated that 'the direction of Lei Feng was correct in the past, it is correct at present and will be always correct in the future.' People's reactions were now mixed with irony and sarcasm. Most irritating was official praise of the PLA's Lei Feng–style activities, promoted to repair the damaged image resulting from its role in suppressing the 4 June movement. Lei Feng also was a PLA soldier and people had little doubt that he would have been among those most eager to support governmental decisions (Schell, 1995: 252).

This notwithstanding, people developed a certain nostalgia for the revolutionary period and the first carefully designed product to combine it with commercial interests was the tape/CD compilation 'The Red Sun – Odes to Mao Tse-tung Sung in a New Beat', released in 1992, and selling millions of copies.[3] Inspired by its success and the growing wave of nostalgia, revolutionary culture entered the realm of commercial popular culture, while China's young generation began to select and define its own 'heroes' and 'idols', often chosen from the fields of popular culture, sports, or from among foreign stars and celebrities (*People's Daily*, 2003). It is in this context that model soldier Lei Feng continued to return every spring and 'learning' from him was promoted under the leadership of Deng Xiaoping, Jiang Zemin, and Hu Jintao.

To promote the Lei Feng spirit, the importance of Lei Feng Day can hardly be overestimated, both in theory and in practice. Public announcements combined the aim of building a 'socialist spiritual civilization' with the spirit of Lei Feng, stating that it perfectly supports the aim of educating young people with the 'Four Haves' (ideals, morals, culture, discipline). 'The spirit of Lei Feng will always exist,' *Renmin Ribao* (1993) was convinced and continued to describe the successful implementation of the Lei Feng spirit in business and work places, among youths, in schools, and within the party apparatus.

The 1990s are also remembered for two extreme developments within Chinese society, namely the increasing importance of religion and spirituality, religious groups, or sects (e.g., Falun Gong) and the rise of a new nationalism. It was 1997, then, that marked not only the year Deng Xiaoping died and the PRC celebrated the 'return' of the British colony Hong Kong, it was also the year when the third Lei Feng film, *The Day Lei Feng Left Us* (*Likai Lei Feng de rizi*), came into the cinemas on Lei Feng Day, followed in summer by China's most expensive movie, *The Opium War*, launched to make audiences rethink the end of imperialist rule in China. *The Day Lei Feng Left Us* is based on the biography of Qi Anshan, the truck driver who accidentally caused the death of Lei Feng. Filled with grief, he literally 'lived' the Lei Feng spirit and promoted it throughout his life. The film, also criticizing egoistic behaviour and the loss of socialist values, was, according to Chinese sources, the most successful movie of the year, bringing in 25 million yuan (Shi Yu and Lin Tao, 2002).

The commercial value of Lei Feng's story and image entered into a new period when China's government was debating and promoting the protection of intellectual property rights a few years later. In this context, one has to look at the story of Zhang Jun (1930–2013), who is credited with having taken the first pictures of Lei Feng in September 1960, when he was instructed to write an article about a soldier who had donated 200 yuan to disaster relief. Until 2003, Zhang Jun's more than 200 Lei Feng photographs had been used by the mass media without any compensation for Zhang himself. At one point, when 'more newspapers or periodicals adopted the photos without affixing his name and some even altered the illustrations,' he felt he had to fight for his rights. In June 2003, he received copyright protection from the copyright administration of Liaoning province. The 73-year-old photographer stated that all payments would be used for publicizing the Lei Feng spirit and volunteer activities (*Xinhua*, 2003).

Earlier that year, on 5 March, *Renmin Ribao* (2003) ran the lead article 'The times are longing for the spirit of Lei Feng – further develop the spirit of Lei Feng and bring it to full expansion.' It explained that millions of people were already consciously practising his spirit and that the young generation, which grew up under the moral guidance of Lei Feng, was eager to further develop this spirit through its activities. However, the Communist Party and society as a whole were called upon to put Lei Feng's spirit into practice and fully develop its main virtues in order to realize the 'Three Represents'.[4] More generally, people were encouraged to 'learn in a highly broadened sense from Lei Feng,' including all kinds of beneficial work, donations of blood, organs, and money, etc. The decisive difference from previous campaigns can be seen in the fact that the focus was not on Lei Feng's communist qualities; rather, emphasis was put on nation-building, a collective spirit, social values, and mutual help. However, probably carried away by eagerness, competition, and rising individualism, people started promoting themselves by listing and promoting the good things they did. The *Southern Daily* (*Nanfang Ribao*) and other media criticized this behaviour and reminded its readers: for Lei Feng, helping others was a personal need, not something that he did to find recognition. It is not important how many good deeds one performs over a given period of time. It is, however, necessary to develop a consciousness which experiences happiness when helping others (Chao Bai, 2004).

To promote exactly this spirit among younger audiences, Shi Yonggang, a public intellectual and author of many books, together with two editors (Liu Qiongxiong and Zhang Jun), published *Lei Feng, 1940–1962* on Lei Feng Day 2006. It was 'one of more than 1000 books that have recorded his good deeds,' but it was the first book that aimed at presenting Lei in a stylish, contemporary, and more accessible fashion. In order to do so, Shi's book 'featured more than 300 never-published photographs of Lei, showing him as a fun-loving young man' (*China Daily*, 2006). The pictures were taken by seven photographers, including Zhang Jun, and clearly present a different image of Lei Feng, showing him, for example, riding on a borrowed motorbike in Tiananmen Square, in fashionable sweaters, in a leather jacket, and wearing a wristwatch. The sheer number of photographs, taken of an ordinary soldier in a politically difficult period, and his almost 'bourgeois' appearance on some of them confirmed speculations about Lei Feng being a construct of propaganda work. The book was, nevertheless, of commercial value when its second edition appeared in 2012.

The year 2006 not only saw the birth of 'fashionable Lei Feng', it was also the time when government institutions engaged in discussions about 'healthy' online games, gaming regulations, control functions, and educational use. Hearn and Willis (2008) identify the phrase 'to use the past to serve the present' as a general feature of promoted online games, which were aimed at strengthening users' patriotic feelings: 'Incorruptible Warrior' mixes past and present Chinese history, introduces heroes and legends, and is basically concerned with fighting corrupt officials. Other games were 'Chinese Heroes' and 'Anti-Japan War Online' – designed to raise the national spirit among young players. 'Learning from Comrade Lei Feng' was another important game in this context. For beginners, 'Sewing and Mending Socks Is the Only Way to Increase Experience and to Upgrade' is a game at the higher levels of which one can upgrade by doing good deeds and fighting secret agents in order to increase one's reputation through skills and loyalty. The final reward is a personal meeting with Chairman Mao (*Shanghai Daily*, 2006). The game is based on the ideal of 'finding pleasure in helping others' (*zhuren weile*) and was aparently not well received (Rosen, 2009: 368). It may, however, have enjoyed some popularity among specific groups, because Chen Kai (2009) felt obliged to analyze the extent to which this online game had a positive effect on moral education. His results were negative, because the main purpose of a game, namely to 'play', is not compatible with the practice of moral education which was at the heart of the 'Learning from Comrade Lei Feng' online game.

Concerns about this popularization of 'heroes', commercial exploitation, and political devaluation have been stressed in various articles throughout the years. One article, entitled 'Protection Laws Proposed for Chinese Heroes', identified five categories of heroes: historical heroes, national heroes, revolutionary leaders, revolutionary martyrs, and model heroes (*China Daily*, 2007). Lei Feng was listed together with Confucius, the Song Dynasty patriot Yue Fei, Dr. Sun Yatsen, and others. The proposers were questioning whether the present 'honour right' for 'natural persons' (real human beings) can also be applied to China's heroes. They particularly mentioned Lei Feng and said 'that it's hard to resort to the related law if Lei Feng's reputation was tarnished, since he has no close relatives to file the lawsuit for him.' One suggestion was to add a Chinese Hero Protection Clause to the existing law. The importance of Lei Feng was again accentuated in 2009, when Liu Jianglong, a member of the Chinese Political Party Consultative Conference, sent a proposal to the government, suggesting it might apply to register 'Lei Feng spirit' as 'UNESCO Intangible Cultural Heritage'. Liu was concerned that today 'as society and culture are rapidly developing, Lei Feng is being increasingly ignored. Many young people don't even know who he is.' And, Liu continues: 'Particularly since the 1990's, learning from Lei Feng has regressed from something that people voluntarily do in the course of their daily lives, to formulaic, commemorative actions' (Liu Jianglong cited in Martinsen, 2009).

In times of increasing computer and Internet access, PRC propaganda clearly had problems updating its hero and attracting young audiences. In summer 2010, therefore, China Central TV (CCTV) launched a 3D animated cartoon series entitled *The Story of Lei Feng* (*Lei Feng de gushi*), consisting of 30 episodes, each 15 minutes long. The production was funded with 21 million yuan and the series was later distributed to all local TV stations.[5] The words of Pang Baochun, Chairman of Shenyang Chunqiu Animation, emphasize both the difficulties the company encountered with this project and the iconic status of its hero: 'How to shoot Lei Feng is a serious question. He has a lot of folk colour, but he's not simply an individual: he's the embodiment of a spirit. So we can't try for comedy, but comedy can't be absent, either. Our production is under a lot of pressure' (Pang Baochun cited in Martinsen, 2009). While Pang Baochun was contemplating how to capture and promote 'the embodiment of a spirit', director Zhao Jing was planning the TV drama series *Lei Feng*. He had a different but in a way somewhat similar problem, because of the diver-turned-actor Tian Liang, who was chosen to play the lead role (2009). Many people protested against this decision, simply because Tian Liang's career and professional life as a 'publicity-seeker' ran counter to the virtues associated with Lei Feng: 'Tian is a good diver. However, he has a totally different life background and experiences compared to Lei Feng. Besides, he is a pop star now. If he does the role of Lei Feng, many people will misinterpret Lei Feng.'[6] The fear that Lei

Feng might be misinterpreted was not new, yet in this case it was ignored. In 2011, *Lei Feng* was screened in 22 episodes of 45 minutes each, with Tian Liang as Lei Feng.

At the time the new Lei Feng projects were in the making and being discussed on China's Internet portals, morality and justice in real life had become highly debated topics as well, especially in social media. Positive images of the Lei Feng spirit were now associated with China's voluntary help force after the Sichuan earthquake and for the Olympics in 2008 and the Shanghai Expo in 2010. The volunteers' 'spirit' was explained with reference to Lei Feng and the volunteers themselves were promoted as the 'new' model citizens. As almost two million volunteers assisted the Olympics, this group also displayed its efficiency and patriotism to an international audience (Chong, 2011). The patriotic movement and violent nationalism directed against France or Japan,[7] however, sent out rather disturbing signals. The organization of events and protests often relied on social media such as Sina-Weibo, and information about whatever affair or scandal was immediately followed by intense online discussions. Between 2006 and 2012, three cases proved to be particularly of interest and are often quoted in articles that either explain the demise of the Lei Feng spirit or argue for its immediate revitalization or for new laws to protect voluntary helpers.[8]

The first is the 'Nanjing Case of Peng Yu' (*Nanjing Peng Yu an*). On 20 November 2006, Peng Yu left a bus and saw an elderly lady, Xu Shuolan, lying on the ground. He helped her to get up, assisted by a Mr. Chen, and Peng then informed her son, a police officer. On the son's request, Peng called a taxi and accompanied her to a hospital. After having arrived at the hospital, Xu Shuolan accused Peng of causing her accident and later went to court. On 5 September 2007, after a public trial, Judge Wang Hao delivered the verdict based on a new 'everyday experience standard', according to which nobody would accompany a stranger to hospital and pay the medical costs, unless he or she had a guilty conscience. Despite any evidence, except for Xu Shuolan's own words, Peng was fined 45,876 yuan, to be paid within 10 days, for the medical bill and Xu Shuolan's suffering and mental distress (*Zhouyi Xinwen*, 2007). What followed was an outcry in China's media, online as well as in print. Nobody supported the judge, who obviously had only listened to the police officer. The case – and what was known about it so far – became so widely known that it undermined morality and prompted people to refuse to help in similar cases.

The second case, the 'Death of Wang Yue' (*Xiao Yueyue shijian*), happened on 13 October 2011. It was recorded by a surveillance camera and was soon circulated on the Internet. A two-year-old girl, Wang Yue, was run over by two trucks in a narrow road in Foshan, Guangdong province. The girl was bleeding on the street for more than seven minutes, but none of the 18 passers-by offered help. An elderly female rubbish scavenger finally helped, yet Little Yue died eight days later in hospital. The case was broadcast by a local media station, posted online, and received worldwide attention. The Communist Party Chief of Guangdong spoke of a 'wake-up call for everybody' and the website Sina-Weibo is said to have received more than 4.5 million posts within a few days. As a result, legal experts in Guangdong discussed drafting a 'Good Samaritan' law, changing existing law, and penalizing people who fail to help in similar situations.[9]

Both cases triggered a new discussion about morality and virtues in China. As Chen Weihua (2011) reported, 'Various surveys in the past weeks have shown that the majority of the people polled believe our morals have suffered a major setback in the past decade.' The shock was even bigger after the state-owned magazine *Dongfang Zhoukan* (*Oriental Weekly*) discovered new material about the Peng Yu case and revealed its findings in January 2012: Peng Yu had confessed to knocking down Xu Shaolin, solicited the media to promote him as a 'Good Samaritan', and agreed on a secret financial settlement with Xu early on in the process. However, the story does not end here, as Minter (2012) reports: 'The revelation that Peng collided with Xu, alone, would have been enough to send China's microbloggers into paroxysms of recriminations. But what made *Oriental Weekly*'s discovery so much more potent, and so much more infuriating, was the revelation that law enforcement officials in Nanjing had received testimony and other evidence to the effect that Peng had knocked over Xu. Why was this testimony and documentation only released this week?'

The two cases and their impact are representative of the speed and sociopolitical power of online media. They shocked the public sphere and irritated people to the extent that they refused to help others. The third case hit China's media in February 2012, when one of the CCP's biggest corruption scandals involved Bo Xilai, a member of the Politbureau and Chongqing's Communist Party secretary, and his wife. Bo, who previously had fought against corruption and initiated the red culture movement in Chongqing, was dismissed from all his party positions in March. In early November, he was expelled from the CCP. This case, among others, led to widespread frustration about the political elite that was also expressed in online media (Zheng Yongnian, 2013).

These are only three cases of many, yet they had an enormous effect on the plausibility of the Lei Feng spirit. Against this background, the CCP and its propaganda organs simply carried on as normal. The public sphere at this time (February 2012) was fully aware of the importance of Lei Feng's message. An analysis of more than 200 newspapers in February showed articles on Lei Feng rising from 7 to 199 per day by the end of the month (Bandurski, 2012). Published in several CCP-run newspapers, one article's headline captured the hero's importance: 'The eternal summons: century symphony for the Lei Feng spirit' (Li Congjun et al., 2012). The Lei Feng spirit is given in a question–answer format, highlighting today's possibilities of putting the spirit into practice, while simultaneously supporting Hu Jintao's vision of a 'harmonious society'. Then, in late February 2012, the CCP organized the ninth forum on the morality of Chinese citizens. During the conference, Liu Yunshan, director of the Publicity Department of the CPC Central Committee, stressed that 'Lei Feng is our model forever, and the Lei Feng spirit is an immortal monument' (*People's Daily*, 2012). As if to emphasize this determination, the opening day of the National People's Congress coincided with Lei Feng Day. Liu Yunshan repeated his efforts in 2013, convinced that 'Re-emphasizing "learning from Lei Feng" can motivate people today to work toward lofty causes, strengthen their patriotism and love for the party and country, and shore up their confidence in socialism with Chinese characteristics' (*Global Times*, 2013a). The 50th anniversary of Lei Feng's death (2012) and of the campaign (2013) surely legitimized even stronger efforts to promote the Lei Feng spirit and a wide range of Lei Feng–related activities.

Lei Feng enthusiasm: activities and propaganda

A campaign promoting the Lei Feng spirit began in 2012. It combined a traditional propaganda set-up with intensified media coverage of various activities. The CCP Central Committee had ordered the major online portals like xinhuanet.com, people.com, and entv.cn to dedicate special sections and microblogging services to Lei Feng–related news and information: 'Mobile phone-compatible short video and text messages will also be used to encourage the public to follow Lei's example ...' (*Global Times*, 2012b). Then, the General Administration of Press and Publication announced its plan to 'release 132 types of Lei Feng-themed publications in memory of the country's icon of altruism' (*China Daily*,

2012). Among them was *The Complete Works of Lei Feng* (*Lei Feng quanji*, 2012), which after 50 years still presented 'a lot of previously unknown content' (Zhang Ran, 2012). People were suddenly aware that not only had Lei Feng left behind a diary, there were also drafts of public presentations, more than 30 poems, 3 unfinished novels, 10 essays, and numerous letters at the time of his death at the age of 22 in 1962. An advert promoting the book stressed 'The historical material is authentic; the content is complete and accurate.' *The Complete Works* is said to have sold 200,000 copies between early February and March 4 (Zhang Ran, 2012). One can order the book via the online store dangdang.com, where the Collector's Edition received 450 reviews, 99.3 per cent of which rated the book as very positive and gave it five stars (*ChinaDaily*, 28 June 2013). The price has since dropped from 35.00 to 20.70 RMB.

Like other campaigns before it, this concentrated on stories from normal people and their individual relationships with the model hero, both online and in print, which can generally be split into three categories: First, oft-repeated stories told by people who had direct contact with Lei Feng, like the musician Zhu Guangdou, who met Lei three times, and the photographers Ji Zeng and Zhang Jun. The latter is famed for the more than 200 pictures he took of Lei Feng. In 2013, at the age of 82, he gave several interviews and was sent on a nationwide tour to promote the Lei Feng spirit. He suddenly died of a heart attack on Lei Feng Day, while delivering a speech to an army audience in the Shenyang Military Region. His last words were reportedly: 'I am devoting my limited life to the limitless cause of "preserving Lei Feng".' During his lifetime he organized 320 photographic exhibitions and gave 1260 lectures (Yu, 2013; Storrar, 2013). The latest information concerns Lei Feng's relationship with a woman. He addressed Wang Peilin as 'elder sister' in his writings and she only revealed herself in July 2012 as a result of much speculation (Becker, 2012).

Apart from people who had direct contant with Lei Feng, there are others who have been 'touched' by Lei Feng or who have a special geographic relationship with him. We point to enthusiastic collectors like Zhao Mingcai, who after decades of intensive work, is said to possess the largest private collection of Lei Feng memorabilia (Lian Hongning and Dong Wanyu, 2009). Another example is 19-year-old Zhang Tiantian, who was born in Liaoning Province (where Lei Feng served the PLA) and who wrote a biographical novel entitled *The Song of Lei Feng* (*Lei Feng zhi ge*) to express the young generation's love and respect for the model soldier. It is suggested that the very closeness to places where Lei Feng has lived or worked not only inspires people but adds to the story's reliability and authenticity. This is further reflected in Lei Feng's hometown Changsha, a city of more than 7 million inhabitants and capital of Hunan province. Changsha is famous for cultivating the spirit of its hero in education, awards, and activities and is said to have about 420,000 active 'Study Lei Feng followers' (*xue Lei Feng zhiyuanzhi*). Several institutions and buildings are named after him. In 2012 the city organized the National Lei Feng Spirit Forum and received permission and funding to establish Lei Feng spirit research (*Lei Feng jingshen yanjiu*) as a special research topic in social sciences (Zhu Min, 2013).

Another example is Guo Mingyi, a 53-year-old steel worker in Liaoning province, who has donated more than 60 litres of his own blood over the past two decades and engages in various charity projects to help children and needy families. The media point out '[b]esides the shared quality of selflessness and kindness, Guo and Lei also seem to share similar trajectories in life. Before joining the army, Lei worked at Guo's current company as a bulldozer driver for more than a year. Lei and Guo were even recruited to the army by the same recruiter.' It is little surprise that Guo mentions that he knows 'a lot of Lei's fellow workers and soldiers, who told me many stories about him. I feel that he has never really left, and this strengthened my belief to follow his example and make more contributions to the country, society and others' (Li Li, 2012). He is, as he described himself, 'nothing more than an ordinary worker, volunteer and person,' and it was also because of this that the CCP honored him as a 'modern Lei Feng' (Huang Yuli and Yang Wanli, 2012).

Guo Mingyi also fits the third category, which concentrates on voluntary services and the new meaning of the Lei Feng spirit. This can be seen, for example, in a report of the Central Committee of the Communist Youth League from August 2001: 'More than 80 million young people have provided over 4.1 billion hours of volunteer services in the last eight years according to incomplete statistics' (*People's Daily*, 2001). More recent examples refer to relief work after the earthquake in Sichuan or other natural catastrophes. Within this group, as pointed out by Butterfield (2012), we see a significant shift in the selection of model workers or heroes. The example discussed is that of Jiang Xiaojuan, a 29-year-old Jiangyou City policewoman. She was photographed in the earthquake area breastfeeding two babies and, a mother herself, 'nursed a total of nine babies among those orphaned or separated from their parents during the earthquake.' The media glorified her as 'China's Mother No. 1' (Butterfield, 2012: 96). This new citizen-hero model has become very popular and differs from the old period insofar as the media select and promote the hero, who may then be honoured by the CCP. It is,

nevertheless, only a rhetorical strategy, as Butterfield (2012: 96) argues, because the image being circulated is still under CCP control. However, for the public this system produces 'real' and emotionally touching heroes taken from current everyday life, and these are more easily accepted than old heroes of the revolutionary era such as Lei Feng. The most recent example is Chen Xianmei, a trash collector, who was the only person trying to help little Wang Yue in the city of Foshan. Her action moved everyone in China and she was given a reward of 20,000 yuan. She did not 'lend a hand for the sake of a reward', as many commentators point out, while criticizing the proposed idea that morality can be increased by offering material benefits.

New heroes and models are selected according to the moral standards defined by the Lei Feng model. The media speak of 'living Lei Feng' (*huo Lei Feng*), 'modern Lei Feng' (*xiandai Lei Feng*), 'female Lei Feng' (*nü Lei Feng*) or, as in one case in Shandong province, 'living Lei Feng of the Hui minority' (*Huimin huo Lei Feng*). These titles fit well with those who identify themselves with the PLA soldier from the 1960s, his spirit, and the propaganda campaigns associated with him. The younger generation may associate itself with the spirit represented by Lei Feng, but not with the way it is promoted and attached to politics and campaigns.

When asked what can be learnt today from Lei Feng, the answers usually refer to his patriotism, spirit, and deeds. Respondents are critical and clearly distinguish between a real and a fake spirit. It is important that someone enjoys helping others, yet there are too many people who offer help only in the expectation of future benefits. It is precisely this behavior that is to be criticized. Helpfulness, modest behavior, and honesty have of course always been appreciated. A decade ago, 80 per cent of pupils at a middle school in South China denied that the spirit of Lei Feng is outdated (*Nanfang Ribao*, 2003). Almost ten years later, the online platform Sina-Weibo posted the question 'Is learning from Lei Feng still necessary?' in a multiple-choice questionnaire. Of the respondents, 39% (377 people) said 'The "Lei Feng spirit" should be updated and promoted'; 37% (357 people) said 'Yes, children should learn. Our society needs people like Lei Feng more than ever'; 24% (231 people) said 'I admire Lei Feng, but he was one of a kind'; 13% (124 people) said 'It doesn't matter. Promoting him as a role model doesn't affect anything'; and only 6% (59 people) said 'No, the "Lei Feng spirit" is out of date'.[10] The results were published in the state-owned *Global Times* and seem to reflect the official position on this topic: Only a minority see the Lei Feng spirit as being irrelevant or even criticize it, the majority – as reflected in the first three categories – consider it important, especially for children, despite wanting to reform his image and promotion techniques.

There are, however, signs reflecting knowledge of Lei Feng is on the wane. According to an online survey carried out by *Southern Weekly* (*Nanfang zhoumo*), of the more than 1000 people surveyed 60 per cent do not remember March 5 as a day to commemorate Lei Feng (Zuo, 2013).

Similar reports came from Beijing, where it was reported that the 'majority of people questioned on Tuesday said they did not realize it was Learn from Lei Feng Day, and had not done any good deeds on purpose.' Comments were, however, generally positive: Lei Feng Day 'might help remind people to help others, particularly in cities like Beijing, where people think twice before they help an elderly person get up after they fall down,' said accountant Sun Xin, 26. Yuan Xishu, a 62-year old worker, was quoted as saying: 'The day is educational to the young, but for us, it means little, we have heard too much about it and don't feel anything anymore' (Zhang Wen, 2013).

Consumption, irony, and commerce

People's ambivalence towards the Lei Feng model is probably best expressed in the world of film and commercial production. To celebrate the 50th anniversary of the Lei Feng campaign, a set of three films was released on Lei Feng Day 2013: *Young Lei Feng* (*Qingchun Lei Feng*), *Lei Feng's Smile* (*Lei Feng de weixiao*), and *Lei Feng 1959* (*Lei Feng zai 1959*). All three films present an updated modern version of Lei Feng, but failed to attract audiences so much so that cinemas in various cities did not even sell a single ticket (Osnos, 2013; Hu Qingyun, 2013a). It was a propaganda disaster, made worse by the fact that the State Administration of Radio, Film and Television (SARFT) had issued a notice (*tongxun*) on 4 March, requesting the relevant movie production enterprises and cinemas in all provinces to do their utmost to properly promote the films.[11]

Clearly people were not willing to spend time and money on a remake of a story they already knew and had difficulties identifying with. While Lei Feng's story was clearly unsuitable for the competitive film market, there is general agreement with Professor Yin Hong from Tsinghua University, who studies China's film and TV industry, that the films should be judged on their educational merit. 'They were not for the market. They should be treated like public-welfare movies and played to the public for free' (Hu Qingyun, 2013a). There is a connect here between the 'successful' Beijing exhibition Forever Lei Feng, in which 'almost all visitors were government workers or schoolchildren, even though municipal officials had sent a text message to millions of cellphone subscribers announcing the show' (Levin, 2013).

Contrary to these state-operated projects, short films under the name *Lei Feng Man* (*Lei Feng xia*) enjoy growing popularity with more than a million visitors from the online community. Filmmaker Ma Shi and producer Zhang Liangliang invented this hero (*xia*), who, filled with Lei Feng's spirit, wears a superhero outfit, rides a rusty bike, and is constantly looking for the possibility of doing something good and beneficial for others. Displaying a mix of irony and humour, he gets involved in all kinds of stressful situations, and in doing so depicts and comments on China's lack of morality. Producer Zhang is not mocking the old hero, but rather providing 'a reinterpretation of Lei Feng, done in an entertaining way' (Valli, 2012).

Indeed, within the realm of popular culture Lei Feng is often portrayed in the context of entertainment and irony. However, comics and cartoons tone down their ridicule of his virtues and instead criticize their absence on the annual return on Lei Feng Day. Yet despite Lei Feng's omnipresence in the Chinese media, cartoons also relay the official fear that the modern pupil may still not know of him or, even worse, may regard him as irrelevant. This fear is embodied in a cartoon that depicts three pupils standing in front of his image, asking 'Who is he?'

Another example is the young photographer and artist Dai Xiang, who in 2007 devoted a New Lei Feng Series of his work to the revolutionary hero. One of his works pictures Lei Feng with a machine gun on Tiananmen Square; another redresses him as Superman flying through the sky and advertising Canon cameras; and yet another shows him reading the *Selected Works of Mao Tse-tung* in a modern coffee house – all of which leaves his image open to many different interpretations (Zhang Dongya, 2010).

Artistic reworking of the model hero is certainly one way of coping with the legacy of Lei Feng. And while young people may agree on virtues such as helpfulness and modesty, the 'spirit of the screw', obedience, and self-restraint are neither perceived as cool nor do they fit the age of individualism. China's youth culture idols changed from rock musicians like Cui Jian in the late 1980s, to Microsoft founder Bill Gates in the 1990s, to several foreign and Chinese stars in the world of sport and entertainment (*People's Daily*, 2003). Today's chosen idols are people such as the 2005 'Supergirl' winner Li Yunchun; China's famous author, race car driver, and blogger Han Han; and Taiwan's pop star Zhou Jielun (Jay Chou) (Fung, 2009; Ling Yang, 2009; Rosen, 2009). Nevertheless, as a comparative study of idol and model worship in Nanjing and Hong Kong revealed, in mainland China 'Lei Feng's persistence in idol worship signals a yearning for appreciation of "inner beauty" characters that are not typically present in the "three stars worship" [pop stars, movie stars, sport stars] culture' (Yue Xao Dong and Cheung Chau-kiu, 2000: 97).

That this longing for 'inner beauty' also matters in the world of pop was felt in August 2007, when Jay Chou, China's most famous music idol, questioned the importance of Lei Feng in an interview with the words: 'Who is Lei Feng? Can he sing?' (*Lei Feng shi shei? Ta hui chang ge ma?*). His comment, together with an image of both him and Lei Feng, was widely circulated on the Internet and music fans were, to put it mildly, disappointed about how little their idol knew about PRC culture. One year later, Jay Chou boosted his image when he donated 500,000 yuan to help earthquake refugees in Sichuan Province. On 24 May 2008, he even organized a charity relief fundraising concert at the Olympics Centre in Chongqing, and donated one million yuan in his own name.[12] One can only speculate about the motives and the rationale behind these activities. This Lei Feng–like gesture was much welcomed and enhanced his image – an important consideration for him since mainland China provides his largest fan base.

There are a lot of 'red' signs, symbols, and sounds in the world of music in China. Lei Feng songs are of course part of the red song repertoire promoted widely through concerts broadcast on TV (Steen, 2013). Lei Feng also appears in Beijing's rock 'n' roll underground. The fact that revolutionary images are frequently redesigned for underground (punk) rock CD covers, and that rock venues in Beijing are given names like 'Mao Live House' or 'Nameless Highland' (*Wuming gaodi*) can also be read as a form of critique directed against today's overwhelming consumerism. As all musicians grew up with the Lei Feng spirit at school, no one is surprised that they remember Lei Feng Day. Yet various interpretations are possible when one has to make sense of an underground Lei Feng remembrance concert containing the lines 'Caring [for] the people around you – let's learn from Comrade Lei Feng' and of a poster advertising the concert, which took place on Lei Feng Day in 2005, showing a distorted image of Lei Feng.[13]

Leaving the world of film and music, it is merchandise like Lei Feng's hat – emblematic of the man – that has had the most widespread commercial success. As Wei Na (2013) reports, 'there are over 500 stores based in Beijing in the online shop Taobao, selling Lei Feng–style cotton hats priced from 16 yuan ($2.5), to mink hats selling at 2,000 yuan.' During a cold winter, up to 300 hats have been known to be sold in a single shop earning profits of more than 15,000 yuan. In the week leading up to Lei Feng Day, sales rise again, and on dangdang.com hats for around 48 yuan are called the 'No. 1. star product'. Asked why young people buy the hat, Wen Ya, a 20-year-old student, said some of her male classmates were buying it just for fun and retro fashion. This also applies to sales of T-shirts, books, and stickers with portraits of Lei Feng in the runup to 5 March (Learn from Lei Feng Day). One seller explains: 'We buy in more stock every year at this time. Sales of hats, books, like Lei Feng's diary, and other products always rise in March' (Wei Na, 2013). These items are also sold overseas, with Lei Feng mink hats having featured in a New York fashion show, and so-called 'ear protection Lei Feng caps' for children being targeted at US purchases by Dion Ltd, Shanghai, for US$5.13 each.[14]

Basketball shoes from Adidas in the series 'adiZero Rose 2.5', called 'Lei Feng', represent the latest commercial trend. With the new shoe Adidas celebrates its growth in Chinese markets in recent years, especially in the basketball sector. Presented in the signature sneaker line of NBA star Derrick Rose, a popular player in China who tours the country every summer, the shoes are said to be a sign of respect and appreciation for the bond formed with China, 'paying tribute to Chinese national icon Lei Feng.' Richard (2012) continues to explain how the characteristics of Lei Feng are inscribed in and reflected through this shoe:

'The "Lei Feng" adidas adiZero Rose 2.5 takes on the characteristics of Lei Feng's famous uniform and the principles he lived by. Military style Strong Olive nubuck and synthetic materials dominate the shoe's upper, while a black faux fur-lined interior reflects the trademark five-pointed star hat he wore. Black also works [for the] GeoFit ankle padding and the Sprint Frame support chassis, while Derrick's Chicago Bulls are represented with Light Scarlet red accenting on the laces and 3-Stripes. Metallic gold, a celebratory color in Chinese culture, appears on the upper lace eyelets, adiZero pinline and lettering on the heel. Lastly, screen emboss screw detailing throughout is symbolic of a journal entry made by Lei in which he expressed his desire to be a "revolutionary screw that never rusts".'

(Richard, 2012)

It remains, however, remarkable that the name of today's most unpopular 'spirit of the screw' from the Maoist period is inscribed on a basketball shoe as a gesture of friendship from Adidas to present day China. On the back of the shoe one can read the golden old-style Chinese characters 'zero three zero five' (ling san ling wu), which none of the reviewers identified. Of course, the figures 03.05 will remind sportsmen of Lei Feng Day. Interestingly, Brandon's article was published on 6 March, promising that 'the shoe will be released this Friday at very select Foot Locker locations in New York City, Los Angeles and Chicago.' Maybe it is an internationally accepted practice that Lei Feng products, including everything from posters and hats, to spirit and shoes, sell best on Lei Feng Day.

Concluding remarks

Were Lei Feng still alive, he would be 73 and enjoying the pension of a retired high official. But there are many other possible scenarios. What if he had continued to follow his honest and incorruptible virtues and the wish to serve the people? Would he have become a victim of the many internal struggles within the CCP or of one of the many campaigns? What if he had had a glorious career within the PLA? Would he have taken action against the students in 1989 – or would he have refused to obey orders? What if he had become a rich businessman during the reform period, due to his technical skills, thirst for knowledge and learning? What if he had rejected every form of career, due to his modest character? Would he have married and enjoyed the life of a lovable but poor worker and grandfather? Thinking of him wearing a fashionable leather jacket and riding around Tiananmen Square on his motorbike, would he have been computer literate, taking advantage of the many possibilities provided by the Internet? Would he be among those controlling it, or would he be running a blog to 'joyfully help the people'? Under all these scenarios, there would probably never have been a Lei Feng campaign. But the reality is he died at the age of 22 and left a legacy called the 'Lei Feng spirit', the promotion, practice, interpretation, and marketization of which has undergone various changes in the past five decades.

Lei Feng's ongoing presence in the PRC is a phenomenon, politically, socially, and culturally. His image, spirit, and material possessions, once defined and controlled for propaganda purposes, are now deeply imbedded in people's minds and (popular) culture. The nature of a resource may limit its use, but 'it cannot limit the creativity of those that use the resource' (Fiske, 2010: 112). Creativity seems to be an important keyword, as it helps to explain the representations and (selected) readings of the Lei Feng spirit over time. Besides, Lei Feng has clearly entered the realm of 'image culture', which Jansson (2002: 26) defined as 'a social arrangement in which media culture and consumer culture are no longer separable categories, and where media images and media influenced commodity-signs are to an increasing extent used as sources for, and expressions of, identity.'

Officially, the Lei Feng spirit is treated as a national treasure, an ideal component of China's national identity. Cheng Hong (2009) concludes that the Lei Feng spirit inherits 5000 years of outstanding traditional virtues of the people of China and is a concrete representation of China's national spirit, epochal spirit, and Communist spirit. As such, Lei Feng represents the essence of Chinese civilization, a remedy for all kinds of social ills, an effective tool and standard that fights corruption and helps students to develop a healthy 'network moral practice' while communicating online (Yan Hui, 2012).

However, official reports commenting on the existence of a positive Lei Feng spirit are difficult to evaluate. The study of Yue Xao Dong and Cheung Chau-kiu (2000: 97) seems to provide a convincing starting point from which to rethink the popularity of Lei Feng. They write, 'idealism, romanticism, and absolutism were more important for selecting idols; whereas realism, rationalism, and relativism were more important for selecting models' as far as China's young people were concerned. This differentiation is a result of China's past campaigns and moral education, helping Lei Feng to survive as an acceptable moral institution. Counterproductive to the hero's popularity is his ongoing deification (Xu Min, 2012), and his close affinity to the CCP and its politics. Several corruption cases over the past years have destroyed trust in the CCP and its officials, rendering its praise of Lei Feng ridiculous in the eyes of many.

In the era of the Internet, *weibo*, and fast speed communication, the officially promoted Lei Feng standard travels fast and is demanding. Ordinary people may use it against corrupt officials, in criminal cases, and to voice their hate against the 'newly rich' and their oft-criticized lifestyles (Gerth, 2011). However, there are other cases discussed in Gerth's article that point at a more general fear of moral decline within Chinese society. Online communication allows people to respond quickly, transfer images and information, and put pressure on governmental institutions, officials, and individuals. The problem is, however, that while 'Lei Feng', model heroes, their images and heritage are protected, those of 'real life heroes' who actually help on the spot are not. As long as the 'Samaritan Law' and people's rights are not clearly defined, it will remain difficult to put the Lei Feng spirit into practice. Li Yijian, for example, wrote with regard to Lei Feng Day: 'Do we need a day to show how selfless we are? We already know we can count on each other for a good deed next time we see a stricken passerby, just as long as they promise not to sue' (*Global Times*, 2013b).

Lei Feng Day will surely be celebrated in the future, and hats, souvenirs, etc. will also be sold. Yet for many people this spirit has already translated into values that are universal in nature (e.g., simply helping those around you who are in need). Voluntary help is what many people seem to associate with a modern Lei Feng spirit, particularly expressed in new private organizations seeking to professionalize it beyond Lei Feng Day (Zhou Ping, 2013). China needs many volunteers, and as *Renmin Ribao* wrote on 5 March 2013: 'You and me, we all have a Lei Feng in us' (*Ni wo xinli dou you yige Lei Feng*).

Let us finish with a few lines from the 67-page lyric long poem *Song of Lei Feng* (*Lei Feng zhi ge*), written by poet He Jingzhi in March 1963. The poem was repeatedly performed, recited nationwide, and became a popular masterpiece of its time. It was the poem most requested by radio audiences and poet Bei Dao recalls 'reciting the poem from the rooftops during his youth' (Crespi, 2009: 160):

> Look, stand up, you are one Lei Feng.
> We will follow you, ten Lei Feng, one hundred Lei Feng,
> One thousand Lei Feng ... all arise, you are at the peak.
> We will follow you, ten peaks, one hundred peaks, one thousand peaks!'

Notes

1. As quoted in (from top to bottom): *Global Times* (2012c); Jacobs (2012); *China Daily*, 2013; Hu Qingyun (2013a).
2. For an introduction to the early Lei Feng campaign see Geist (1992), Reed (1991, 1998), Sheridan (1968). Especially recommended is the three-part Lei Feng Poster Collection available at Stefan Landsberger's homepage (see also Landsberger, 2011). Available from: *http://chineseposters.net/themes/leifeng.php* [accessed 31 July 2013].
3. In Chinese: *Hong taiyang – Mao Tse-tung songge xin jiezou lianchang* (see Barmé, 1996: 192).
4. The 'Three Represents' (called somewhat more grammatically the 'Three Representations' by Steen) was the guiding sociopolitical ideology of the Communist Party of China under Jiang Zemin. It was launched at the Sixteenth Party Congress in 2002 and stands for (1) advanced social productive forces (i.e., economic production), (2) the progressive course of China's advanced culture (i.e., cultural development), and (3) the fundamental interests of the majority (i.e., political consensus).

5. For more information see *http://baike.baidu.com/view/337620.htm#sub5110258*

6. See Du Guodong (2009).

7. During the Olympics there was anti-French sentiment due to Paris bestowing honorary citizenship on the Dalai Lama, culminating in protests outside the French Embassy and Carrefour supermarkets. There was also anti-Japanese sentiment based both on the Japanese attack during the Pacific War/WW2 and more recent disagreements over the Diaoyu/Senkaku Islands. During the opening ceremony of the Olympics the stadium crowd went silent when the Japanese representatives were announced, while massive applause and cheering greeted the Hong Kong and Taiwanese representatives.

8. For example, see *Global Times* (2012a).

9. For more information on the case see *http://en.wikipedia.org/wiki/Death_of_Wang_Yue* [accessed 31 July 2013].

10. See (2012a). Available from: *http://www.globaltimes.cn/content/697218.shtml* (accessed 25 June 2013).

11. The notice is accessible via the SARFT homepage at *http://www.sarft.gov.cn/articles/2013/03/05/20130305173548980088.html* (accessed 22.06.2013).

12. See his homepage *http://jaychoustudio.com/archives/jay-chou-gives-another-1-million-hopes-he-can-support-the-disaster-area-more/780* (accessed 28 June 2013).

13. The concert poster is available from *http://www.flickr.com/photos/azchael/725441010/lightbox/* [accessed 31 July 2013].

14. See *http://www.dhgate.com/product/ear-protection-lei-feng-cap-children-plus/151867073.html*

8

Advertising and China: How does a love/hate relationship work?

Giovanna Puppin

Abstract: Despite its ubiquity as the main tool to promote the so-called 'consumer revolution' in contemporary mainland China, commercial advertising has not always been welcomed by the Chinese authorities. On the contrary, following a short and intense development in the 1920s and 1930s, its growth was abruptly interrupted by the ascent of Mao Zedong and the Chinese Communist Party (CCP). The reintroduction of advertising began in 1979, in concomitance with the process of reform and opening up initiated by Deng Xiaoping and the publication of the famous article 'Restoring the good name of advertising' by Ding Yunpeng (1979). Undoubtedly, the Chinese authorities had to find a set of rhetorical strategies in order to legitimize the 'unexpected' return of a phenomenon that not long before was accused of being 'the Bible of capitalism'. In order to show substantial adherence to Marxism and its critical position towards advertising, Chinese official sources of that time recalled the necessity of developing *socialist advertising* or even *socialist advertising with Chinese characteristics*. These requirements had to be met by the academics and operators of the 'new' Chinese advertising industry, but soon turned out to be too ambiguous and contradictory, and this coveted phenomenon ended up being very difficult to put into practice. The efforts carried out in the 1980s and 1990s have not come to an end though, and China continues to struggle to find its own advertising form even today.

Rather than focusing on the recent consumer expenditure boom in contemporary China, this chapter concentrates on the 'collateral effects' of the country's growing consumerism, shedding light on the ongoing ambivalence of the Chinese authorities towards advertising, by adopting a diachronic perspective and by making extensive use of Chinese-language sources. First, this chapter goes back in history to provide an overview of the origins, rise, and decline of advertising in China before 1979 and takes account of key elements in the political, economic, and societal context. Second, it describes the uneasy return of advertising in China after the Maoist era and stresses the ideological implications; more specifically, an in-depth analysis of the key concepts of *socialist advertising* and *socialist advertising with Chinese characteristics* will be carried out. Third, this chapter identifies and investigates some contemporary trends in China's advertising culture – namely, the emphasis on *creativity* and the need for an advertising *with Chinese elements* – which spread following China's outward-looking policy, its entrance into the World Trade Organisation (WTO), and its emergence on the global scene. The conclusions drawn at the end of this chapter argue that the new call for *creative advertising with Chinese elements* can be understood as a continuation of the campaign aimed at differentiating Chinese (socialist) advertising from Western (capitalist) advertising – or to keep a 'Chinese way' of advertising – which started some decades ago. This 'new' advertising has its own distinctive rationality, characteristics, and aims, and is explicitly being promoted through the use of a more modern and less political terminology.

Key words: capitalist advertising, Chinese advertising, Chinese characteristics, Chinese elements, creativity, socialist advertising, Western advertising.

Guess who's back?

On 4 January 1979, the Chinese newspaper *Tianjin Daily* printed an ad promoting some local products. The headline 'Description of *Tianjin Toothpaste* main products' was followed by a black-and-white visual depicting the wide range of toothpastes produced by the local company. The visual comprised some extremely simple drawings, such as those of a little girl washing her teeth and a woman smiling, and some informative text.[1] Compared with today's colourful and attractive ads – let alone the even more eye-catching TV commercials that we have become familiar with – this ad appears old fashioned and bland, and would probably not succeed in getting our attention. Yet, this same ad 'opened the prelude' (Chen Pei'ai, 2009: 115) to commercial advertising in mainland China. It was the first commercial ad to appear in the country after the process of reform and opening up initiated by Deng Xiaoping at the Third Plenum of the 11th Central Committee of the Chinese Communist Party (CCP), held over 18–22 December 1978. It is not the first example of advertising in China though, the origins of which are commonly dated back to ancient times.

In relation to the history of commercial advertising in general, Raymond Williams in his pioneering essay 'Advertising: the Magic

System' highlighted that every account is usually accompanied by a 'pleasant little ritual' (Williams, 1980: 170), which consists in placing the birth of the phenomenon as early as possible. Chinese studies conducted on the history of autochthonous advertising are no exception to this trend: on the contrary, they go much further back into history than is usual for those carried out in the West. As a matter of fact, according to the majority of advertising textbooks currently used as teaching materials in university courses in mainland China, the first examples of advertising in the country can be traced back to the beginnings of primitive society: Zhao identifies advertising with the clan and tribal totems before the mythical early dynasties of Xia and Shang (Zhao Chen, 2005: 1–2), while Ni even dates them back to 3000 BCE and the slave and feudal society that followed, when *physical advertising* (*shiwu guanggao*) started to appear together with the first trade activities (Ni Ning, 2001: 36).[2]

It goes without saying that these forms of advertising were very different from advertising in the modern sense. The latter, referred to in Chinese-language sources as *xiayi guanggao* (advertising in a strict sense), *shangye guanggao* (commercial advertising), or more simply *guanggao* (advertising), is believed to have begun in the first half of the nineteenth century. This was precisely the time that China witnessed a boom in arrivals and settlements of foreigners, who were driven by commercial and religious motivations. With the aim of spreading their religious faith, as well as selling their goods and making business with the local population, they began to employ a persuasive promotional technique: *advertising* (Cheng Hong, 1996: 75–6). It is not by chance, therefore, that the first examples of modern ads in China appeared in the pages of foreign-run newspapers published in the country's coastal cities: *Canton Register* (1827, in English) and *Dongxi yangkao meiyue tongji zhuan* (1833, in Chinese, also known as *Eastern Western Monthly Magazine*).[3]

As a direct consequence of the Opium Wars (1839–42 and 1856–60) and the Unequal Treaties, the foreigners not only imposed a commercial imperialism that drastically changed the flow of goods and capital to their advantage, but also exerted an 'advertising imperialism', defined by Michael H. Anderson as 'a particular type of communication exchange that fosters a general structural relationship that keeps some nations and some groups in harmony and others in conflict' (Anderson, 1984: 13–14). Selling foreign goods to Chinese consumers, therefore, proved to be an uneasy task, especially due to periodic nationalistic boycotts that spread in the early part of the ninetheenth century and promoted consumer nationalism (see Gerth, 2003: 125–200).

Just a few decades later, in the 1920s and 1930s, advertising witnessed its so-called 'golden age' before the revolution: economic stability fostered the birth and development of the first advertising agencies, such as the Big Four of the time (namely, Carl Crow Inc.; Millington's Advertising Co.; China Commercial Advertising Agency; and Consolidated National Advertising Co.) (Wang Jian, 2000: 27). Advertising appeared in a wide variety of media, from newspapers to billboards, from radio to electronic displays. More specifically, the advertising activities were concentrated in the city of Shanghai and the most popular advertising images became those of calendar posters (*yuefenpai*), depicting young Chinese beauties in modern and Westernized postures.[4] However, this era would not last long, due to the outbreak of anti-Japanese resistance (1937–45) and the civil war between nationalists and communists (1945–9), during which advertising continued to exist even if it gradually lost the crucial role it had played in the previous years.[5]

With the foundation of the People's Republic of China (PRC) on 1 October 1949, advertising started to gradually decline.[6] In China, as in every other socialist country, commercial advertising constituted an uncomfortable presence; it was dismissed as incompatible with socialist ideals and useless in state-controlled economies, in perfect accordance with the traditional Marxist view.[7] The first years after the founding of the PRC actually witnessed the survival of the phenomenon, even though the participation of foreign companies came to an end. From January 1956, the advertising industry also started to be affected by the ongoing construction of a socialist economy, and within just a few years all the agencies operating on Chinese soil became state run; for example, the 108 agencies present in Shanghai merged into the Shanghai Advertising Corporation (SAC) (Cheng Hong, 1996: 77–8). The importance and legitimacy of advertising in a country like China was confirmed during the Conference of Advertising Workers in Socialist Countries, held in Prague in 1957: the outcome was a real push in order to develop *socialist commercial advertising* (*shehui zhuyi shangye guanggao*), which had to be 'ideological, truthful and concrete in nature'.[8] By 1958, advertising in communist China even ventured into previously unthinkable media, such as 'railroad trains in which poker card boxes, lunchboxes, chessboards, passenger magazines, and decorative hangings were all allowed to display commercial messages' (Wang Jing, 2008: 7).

This tolerant phase was soon followed by one of sudden closure: during the so-called 'dark years' of the Cultural Revolution (1966–76) intolerance towards commercial advertising reached its peak:

'When the Cultural Revolution began, neon signs were first smashed by "red guards". Advertisements disappeared from newspapers, except those showing and staging the eight "model dramas". All shop windows were pasted with "big character posters" and all shop names were changed. There were only political slogans on billboards.'

(Cheng Hong, 1996: 78)

In those years, advertising was accused of being 'the result of capitalism' (*ziben zhuyi de chanwu*), 'an imported product for the adoration of things foreign' (*chongyang meiwai de holaipin*) and 'a manifestation of capitalist waste and corruption' (*ziben zhuyi fuxiu he langfei de biaoxian*) (Chen Pei'ai, 1997: 77). Even linguistically, the word 'advertising' became a taboo and gradually disappeared, together with other names of products, brands and shops.[9] For example, the creative and 'capitalist' names of Wangfujing Department Store, the famous Quanjude Peking Roast Duck restaurant, the watch shop Xiangdeli, and the clothes shop Xushunchan were modified by revolutionary staff and Red Guards into the more politically correct Beijing Department Store, Peking Roast Duck Restaurant, Capital Watch Shop, and East Wind Clothes' Shop (quoted in Chen Pei'ai, 1997: 78–9). This low point in the uneven history of commercial advertising in China was brought about by a series of intertwined factors that went beyond the divide of socialist/capitalist ideology and led advertising to lose its main *raison d'être*: a planned economy that did not account for consumers' needs and demands; the stress on heavy industry rather than the service sector; the nationalization of private enterprises and the subsequent lack of competition; the rationalization of food staples and other daily necessities, which slowed down consumption; limited trade with Western countries. In addition, the media were requested to act exclusively as 'the mouthpiece of the Party', and they too became state owned.[10]

Different views are held by Chinese scholars as to whether advertising survived in those years: some argue that the phenomenon was neglected (Chen Pei'ai, 1997: 79; Ni Ning, 2001: 47); others hint that it was actually replaced by other forms of communication that were more similar to political propaganda than commercial propaganda (Xu Junji, 2006: 227–8; Sun Shunhua, 2007: 71–2); others prefer not to consider this page of history and skip from the early nationalist period to the reform and opening period (Fan Zhiyu, 1998: 36–7). Nonetheless, despite the attack on different forms of advertising, it was never officially banned or censored during the Cultural Revolution. There is unanimity of opinion that the phenomenon made its official reappearance in China in 1979, in the form of the *Tianjin Toothpaste* ad as described earlier.

Capitalist or socialist, that is the question

As anticipated earlier, the return of advertising in the country was possible only thanks to the reform and opening-up process inaugurated at the Third Plenum at the end of 1978: a new phase in the history of China began, one with more emphasis on modernization and development of the country, rather than stressing ideology, as expressed in the famous maxim by Deng Xiaoping: 'Black cat or white cat, as long as it catches mice, it's a good cat' (Li Kwok-sing, 1995: 12–14). The reflourishing of advertising activities was helped by new policies that allowed gradual privatization and growing competition, fast economic development by means of 'socialism with Chinese characteristics' and adoption of a 'socialist market economy', an improvement in living standards and an increase in the availability of consumer goods, the expansion of foreign business, the progressive commercialization of media, etc.[11] Very soon, advertising reappeared in the media and became the protagonist of a long and complex process of regulation.[12] Some of the biggest foreign advertising agencies – such as Dentsu, Young & Rubicam, McCann-Erickson, Ogilvy & Mather, and Leo Burnett – began negotiations with the Chinese government and entered the country, mainly focusing on international accounts. In this context, advertising refound the basic conditions necessary for its existence and carried out its main purpose: to increase demand and to promote consumerism. This is how advertising returned to China – and it was there to stay.

At this point, it is quite reasonable to ask: How did a phenomenon that only a few years before had been dismissed as the vital lymph of capitalist culture become reintroduced as a useful tool in reform and opening up, as well as in the Four Modernizations process?[13] Who was behind the campaigning for the return of advertising and how was this carried out? As a matter of fact, the return of advertising was not a smooth process, as it required the Chinese authorities to solve an ideological impasse: 'to sell the legitimacy of selling' (Stross, 1990: 485). In this new context, it was precisely advertising that had to be sold, not only to the new professionals in the communication industry, but also to the new scholars and academics and, moreover, to those meant to be the new Chinese consumers – the masses.[14]

It is not surprising that the document that legitimized the return of advertising on Chinese soil was entitled 'Restoring the good name of advertising' (*Wei guanggao zhengming*). This article, written by Ding Yunpeng, the former chief of the SAC,[15] and published by the newspaper *Wenhui Daily* on 14 January 1979, rehabilitated the phenomenon by listing a series of arguments in support of the reintroduction of advertising in the country. The most significant were: the absence of advertising on Chinese television had to be considered 'a huge waste' (*hen da langfei*) in economic terms; advertising could no longer be accused of deceiving (*bai xuetou*) or exaggerating (*chui niupi*), as Lin Biao and the Gang of Four had been keen to do; advertising had to be considered a 'form of knowledge' (*xuewen*), capable of promoting commercial exchanges and improving business management. The author went on to highlight the necessity of making a distinction between advertising as 'the Bible of capitalism' (*ziben zhuyi de Shengyijing*), and an alternative version of it; that is, differentiating *capitalist advertising* from *socialist advertising*. He also urged the Chinese to learn from foreign countries and put into practice the famous principle 'to make foreign things serve China' (*yang wei Zhong yong*).[16] In addition, he mentioned a form of advertising that was not limited to the promotion of business (Ding Yunpeng, 1979).

The merits of the reintroduction of advertising enumerated in Ding Yunpeng's article – which clearly did not reflect the personal opinion and ideas of a single individual but made public a decision that had already been taken by the authorities (Stross, 1990: 486) – have been subsequently diffused in all the essays and books published from the 1980s onwards. *Socialist advertising* (*shehui zhuyi guanggao*), sometimes even referred to as *socialist advertising with Chinese characteristics* (*you Zhongguo tese de shehui zhuyi guanggao*), first had to serve the purpose of building a socialist market economy; second, it not only had to be true, it had to be able to guide consumers, beautify cities, serve the masses, be ideologically correct, etc. An unusual characteristic was that it could not be creative: creativity was, in fact, conceived to be a feature of capitalist advertising (Zhang Nanzhou, 1986; Zhao Yuji, 1987).

In the introduction to the *neibu* (internal) publication *Shehui zhuyi guanggaoxue* (The Discipline of Socialist Advertising), the author summarized the priorities set out by the rhetoric of the time in order to legitimize the phenomenon:

'Having to deal with the prejudices held by some people towards advertising, "the discipline of Chinese socialist advertising" should first of all implement the process of rectifying the name of socialist advertising, ending up in satisfying the need of many theoreticians and advertising professionals to promote the name and the status of the phenomenon.'

(Song Shunqing, 1983: 4)

Later on, it was stressed that socialist advertising had to be true, in contrast to capitalist advertising; it had to follow the principles of production and serve the people, the proletarian cause, and socialist culture; it had to stress economic profit; more importantly, it had to reflect socialist material and spiritual civilizations (Song Shunqing, 1983: 6–7). While material civilization refers to economic development, spiritual civilization is more complex, as it finds its guiding principle in Marxism–Leninism–Mao Zedong thought, adheres to the Four Cardinal Principles,[17] and sticks to the modernization, reform, and Open Door policy; moreover, it also embraces other values, such as moral education, patriotism, the fight against corruption, and so on.[18]

Xu Baiyi, who is considered the 'father' of Chinese advertising theory, identifies the principal differences between advertising in capitalist and socialist countries as follows: in capitalist countries, where production is private, advertising mainly serves the purpose of maximizing profits for shareholders and groups who hold the monopoly (while advertising in China aims at maximizing profits for the state and through the state enhancing people's lives); in capitalist countries advertising is completely divorced from government actions and often uses a high degree of technology (while Chinese advertising is part of the planned economy, and therefore has to be aligned with government policies; even though different products are in competition with one another, the final aim is to promote the best product to the detriment of the worst, therefore advertising is useful for consumers and all of society); in capitalist countries advertising is concerned with how to attract people's attention, consequently it contains exaggerations, untrue content, is often in bad taste, and uses sex to promote products (while in China advertising helps to build a socialist spiritual civilization, one that is healthy and raises the moral quality, *suzhi*, of the people) (Xu Baiyi, 1988: 34–5).[19]

The intrinsic properties of Chinese socialist advertising involved the so-called 'three natures, one style' (*sanxing yige*): it had to be ideological, true, and artistic in nature as well as national in style.[20] An alternative was 'four natures, one style' (*sixing yige*): ideological, political, true, and artistic nature as well as being national in style.[21] Another was 'five natures, one style' (*wuxing yige*): ideological, informative, true, scientific, and artistic in nature as well as national in style.[22]

As highlighted in previous studies (Stross, 1990; Hong Junhao, 1994; Gao Zhihong, 2003), the rhetoric used by the Chinese authorities to distinguish socialist advertising from capitalist advertising fell on deaf ears: the arguments were not convincing enough and sometimes were even contradictory; practical examples of how to put these guidelines into practice were never provided, therefore the theoretical load ended up being too complex and intricate. Furthermore, since its reintroduction, commercial advertising has had to face some particularly harsh challenges such as the Anti-Spiritual Pollution Campaign (1983–4), during which domestic advertising was accused of pursuing profit in a way that was too similar to Western advertising, and the Anti-Bourgeois Liberalization Campaign (1987), during which dozens of outdoor ads were removed (Wang Jian, 2000: 42). According to Gao Zhihong (2003), these were the 'primary means' used by the Chinese government to fight the negative social effects of advertising, identifiable mainly by fake advertising, unfair competition, and ideological pollution, the latter being expressed as hedonism, individualism, and sexuality.

Despite these sporadic campaigns, the Chinese authorities and scholars were busy restoring the good name of advertising throughout the 1980s: while much emphasis was placed on differentiating *socialist advertising* from *capitalist advertising* (worth studying as a phenomenon typical of modern societies), less stress fell on how to find a coherent critical attitude towards the latter, and to propose a consistent practice of *socialist advertising with Chinese characteristics*. Nevertheless, advertising continued its tormented journey in China.

Dancing with wolves

By 2013 China had grown to become the world's second largest advertising market, after the US. By the end of 2012, the number of advertising agencies in China reached 377,800, they had 2.18 million employees and business revenues of 469.8 billion yuan (US$75.52 billion), as recently announced by Zhang Mao, the head of China's State Administration for Industry and Commerce (SAIC), the authority in charge of advertising regulation. The advertising industry has been one of the fastest growing sectors in China, with revenues rising 30 per cent every year.[23] These mind-boggling figures clearly show the advertising industry booming. Moreover, the improvements in advertising quality and creativity have resulted in significant international visibility and recognition: in 2008, for example, the Cannes International Advertising Festival dedicated a special section to showcase Chinese advertising.[24] In 2012, another significant event took place with Lo Sheung Yan, from JWT Shanghai, becoming the first Chinese jury president at the Cannes Festival.[25] Nevertheless, as highlighted by Mr. Zhang in his speech revealing the latest data on Chinese advertising, the industry is not as professional, organized, and innovative as in developed countries as a result of a dearth of top professional talents.[26] What are the main reasons behind this negative attitude towards Chinese advertising?

The first time a Chinese delegation visited the Cannes International Advertising Festival was 1996 and represented the first formal encounter between Chinese and international advertising. While the outcome of the encounter was possibly far worse than expected, it provided an opportunity for China's advertising professionals to carry out some self-reflection and critique. The members of the delegation, who came from local media, advertising agencies, and governmental bodies, 'were surprised by the wide gap between China's advertising and foreign advertising' (Hu Xiaoyun, 2006: 46), and went back to their country somewhat 'crestfallen' (Hu Xiaoyun, 2006: 48). As far as members of the international jury were concerned, great perplexity spread regarding the decodification of the Chinese elements. Some of the delegates blamed recurrent elements in China's national adverts as being cultural barriers that prevented the country from winning prizes and awards. As a result of this visit, China's authorities, practitioners, and scholars of advertising became concerned with the issue of 'creativity' (*chuangyi*) in advertising, which had been left far behind as a result of the main priority being ideological orientation. As the years went by, their concerns began to increase.

Cang Zhenhua was one of China's delegates to Cannes back in 1996, and proffered some interesting insights and ideas. In his opinion, participating in international advertising events was crucial for China, but more emphasis had to be given to the cultural content diffused by the adverts; Chinese advertising needed to learn how to manage cultural content more effectively if it wanted to be understood by an international jury and meet international standards. The maxim 'Western substance, Chinese function' (*Xiti Zhongyong*)[27] was mentioned. On the one hand, China had to learn from the West, gain more technological competence, and adopt the international advertising language; on the other hand, it should avoid employing an international style just to please an international jury and win prizes, and promote instead so-called 'outstanding national culture' (*minzu youxiu wenhua*). In a new epoch where commercial exchanges between China and the West were becoming more frequent and the advertising sector increasingly globalized, Cang called for a new kind of advertising: 'advertising with Chinese characteristics' (*you Zhongguo tese de guanggao*). This time the adjective 'socialist' was not to appear. Cang urged his colleagues to understand that the shift towards international advertising was necessary and that there was no need to fear foreign products or ad people (Cang Zhenhua, 1996). To meet this new challenge, it was felt that education programmes should be aimed at training skilled professionals, but in the meantime more emphasis should fall on the internal market. As far as *Chinese characteristics* were concerned, adverts should enhance the outstanding national culture: its theories, values, aesthetics, and civilization (Cang Zhenhua, 1996). Cang's opinion is representative of the cultural turn that took place in advertising in the 1990s. Several scholars argued that 'Chinese characteristics' in advertising were to find creative inspiration in the country's rich and fertile national culture, driven both by a revival of interest in the Chinese essence and a protectionist attitude towards interference from the West. But what were the factors that led to this inward-looking mood?

Since the reform and opening up, transnational advertising agencies (TNAAs) have found the prospect of selling to the biggest market in the world very appealing and, by seizing the right moment, successfully managed to make foreign brands attractive to Chinese consumers through ads.[28] Compared with their foreign counterparts, Chinese agencies were still technologically inferior, lacked professionals, and unable to produce high-quality ads (Hong Junhao, 1994: 335–6). The situation almost exclusively favoured foreign advertising agencies. This uneven situation sounded all too familiar to the Chinese people: it brought back memories of the advertising imperialism that spread in the middle of the nineteenth century and the impacts that accompanied it, such as the export of Western advertising and its professionalism, the transnationalization of consumer culture, and the commercialization of local mass media (Wang Jian, 2000: 12–13). Even today, the memory of that time of usurpations is still vivid and fuels China's anti-imperialist and nationalist discourses as well as the country's determination to rid itself of a past of abuses by Western countries, commonly referred to as 'the century of humiliation' (*bainian guochi*).[29] This applies also to the advertising sphere.

China's decision to join the World Trade Organisation (WTO), while significant, brought with it many new concerns and worries. China was accepted as a member on 11 December 2001 and made a commitment to lift within four years the restriction that confined foreign advertising companies to operate only through joint ventures with local companies, and another restriction on foreign ownership not exceeding 49 per cent.[30] On a practical level, this meant opening the doors to TNAAs which were much bigger and had greater experience, top-quality professionals, economic strength, and other advantages.

Concerned by these prospects, Chinese agencies considered many possible future scenarios and ways of ensuring their companies could continue to exist and be profitable. Han Wengen (2002), for example, argued that there was going to be an increase in the number of foreign sponsors, as well as products and brands, leading to an increase in advertising expenditure. For Chinese local advertising agencies, the only way to survive would be to compete with foreign TNAAs, and at the same time sell national products to the internal market, in order to keep their market share. Similarly, Yao Jie (2002) foresaw robust competition between foreign and Chinese advertising agencies as well as brands. At first, he argued that the big multinational advertising agencies – such as Ogilvy, JWT, Saatchi & Saatchi, and DDB – which were already present in China would take over and threaten the existence of smaller and less powerful Chinese agencies. To be more convincing, he employed a quite effective metaphor: 'the wolves' (meaning 'the foreigners'). If the wolves come, he argued, there is only one way out: that is to 'dance with the wolves', with the final aim of becoming a good wolf handler (Yao Jie, 2002: 268):

'We can learn from the others, learn from their creativity, learn from their planning, learn from their brand management, learn from their print design, learn from their market analysis. Once we have learnt their skills, our feathers will be thicker, our wings will be harder, and we will hold the balance. When that day will come, we "can say no" also to foreign advertising agencies.'

(Yao Jie, 2002: 269)

The expression 'can say no' (*keyi shuo bu*) is highly meaningful, as it makes an explicit reference to the title of a best-seller, *China Can Say No: Political and Emotional Choices in the Post Cold War Era*, written by a group of intellectuals in 1996. The book is highly nationalistic and the first part of the title – 'China Can Say No' (*Zhongguo keyi shuo bu*) – very quickly became a slogan in various anti-foreign demonstrations, such as those fuelled by the bombing of China's embassy in Belgrade in 1999.[31] The 'extreme' positions illustrated above are clear signals that the wave of anti-imperialism and nationalism towards Western advertising has continued up to more recent years. At the turn of the twenty-first century, Chinese advertising was facing a set of new challenges: How could this industry survive the robust competition set by foreign multinationals? How could it create ads to reflect national culture, while at the same time attract a foreign audience? There seemed to be only one solution and, paradoxically, the 'Chinese way' to choose was indicated by the Westerners (even though indirectly or unwillingly).

While it was true that Chinese consumers were fascinated by foreign-sounding brand names and Western testimonials, as well as appreciating international styles and techniques, a new trend in advertising in China began to spread. This involved increasing use of *Chinese elements* (*Zhongguo yuansu*), even in the advertising campaigns of transnational agencies for the promotion of foreign products. Following disenchantment with theories promoting standardized marketing campaigns, the emerging new motto for transnational corporations (TNCs) became 'Think *locally*.' As Kevin Roberts, CEO of Saatchi & Saatchi worldwide, perceptively put it in 2002:

> 'Anyone who wants to go global has to understand the local – their own local and the locals of their consumers. People live in the local. I've never met a global consumer. I never expect to. We define ourselves by our differences. It's called identity – self, family, nation.'

> (Quoted in de Mooij, 2004: 16)

Speaking about self, family, nation, and localization of advertising campaigns in China, the standard bearer of the 'Think Local, Act Local' strategy, Coca-Cola, probably set the best example. Contrary to expectations, Chinese consumers seemed to prefer the way the US giant stimulated *guoqing* (national sentiment) than the nationalistic and patriotic styles used by its Chinese counterpart (*Feichang Kele*, Future Cola, produced by Wahaha) (Wang Jing, 2003: 252). The most famous Coca-Cola commercial is arguably one shot in 2005, which portrayed the Chinese athlete Liu Xiang walking down the streets of Paris, all alone on Chinese New Year's Eve. He had just phoned home to tell his family he could not be there to celebrate. He entered a restaurant in a desperate attempt to cheer himself up, but a disappointing plate of *jiaozi* (dumplings) made him feel even worse. Then he ordered a can of Coca-Cola. Once opened, two cartoon-style children – *afu* and *axi*, two auspicious traditional symbols – magically appeared and brought him home.

Not all campaigns proved to be so positive, though. On the contrary, a list of not-so-exemplary foreign campaigns appeared in many articles published in magazines and books on advertising. For example, Toyota ran a print ad in which two stone lions bowed to and paid respect to a Prado SUV (Saatchi & Saatchi, 2003); Nippon Paint ran a print ad depicting a freshly painted pillar with a dragon sliding down Japanese paint (Leo Burnett, 2004); and Nike ran a commercial starring the NBA player James LeBron fighting and defeating a variety of symbols of Chinese traditional culture, such as a kung-fu master, some fascinating Apsaras, and a pair of dragons (Wieden & Kennedy, 2004). In all the above cases, the ads were pulled and the companies had to apologize.[32] In light of these embarrassing blunders China's ad agencies saw the opportunity to gain the moral high ground by using Chinese traditional elements and positioning themselves as the real depositories of Chinese culture. After all, if the American giant Coca-Cola chose to localise its communication campaigns in China and decided to exploit elements of the Chinese tradition, the Chinese naturally should not only be able to do it too but possibly do it better.[33]

A new form of advertising was required and the so-called *creative advertising with Chinese elements* (*Zhongguo yuansu chuangyi guanggao*) seemed to fit the bill. In order to provide a platform for its development, a dedicated competition was set up called the 'Chinese Element International Creative Award' (*Zhongguo yuansu guoji chuangyi dasai*). The competition began in October 2006 in the city of Kunming (Yunnan) and attracted 5000 adverts, from 40 different countries (Jiang Haiying, 2006: 82).[34] The objectives of this new trend were to reinvigorate Chinese culture, to stress the importance of cultural components in advertising creativity, to help national brands in the internationalization process, and to enhance China's soft power.[35,36] Indeed, a series of publications and events were dedicated to investigating the meaning of *Chinese elements* and how best to represent them, becoming as a result a hot topic in advertising circles.[37] Gao Jun, president of the jury, explained the need for this competition as the lack of self-esteem of China's creative people. He mentioned the sad episode of the first Chinese delegation to Cannes highlighting the substantial lack of understanding of Western standards, and initiating a call to develop a Chinese style. In this sense, 'Chinese elements' must be conceived as a drive to stimulate creativity, as well as to promote the national spirit and the correct intercultural communication between China and the rest of the world (Jiang Haiying, 2006: 82). Zhu Hailiang, from JWT Shanghai, admitted that, up until the first stage of the competition, the definition of 'Chinese elements' was too restricted. In his opinion, both figurative and imaginative components should be part of it: not just the widespread symbols of Chinese culture, such as the dragon, the Great Wall, calligraphy, etc., but also the spirit, values, and habits of the people (Zhou Ying, 2007: 54). A Singapore-based advertising professional, Huang Guoxiong, argued that the label 'Chinese elements' was going to replace the label 'Created in China' (which, in its turn, replaced 'Made in China'),[38] in a sort of escalation that could lead China and its cultural elements to become recognized internationally and even become mainstream (Zhou Ying, 2007: 55).

The term 'Chinese elements' was initially defined as 'the condensed manifestation of Chinese traditional culture' (*Zhonghua minzu chuantong wenhua de jizhong tixian*) (Chen Pei'ai and Zhang Liping, 2010: 1), but it soon became clear that the adjective 'traditional' (*chuantong*) seemed to act more as a limit, a restriction to the variety and richness of Chinese culture (Ji Jianxiu, 2006). It could be argued that what was constructed as the most powerful advertising form in Chinese-language sources ended up being lost in its own definition.

The show must go on

It is now more than 30 years since the reintroduction of advertising in China, and despite the mind-boggling figures (number of agencies, employees and turnover) surrounding the industry, its existence is far from harmonious and its development far from smooth. Maybe it is because the phenomenon on occasion is too similar to Western advertising and ends up blurring the boundaries of socialist/capitalist advertising? Or maybe it is because it has still not been able to surpass Western advertising from both a qualitative and a creative standpoint? There seems to be more to it than this though.

Chinese advertising is a subject that has attracted scholars who agreed in describing it as a complex, controversial, paradoxical phenomenon: it constantly reminds the Chinese authorities of the country's contradictions, including the desire to protect national culture and the need to open up to the Western world (Gao Zhihong, 2003); it is thought to have fuelled new hungers for better living conditions and even political change (Stross, 1990: 501); it is considered risky, because the uneven development of the industry could increase the gap among urban and rural citizens (Yu Xuejun, 1991: 26).

Throughout the years, Chinese advertising has been shown to be suffering from the same evils as Western capitalist advertising. These are exactly the same evils it was told to avoid when it was reintroduced in China. For instance, it often suffers from lack of truth or sincerity (as evidenced by the long list of illegal and deceptive ads that are denounced on a yearly basis); it plays with embarrassing homophones and breaks sexual taboos; it fails on many occasions to respect the standard language, etc.[39] In 2011, the Beijing office of the SAIC issued a ban on ads promoting luxury goods, as they appeared to contribute to the already visible gap between the wealthy and the less wealthy.[40] One year later, the State Administration of Radio, Film and Television (SARFT) banned some TV commercials after accusing them of promoting what is termed the 'gift culture' in which expensive luxury items are given in exchange for favours.[41] It is too late now for the state to go back, as it has become indispensable to the economy and to the commercialization of media. The ambivalent attitude of China's authorities towards advertising, as well as the highly contradictory relationship with foreigners, proved to be two recurrent themes in more recent years: new attacks on advertising recall the neglect that spread during the Cultural Revolution and the anti-corruption campaigns carried out in the 1980s. Ideological concerns are still present.

As a consequence of China's membership of the WTO and its growing role on the global scene, a new campaign with an emphasis on advertising *with Chinese characteristics* has been employed from both a protectionist and a nationalist perspective: on the one hand, embracing the challenges set by the big multinationals and, on the other hand, reasserting China's legitimacy to use symbols of its own culture. Being part of an ongoing project by the author, this chapter is not exhaustive on the topic, but rather has tried to fill a gap in existing studies, deliberately leaving out of the picture another form of advertising (public service advertising, *gongyi guanggao*) which the author intends to address in depth in forthcoming research.[42] Rather than love at first sight, the relationship between advertising and China shows the symptoms of a love/hate relationship that, despite the best efforts, is difficult to maintain.

Notes

1. A graphic reproduction of this print ad can be found in Liu Libin (2004: 8).
2. This 'pleasant little ritual' of the origins of advertising in China is shared by other scholars, such as Chen Pei'ai (1997: 9–18), Liu Jialin (2000: 6–17), Yao Xi and Jiang Yibing (2006: 39–41), and Xu Junji (2006: 3–5).
3. See Liu Jialin (2000: 153), Huang Yong (2003: 76), and the list of newspapers and magazines carrying advertising provided by Wang Jian (2000: 24–5).

4. See Dal Lago (2000) and Hestler (2005).

5. See Yao Xi and Jiang Yibing (2006: 142, 145–6) and Wang Jian (2000: 34).

6. Meisner (1977), Schoenhals (1996), and Cheek (2002) offer comprehensive accounts of China under Mao's rule.

7. 'Socialists never liked the advertising industry,' this is how Hanson's book on the spread of commercial advertising in the Soviet Union, Poland, Hungary, and Yugoslavia begins (Hanson, 1974: 1).

8. See Xu Baiyi (1988: 35–6) and Chen Pei'ai (1997: 73–4).

9. For example, the SAC was renamed the Shanghai Fine Arts Company, and many brands were required to adopt new names like 'Red Guard', 'People', and 'Workers and Peasants' (see Wang Jian, 2000: 35).

10. The works by Lee Chin-Chuan (1994), Zhao Yuezhi (1998), and Lynch (1999) offer an exhaustive overview and analysis of Chinese media both in the pre-Mao and post-Mao years.

11. For detailed accounts of the main transformations that occurred during Deng's China see Evans (1993), Meisner (1996), Goldman and MacFarquhar (1999), and Vogel (2011).

12. For contributions on advertising regulation in China see Yu Xuejun (1991), Gao Zhihong (2007), and Gao Zhihong and Kim Sion (2009).

13. The Four Modernizations were proposed by Zhou Enlai in 1963 and related to agriculture, industry, defence, and science and technology. They were enacted by Deng Xiaoping in 1978.

14. For an investigation of the so-called consumer revolution in China see Davis (2000) and Croll (2006b). Specific studies on the promotion of foreign brands to Chinese consumers are provided by Wang Jian (2000) and Tian and Dong (2010).

15. The SAC was established in 1962, it disappeared under pressure from the Gang of Four, and reopened in 1978 (see Anderson, 1984: 279).

16. This slogan – whose long version is 'To make the past serve the present and foreign things serve China' – is attributed to Mao Zedong, who launched it in 1957, in concomitance with the campaign 'Let a hundred flowers bloom and a hundred schools of thought contend.'

17. The Four Cardinal Principles were introduced in 1979 by Deng Xiaoping and could not be debated within the PRC. The principles upheld 'the socialist path', 'the people's democratic dictatorship', 'the leadership of the Communist Party of China', and 'Mao Zedong thought and Marxism–Leninism'.

18. The expression 'socialist spiritual civilization' was introduced in 1979 by Ye Jianying, a Chinese Communist General and Chairman of the Standing Committee of the National People's Congress (1978–83),

and became an official catchphrase thanks to the CCP General Secretary Hu Yaobang, who used it in a famous speech delivered at the 12th CCP National Congress (September 1982).

19. More on the requirements socialist advertising with Chinese characteristics had to meet can be found in Tao Yongkuan and Hu Zuyuan (1984) and Ding Yunpeng (1985).

20. See Zhang Nanzhou (1986: 143–4) and Fu Hanzhang (1988: 39–42).

21. See Ding Yunpeng (1985); an alternative version is provided by Zhao Yuji (1987).

22. See Xu Baiyi (1988: 37–8), Huang Yong (2003, 88–9), and Huang Yanqiu and Yang Dongjie (2006: 8).

23. *Xinhua* (2013a).

24. Sweney (2008).

25. Canneslions (2011).

26. *Xinhua* (2013a).

27. This slogan is attributed to the philosopher Li Zehou, whose intent was to embrace global modernity and apply it in a Chinese way (Li Zehou, 1987). Linguistically, it corresponds to the opposite of *Zhongxue weiti, Xixue weiyong* (Chinese learning for substance, Western learning for function), which was advocated by Zhang Zhidong in his major work *Exhortation to Study* (*Quanxue pian*), published in 1900, and reflected the necessity to keep a Chinese core while importing science and technology from the West.

28. See three manuals on how to target one billion consumers written by Xu Baiyi (1990), Davison (2006), and Doctoroff (2007).

29. For an updated account of the crucial role played by the ongoing rhetoric of 'the century of humiliation' in China see Wang Zheng (2012).

30. For an analysis of the challenges set by China's membership of the WTO's advertising sector see Keane and Spurgeon (2004) and Wang Jing (2008: 40–51).

31. On the sensation caused by publication of *China Can Say No* see Gries (2004: 180–94).

32. The didactic intention is pretty explicit: 'These widely publicized incidents vividly demonstrate the idiosyncrasies of the Chinese advertising market … they also highlight the insensitivity among Western advertising professionals toward Chinese politics and culture. So … it is important to take a closer look at Chinese history so that lessons can be learned from the past to prevent future mistakes' (Gao Zhihong, 2007).

33. See Guo Yingjie (2004: 109–32).

34. The competition, which takes place yearly and is still running, is organized by the SAIC and the Chinese Advertising Association (CAA).
35. 'Soft power' is a term describing the ability to attract and co-opt and stands in stark contrast to coertion, the use of force, or bribery. It was first used by Joseph Nye of Harvard University.
36. See Chen Pei'ai and Zhang Liping (2010) and Liu Yiqing (2010).
37. For example, the two books entirely dedicated to advertising 'with Chinese elements' by Chen Pei'ai (2010) and Guo Youxian and Hao Dongheng (2010).
38. An explanation of the difference between 'Made in China' and 'Created in China' is offered by Keane (2007).
39. See Chu Guangzhi (2005), Hu Xiaoyun and Xie Jinyu (2005), and Wang Lan and Huang Heshui (2005).
40. Moore (2011).
41. *Xinhua* (2013b).
42. This is the topic of my PhD thesis, 'What's in a name?: on China's Search for Public Service Advertising (*gongyi guanggao*),' 2009, Ca' Foscari University of Venice (unpublished).

References

Abarca, M. (2006) *Voices in the Kitchen: Views of Food and the World from Working-Class Mexican and Mexican American Women.* Austin, TX: University of Texas Press.

Agamben, G. (1998) *Homo Sacer: Sovereign Power and Bare Life.* Stanford, CA: Stanford University Press.

Ames, R.T. (2011) *Confucian Role Ethics: A Vocabulary.* Hong Kong, China: Chinese University Press.

Ames, R.T. and Rosemont, H., Jr. (Transl.) (1998) *The Analects of Confucius: A Philosophical Translation.* New York: Ballantine Books.

Anderson, M.H. (1984) *Madison Avenue in Asia: Politics and Transnational Advertising.* London: Associated University Press.

Arlt, W.G (2012) *China Outbound Tourism Research Institute Yearbook (CORTI).* London: Peter Lang Verlag.

Badiou, A. (2011) *Being and Event.* London: Continuum

Baehr, P. (2001) 'The "iron cage" and the "shell as hard as steel": Parsons, Weber, and the Stahlhartes Gehäuse metaphor in The Protestant Ethic and the Spirit of Capitalism,' *History and Theory,* **40**, 153–69.

Bain & Company (2011) *China Luxury Market Study.* Boston, MA: Bain & Company.

Bain & Company and Kantar Worldpanel (2012) 'What Chinese shoppers really do but will never tell you,' *China Shopper Report,* **2**. Available from: *http://www.bain.com/Images/BAIN_REPORT%20_Chinas_shoppers_Do_city_tier_lifestage_ and_category_matter.pdf*

Bandurski, D. (2012) 'Old propaganda for a new era,' China Media Project, Hong Kong, 1 March 2012. Available from: *http://cmp.hku.hk/2012/03/01/19852/* [accessed 18 June 2013].

Barlow, T. (1994) 'Theorizing woman: *funü, guojia, jiating.*' In: A. Zito and T.E. Barlow (Eds.), *Body, Subject and Power in China.* Chicago: University of Chicago Press.

Barlow, T. (2004) *The Question of Women in Chinese Feminism.* Durham: Duke University Press.

Barlow, T. (2012) *Wang Guangmei's Qipao,* forthcoming.

Barmé, G. (Ed.) (1996) *Shades of Mao: The Posthumous Cult of the Great Leader.* Armonk, NY: M.E. Sharpe.

Baumann, Z. (2005) *Work, Consumerism and the New Poor,* Second Edition. Maidenhead, UK: Open University Press.

BCCC/CBBC (2011) *China's Twelfth Five Year Plan.* Available from: *http://www.britishchamber.cn/content/chinas-twelfth-five-year-plan-2011-2015-full-*

english-version [accessed 4 May 2013] [British Chamber of Commerce in China/ China–Britain Business Council].

Becker, J. (2012) 'Lei Feng's mystery girlfriend revealed,' *South China Morning Post*, 23 July 2012. Available from: *http://www.scmp.com/article/188365/lei-fengs-mystery-girlfriend-revealed* [accessed 12 June 2013].

Behuniak, J., Jr. (in press) 'Two challenges to market Daoism.' In: R.T. Ames and P. Hershock (Eds.), *Value and Values: Economics and Justice in an Age of Global Interdependence*. Honolulu, HI: University of Hawaii Press.

Bell, D. (2008) *China's New Confucianism: Politics and Everyday Life in a Changing Society*. Princeton, NJ: Princeton University Press.

Benjamin, W. (2000, [1936]) 'The work of art in the age of mechanical reproduction,' *The Continental Aesthetics Reader*. London: Routledge.

BHT (2013) *Ai Wei Wei Seeds Appeal*. Available from: *http://www.bexley heritagetrust.org.uk/ai-wei-wei-seeds-appeal* [accessed 8 April 2013] [Bexley Heritage Trust].

Blumer, H (1969) 'Fashion: from class differentiation to collective selection,' *The Sociological Quarterly*, **10**(3).

Bo, Z. (2012) 'From gongren to gongmin: a comparative analysis of Ai Weiwei's Sunflower Seeds and Nian,' *Journal of Visual Art Practice*, **11**(2/3), 117–33.

Bourdieu, P (1984) Distinction: A Social Critique of the Judgment of Taste. Cambridge, MA: Harvard University Press

Bourdieu, P. (1997) 'The forms of capital.' In: A. Halsey, H. Lauder, P. Brown, and A.S. Wells (Eds.), *Education: Culture, Economy and Society*. Oxford: Oxford University Press.

Boyer, D. (2003) 'The medium of Foucault in anthropology,' *The Minnesota Review*, [e-journal], 58–60. Available from: *http://www.theminnesotareview.org/ journal/ns58/boyer.htm* [accessed 28 May].

Brandon, R. (2012) 'Closer look: Adidas adiZero Rose 2.5 "Lei Feng",' 6 March 2012. Available from: *http://solecollector.com/news/closer-look-adidas-adizero-rose-2-5-lei-feng-/* [accessed 28 June 2013].

Burke, T. (1996) *Lifebuoy Men, Luxe Women: Commodification, Consumption and Cleanliness in Modern Zimbabwe*. Durham: Duke University Press.

Butler, J. (1994) 'Against proper objects,' *Differences: A Journal of Feminist Cultural Studies*, **6**, 1–26.

Butterfield, R. (2012) 'Rhetorical forms of symbolic labor: the evolution of iconic representations in China's Model Worker Awards,' *Rhetoric & Public Affairs*, **15**(1), 95–125.

Cang Zhenhua (1996) '*Gana guoji guanggaojie de ganshou yu qishi*' ('Impressions and admonishments from Cannes International Advertising Festival'), *Zhongguo guanggao*, **4**, 41–2.

Canneslions (2011) 'Cannes Lions appoints first Chinese jury president: Lo Sheung Yan to chair outdoor category,' 10 November 2011. Available from: *http://www.canneslions.com/press/press_story.cfm?article_id=250* [accessed 30 April 2013].

Cao Nanklai (2011) *Constructing China's Jerusalem: Christians, Power and Place in Contemporary Wenzhou*. Stanford, CA: Stanford University Press.

Cao, X. (1973) *The Story of the Stone*, Vol. 1. New York: Penguin [originally published in the eighteenth century].

Cha Jianying (1995) *China Pop*. New York: New Press.

Chan Koonchung (2014) *The Unbearable Dreamworld of Champa the Driver*. Doubleday, New York.

Chan, W. (1963) *A Source Book in Chinese Philosophy*. Princeton, NJ: Princeton University Press.

Chang, E. (2005) 'A chronicle of changing clothes.' In: A. Jones (Ed.), *Written on Water*. New York: Columbia University Press.

Chao Bai (2004) '*Jintian shi 'xiang Lei Feng xuexi' 41 zhou nian: Women gai xuexi shenme?*' ('Today is the 41st anniversary of "Learning from Lei Feng": What shall we learn?),' 5 March 2004. Available from: *http://www.chinanews.com/n/2004-03-05/26/409871.html* [accessed 22 June 2013].

Chao Chung-fan (1974) 'Fight a people's war of criticizing Lin Biao and Confucius,' *Workers, Peasants and Soldiers Criticize Lin Piao and Confucius*. Available from: *http://www2.kenyon.edu/Depts/Religion/Fac/Adler/Reln471/Criticize.htm* [accessed 11 April 2013].

Cheek, T. (2002) *Mao Tse-tung and China's Revolution: A Brief History with Documents*. New York: Palgrave Macmillan.

Chen Kai (2009) ' "*Xue Lei Feng*" *wangluo youxi nengfou chengwei deyu de yiji liangyao?*' ('Can the online game "Learning from Lei Feng" become a good medicine for moral education?'), *Xiandai zhongxiaoxue jiaoyu*, 3, 14–16.

Chen Ming (2011) 'The fighting of the two tigers,' on Sina.com (18 March 2001). Available from: *http://auto.sina.com.cn/ news/2011-03-18/0739737978.shtml* [accessed 28 May 2013].

Chen Pei'ai (1997) *Zhongwai guanggaoshi (A History of Chinese and Foreign Advertising)*. Beijing: Zhongguo wujia chubanshe.

Chen Pei'ai (2009) *Zhongwai guanggaoshi xinbian (A New History of Chinese and Foreign Advertising)*. Beijing: Gaodeng jiaoyu chubanshe.

Chen Pei'ai (2010) *Zhongguo yuansu yu guanggao yingxiao (The Chinese Elements and Advertising Promotion)*. Xiamen, China: Xiamen daxue chubanshe.

Chen Pei'ai and Zhang Liping (2010) ' "*Zhongguo yuansu*" *yu guojia ruanshili jingzheng: yi guanggao yu pinpai chuangyi weilie*' ['"The Chinese Elements" and national soft power: examples from advertising and brand creation'), *Journal of Shenyang Normal University (Social Science Edition)*, 34(2), 1–5.

Chen Weihua (2011) 'Reclaiming moral ground key to nation,' *China Daily Online*, 1 November 2011. Available from: *http://www.chinadaily.com.cn/opinion/2011-1/01/content_14012721.htm* [accessed 5 June 2013].

Cheng Hong (1996) 'Advertising in China: a socialist experiment.' In: K.T. Frith (Ed.), *Advertising in Asia: Communication, Culture and Consumption*. Ames, IA: Iowa State University Press.

Cheng Hong (2009) '*Mao Tse-tung de tici yu xue Lei Feng de huodong*' ('Mao Tse-tung's calligraphic inscription and the campaign of learning from Lei Feng'), *Shijiqiao*, 3, 9–13.

Cheng Yan (2010) *Tourism Media Dynamics: Narratives of the Nation-state*. Champaign, IL: University of Illinois Press.

China Daily (2007) 'Protection laws proposed for Chinese heroes,' 20 May 2007. Available from: *http://www.chinadaily.com.cn/china/2007-05/20/content_876314.htm* [accessed 12 June 2013].

China Daily (2012) 'Lei Feng-themed publications to boost altruism,' 4 March 2012. Available from: *http://www.chinadaily.com.cn/china/2012-03/04/content_14750145.htm* [accessed 20 May 2013].

China Daily (2013) 'Weibo buzz: significance of Lei Feng spirit,' 3 May 2012. Available from: *http://www.chinadaily.com.cn/opinion/2012-03/05/content_14759082.htm* [accessed 27 June 2013].

Chio, J. (2009) 'Landscape of travel: tourism, media and identity in Southwest China.' PhD dissertation, UC Berkeley.

Chong, G.P.L. (2011) 'Volunteers as the "new" model citizens: governing citizens through soft power,' *China Information*, 25(33), 33–59.

Chu Guangzhi (2005) '*Zhili xujia guanggao yu guanggao hangye zilü*' ('The management of false advertising and industry self-regulation'). In: Ding Junjie and Dong Lijin (Eds.), *Hexie yu chongtu: guanggao chuanbo zhong de shehui wenti yu chulu (Harmony and Conflict: Social Problems and Resolutions in Advertising)*. Beijing: Zhongguo chuanmei daxue chubanshe.

CNBS (2005) 'China's middle class defined by income,' *People's Daily*, 20 January 2005) [in Chinese] [China's National Bureau of Statistics].

CNN (2011) *China's Most Ambitious Replica: Manhattan*, CNN, 9 August 2011. Available from: *http://travel.cnn.com*

Conner, P. (1999) 'Lamqua, Western and Chinese painter,' *Arts of Asia*, 29(2), March/April, 46–64.

CPA (2009) *Jianzheng: Gaige kaifang sanshinian (Witness: China's Thirty Years)*. Hong Kong: Oxford University Press [*Zhongguo shyingshi xiehui* (China Photographers' Association)].

Crandon-Malamud, L. (1993) *From the Fat of Our Souls: Social Change, Political Process, and Medical Pluralism in Bolivia*. Berkeley, CA: University of California Press.

Crespi, J. (2009) *Voices in Revolution: Poetry and the Auditory Imagination in Modern China*. Honolulu, HI: University of Hawaii Press.

Croll, E.J. (2006a) 'Conjuring goods, identities and cultures.' In: K. Latham, S. Thompson, and J. Klein (Eds.), *Consuming China: Approaches to Cultural Change in Contemporary China*. London: Routledge.

Croll, E. (2006b) *China's New Consumers: Social Development and Domestic Demand*. London: Routledge.

Dai Jinhua (1997) 'Imagined nostalgia,' *Boundary 2*, 24(3), 143–61.

Dai Jinhua (1999) *Yixing shuxie: Jiushi niandai zhongguo wenhua yanjiu (Invisible Writings: Chinese Cultural Studies in the 1990s)*. Nanjing, China: Jiangsu Chubanshe.

Dai Jinhua (2004) 'Class and gender in contemporary Chinese women's literature.' In: Jie Tao, Bijun Zheng, and S.L. Mow (Eds.), *Holding Up Half the Sky: Chinese Women Past, Present, and Future*. New York: CUNY/Feminist Press.

Dal Lago, F. (2000) 'Crossed legs in 1930's Shanghai: how "modern" is the modern woman,' *East Asian History*, 19, 103–44.

Das, V. and Poole, D. (Eds) (2004) *Anthropology in the Margins of the State*. Santa Fe, NM: School of American Research Press.

Davis, D. (2000) 'Introduction.' In: D. Davis (Ed.), *The Consumer Revolution in Urban China*. Berkeley, CA: University of California Press.

Davis, D. (2005) 'Urban consumer culture,' *China Quarterly*, **183**, September, 692–709.

Davison, L. (2006) *Serving the New Chinese Consumer*. New York: McKinsey & Co.

de Mooij, M. (2004) *Consumer Behaviour and Culture: Consequences for Global Marketing and Advertising*. London: Sage.

Dicks, B. (2003) *Culture on Display: The Production of Contemporary Visitability*. Maidenhead, UK: Open University Press.

Dickson, B. (2003) *Red Capitalists in China: The Party, Private Entrepreneurs, and Prospects for Political Change*. Cambridge, UK: Cambridge University Press.

Ding Mingtang (Ed.) (1994) *Lei Feng songge: Gequ zhuanji (Odes to Lei Feng: Song Collection)*. Qingdao, China: Qingdao Publishing Group.

Ding Yunpeng (1979) '*Wei guanggao zhengming*' ('Restoring the good name of advertising'), *Wenhui bao*, 14 January 1979, p. 2.

Ding Yunpeng (1985) '*Woguo shehui zhuyi guanggao tezheng chuyi*' ('My opinion on the characteristics of Chinese socialist advertising'), *Zhongguo guanggao*, **1**, 4–5.

Dirlik, A. and Xudong Zhang (Eds.) (2000) *Postmodernism and China*. Durham, NC: Duke University Press.

Doctoroff, T. (2007) *Billions: Selling to the New Chinese Consumer*. New York: Palgrave Macmillan.

Dong, M. (2006) '*Shanghai's China Traveler*', in *Everyday Modernity in China*. Washington, DC: University of Washington Press.

Du Guodong (2009) 'Protest over Tian's Good Samaritan role,' *Global Times*, 6 May 2009.

Englehart, N.A. (2000) 'Rights and cultures in the Asian values argument: the rise and fall of Confucian Ethics in Singapore,' *Human Rights Quarterly*, **22**, 548–68.

Evans, H. (2006) 'Fashions and feminine consumption.' In: K. Latham, S. Thompson, and J. Klein (Eds.), *Consuming China: Approaches to Cultural Change in Contemporary China*. London: Routledge.

Evans, R. (1993) *Deng Xiaoping and the Making of Modern China*. London: Hamish Hamilton.

Fan Zhiyu (1998) *Shijie guanggao shihua (The History of World Advertising)*. Beijing: Zhongguo youyi chubanshe.

Fan, F. (2004) *British Naturalists in Qing China: Science, Empire, and Cultural Encounter*. Cambridge, MA: Harvard University Press.

Fan, R. (2010) *Reconstructionist Confucianism: Rethinking Morality after the West*. Dordrecht, The Netherlands: Springer Verlag.

Farquhar, J. (1994) *Knowing Practice: The Clinical Encounter of Chinese Medicine*. Boulder, CO: Westview Press.

Farquhar, J. (2002) *Appetites: Food and Sex in Post-socialist China*. New York: Duke University Press.

FBIC (2013) *Luxury Market in China: Huge Growth Potential Ahead*. Shanghai, China: Fung Business Intelligence Centre.

Ferguson, J. (1994) *The Anti-politics Machine: 'Development', Depoliticization, and Bureaucratic Power in Lesotho*. Cambridge, UK: Cambridge University Press.

Finnane, A. (2008) *Changing Clothes in China: Fashion, History, Nation.* New York: Columbia University Press.

Fiske, J. (2010, [1989]) *Understanding Popular Culture*, Second Edition. New York: Routledge.

Foucault, M. (1991) 'Governmentality.' In: G. Burchell, C. Gordon, and P. Miller (Eds.), *The Foucault Effect: Studies in Governmentality.* Chicago, IL: University of Chicago Press.

Foucault, M. (1994) *The Birth of the Clinic: An Archaeology of Medical Perception* (translated by A. Sheridan). New York: Vintage.

Fu Hanzhang (1988) '*Shehui zhuyi guanggao tixi tantao*' ('On the system of socialist advertising'), *Xinjiang shehui kexue*, **3**, 39–42.

Fung, A.Y.H. (2009) 'Fandom, youth and consumption in China,' *European Journal of Cultural Studies*, **12**, 285–303.

Fussell, P. (1992) *Class: A Guide Through the American Status System.* New York: Simon & Schuster.

Gao Zhihong (2003) 'What's in a name? On China's search for socialist advertising,' *Advertising & Society Review*, **4**(3). Available from: *http://muse.jhu.edu/* [accessed 30 April 2013].

Gao Zhihong (2007) 'The evolution of Chinese advertising law: a historical review,' *Advertising & Society Review*, **8**(1). Available from: *http://muse.jhu.edu/* [accessed 30 April 2013].

Gao Zhihong and Kim Sion (2009) 'Advertising law and regulation in China.' In: Cheng Hong and Chan Kara (Eds.), *Advertising and Chinese Society: Impacts andIssues.* Gylling, Denmark: Copenhagen Business School Press, pp. 134–60.

Geist, B. (1992) 'Lei Feng and the Lei Fengs of the eighties,' *Papers on Far Eastern History*, **42**, 97–124.

Gerth, K. (2003) *China Made: Consumer Culture and the Creation of a Nation.* London: Harvard University Asia Center.

Gerth, K. (2010) *As China Goes, So Goes The World.* New York: Hill & Wang.

Gerth, K. (2011) 'Lifestyles of the rich and infamous: the creation and implications of China's new aristocracy,' *Comparative Sociology*, **10**, 488–507.

Ghimire, K. (2001) 'The economic role of national tourism in China.' In: K. Ghimire (Ed.), *The Native Tourist.* Oxford, UK: Earthscan.

Gillette, M.B. (2000) *Between Mecca and Beijing: Modernization and Consumption among Urban Chinese Muslims.* Stanford, CA: Stanford University Press.

Global Times (2012a) 'When Lei Feng meets non-believers,' 5 March 2012. Available from: *http://www.globaltimes.cn/content/697218.shtml* [accessed 12 May 2013].

Global Times (2012b) 'China to step up "Learning from Lei Feng" campaigns,' 3 March 2012. Available from: *http://www.globaltimes.cn/content/698386.shtml* [accessed 20 May 2013].

Global Times (2012c) 'Full text of Hu Jintao's report at the 18th Party Congress,' 18 November 2012.

Global Times (2013a) 'Liu Yunshan urges learning from Lei Feng,' 2 March 2013. Available from: *http://www.globaltimes.cn/content/765271.shtml* [accessed 26 June 2013].

Global Times (2013b) 'Letters: Is Lei Feng Day necessary?' 6 March 2013. Available from: *http://www.globaltimes.cn/content/766346.shtml* [accessed 20 June 2013].

Goldman, M. and MacFarquhar, R. (Eds.) (1999) *The Paradox of China's Post-Mao Reforms*. Cambridge, MA: Harvard University Press.

Goodman, D.S.G. (1999) 'The new middle class.' In: M. Goldman and R. MacFarquhar (Eds.), *The Paradox of China's Post-Mao Reforms*. Cambridge, MA:Harvard University Press.

Greenhalgh, S. and Winckler, E. (2005) *Governing China's Population: From Leninist to Neoliberal Biopolitics*. Stanford, CA: Stanford University Press.

Gries, P.H. (2004) 'Popular nationalism and state legitimation in China.' In: P.H. Gries and S. Rosen (Eds.), *State and Society in 21st-century China: Crisis, Contention, and Legitimation*. New York: Routledge.

Guo Moruo (1964) '*Bu'ai hongzhuang ai wuzhuang*' ('Don't like red dress, like military uniform'), *Renmin Ribao (People's Daily)*, 25 April 1964.

Guo Yingjie (2004) *Cultural Nationalism in Contemporary China: The Search for National Identity under Reform*. London: Routledge/Curzon.

Guo Youxian and Hao Dongheng (2010) *Zhongguo yuansu yu guanggao chuangyi (The Chinese Elements and Advertising Creativity)*. Beijing: Beijing daxue chubanshe.

Han Wengen (2002) '*WTO yu Zhongguo guanggaoye*' ('WTO and China's advertising industry'). In: Qiao Jun, Cheng Zhuangzhuang, and Dong Lijin (Eds.), *Zhongguo guanggao hangye jingzhengli yanjiu (Research on China's Advertising Industry Competitiveness)*. Chengdu, China: Xinan caijing daxue chubanshe, pp. 259–73.

Han Xu (2012) '*Lei Feng jingshen' 50 nian yanjiangshi: 21 shiji Lei Feng daibiao shenme*' ('50 years of evolutionary history of the Lei Feng Spirit: What does Lei Feng represent in the 21st century?') *Renmin Wang*, 20 February 2012. Available from: *http://culture.people.com.cn/GB/87423/17157459.html* [accessed 18 May 2013].

Hansen, V. (2000) *The Open Empire: A History of China to 1600*. New York: W.W. Norton & Co.

Hanson, P. (1974) *Advertising and Socialism*. London: Macmillan.

Harrell, S. (1995) 'Introduction.' In: S. Harrell (Ed.), *Cultural Encounters as China's Ethnic Frontiers*. Seattle, WA: University of Washington Press.

He Ma (2011) *The Tibet Code*. Chongqing, China: Chongqing Press [in Chinese].

Hearn, K. and Willis, A (2008) 'Lei Feng lives on in cyberspace,' paper presented at *DIMEA '08 Proceedings of the Third International Conference on Digital Interactive Media in Entertainment and Arts*, New York: ACM, pp. 248–55. Available from: *http://dl.acm.org/citation.cfm?doid=1413634.1413682* [accessed 20 May 2013].

Heinrich, L. (2008) *The Afterlife of Images: Translating the Pathological Body between China and the West*. Durham, NC: Duke University Press.

Helgason, E. (2011) 'The troubled history of the harp: the billionaire who wanted to rebuild Reykjavik, a house of glass and a very good orchestra,' *The Reykjavík Grapevine*, 18 May. Available from: *http://www.grapevine.is/Author/Read Article/The-Troubled-History-Of-The-Harp* [Accessed: 1 May 2013].

Hestler, A. (2005) *Shanghai Posters: The Power of Advertising*. Hong Kong, China: FormAsia.

Hockx, M. (2005) 'Virtual Chinese literature: a comparative study of online poetry communities,' *China Quarterly*, **183**, 670–91.

Hollinshead, K. and Hou Chun Xiao (2012) 'The seduction of "Soft Power".' *Journal of China Tourism Research*, **8**, 227–47.

Hong Junhao (1994) 'The resurrection of advertising in China: developments, problems, and trends,' *Asian Survey*, **34**(4), 326–42.

Honig, E. and Hershatter, G. (1988) *Personal Voices: Chinese Women in the 1980's*. New York: Stanford University Press.

HRW (2013) *China: 'Benefit the Masses' Campaign Surveilling Tibetans: Cadre Teams in Villages Collecting Political Information, Monitoring Opinions*. New York: Human Rights Watch, 19 June 2013.

Hu Qingyun (2013a) 'Lei Feng's last words?' *Global Times*, 11 March 2013. Available from: *http://www.globaltimes.cn/content/767356.shtml#. UcBIzZwXF9Y* [accessed 17 May 2013].

Hu Qingyun (2013b) 'Despite orders Lei Feng films bomb,' *Global Times*, 7 March 2013. Available from: *http://www.globaltimes.cn/content/766438.shtml* [accessed 17 May 2013].

Hu Xiaoyun (2006) 'Theoretical studies of advertising in modern China: the history and the actuality.' *China Media Research*, **2**(2), 44–57.

Hu Xiaoyun and Xie Jinyu (2005) '*Qingse guanggao tupo seqing jinqu*' ('Sex in advertising breaks the taboos'). In: Ding Junjie and Dong Lijin (Eds.), *Hexie yu chongtu: guanggao chuanbo zhong de shehui wenti yu chulu (Harmony and Conflict: Social Problems and Resolutions in Advertising)*. Beijing: Zhongguo chuanmei daxue chubanshe, pp. 125–9.

Huang Yanqiu, and Yang Dongjie (2006) *Zhongguo dangdai shangye guanggaoshi (The History of Chinese Contemporary Commercial Advertising)*. Kaifeng, China: Henan daxue chubanshe.

Huang Yong (2003) *Zhongwai guanggao jianshi (A Brief History of Chinese and Foreign Advertising)*. Chengdu, China: Sichuan daxue chubanshe.

Huang Yuli and Yang Wanli (2012) 'Lei Feng continues to lead by heroic example,' *Qiushi Journal*, 5 March 2012. Available from: *http://english.qstheory.cn/ society/201203/t20120305_143197.htm* [accessed 17 May 2013].

Huang, S. and Liu, S. (2012) 'De-centering China: the Southwest as the core,' paper presented at *AAA San Francisco*.

Huntington, S.P. (2000) 'Foreword: cultures count.' In: L.E. Harrison and S.P. Huntington (Eds.), *Culture Matters: How Values Shape Human Progress*. New York: Basic Books.

Hyde, S. (2001) 'Sex tourism practices on the periphery.' In: N. Chen (Ed.), *China Urban*. New York: Duke University Press.

International Business (2012) 'Chinese dissident Ai Weiwei's Sunflower Seeds pull in $782,000,' 11 May 2012. Available from: *http://www.ibtimes.com*

Jacobs, A. (2012) 'Chinese heroism effort is met with cynicism,' *New York Times*, 5 March 2012. Available from: *http://www.nytimes.com/2012/03/06/world/ asia/lei-feng-day-draws-chinese-cynicism.html?ref=asia* [accessed 20 June 2013].

Jansson, A. (2002) 'The mediatization of consumption: towards an analytical framework of image culture,' *Journal of Consumer Culture*, **2**(5), 5–31

Ji Jianxiu (2006) '*Yong Zhongguo yuansu hongyang Zhongguo wenhua*' ('Use Chinese elements to promote Chinese culture,' *Guanggaoren*, **9**, 2.

Jia Zhaoquan (1986) 'Party Membership and Wearing Dresses', *People's Daily*, 2 December 1986)

Jia Zhaoquan (1986) '*Rudang yu chuan qunzi*' ('Party membership and wearing dresses'), *Renmin Ribao (People's Daily)*, 2 December 1986.

Jiang Haiying (2006) '*Zhongguo de, shijie de! Ji shoujie Zhongguo yuansu guoji dachuangyi dasai*' ('Of China, of the World! Reporting the first edition of the Chinese Element International Creative Award,' *Guanggao daguan zongheban*, **12**, 82–7.

Jingji Ribao (Economic Daily) (1992) '1985–2000 Aspects of Chinese women taken in 1992 in Wuxi, Jiangsu,' 3 June 1992.

Johanson, M. (2012) 'China: Tibet theme park will promote harmony,' *International Business Times*. Available from: *http://www.ibtimes.com/articles/361043/ 20120709/china-tibet-theme-park-lhasa.htm* [accessed 9 July 2012].

Juanjuan Wu (2009) *Chinese Fashion: From Mao to Now*. Oxford, UK: Berg.

Kahn, H. (1979) *World Economic Development: 1979 and Beyond*. London: Croom Helm.

Kaiman, J. (2013) 'China arrests 900 in fake meat scandal,' *Guardian*, 3 May 2013). Available from: *http://www.guardian.co.uk* [accessed 3 May 2013].

Keane, M. (2006) 'From Made in China to Created in China,' *International Journal of Cultural Studies*, **9**, 285–96.

Keane, M. (2007) *Created in China: The Great New Leap Forward*. New York: Routledge.

Keane, M. and Spurgeon, C. (2004) 'Advertising industry and culture in post-WTO China,' *Media International Australia*, **11**, 104–17.

Kennady, M. (2011) 'Ai Weiwei's Sunflower Seeds to go on sale at Sotheby's,' *Guardian*, 26 January 2011. Available from: *http://www.guardian.co.uk*

Kinder, C. (2011) 'China's Manhattan knock-off,' *The Atlantic*, 4 August 2011. Available from: *http://www.theatlantic.com*

Klein, N. (2007) *The Shock Doctrine: The Rise of Disaster Capitalism*. London: Penguin Books

Kleinman, A. (1997) *Writing at the Margin: Discourse between Anthropology and Medicine*. Berkeley, CA: University of California Press.

Kleinman, A. and Watson, J. (2005) *SARS in China: Prelude to Pandemic?* Stanford, CA: Stanford University Press.

Kleutghen, K. (2010) 'Ai Weiwei Sunflower Seeds,' *Modern Art Asia*, 5 November 2010. Available from: *http://modernartasia.com/ai-wei-wei-sunflower-seeds-5/* [accessed 17 April 2013].

Kotler, P. and Armstrong, G. (2010) *Principles of Marketing*, 13th Edition. Upper Saddle River, NJ: Pearson.

KPMG (2013) *Global Reach of China Luxury*. North Holland, The Netherlands: KPMG.

Landsberger, S. (2011) 'Learning by what example? Educational propaganda in twenty-first-century China,' *Critical Asian Studies*, **33**(4), 541–71.

Lee Chin-Chuan (1994) *China's Media, Media's China*. Boulder, CO: Westview.

Leung, M. (2013) *Made in Hong Kong*. Available from: *http://www.lmp.hk/workdetail.php?id=29* [accessed 4 April 2013].

Levin, D. (2013) 'In China, cinematic flops suggest fading of an icon,' *New York Times*, 11 March 2013. Available from: *http://www.nytimes.com/2013/03/12/world/asia/in-china-unpopular-films-suggest-fading-of-icon.html?hp&pagewanted=all&_r=0* [accessed 26 June 2013].

Li Chi: Book of Rites (1967) Volumes 1 and 2. Translated by J. Legge. New York: University Books.

Li Chunling (2003) 'The composition and proportion of the present Chinese middle class,' *Chinese Journal of Population Science*, 6, 25–32.

Li Chunling (2004) 'Middle stratum: the group of the Chinese society needs attention.' In: Zai Ruxin (Ed.), *The Analysis and Forecast of the Condition of the Chinese Society*. Beijing: Social Science Documentation Publishing House [in Chinese].

Li Congjun, Zhang Yanping, Zhao Cheng, and Xiao Chunfei (2012) '*Tongxun: Yonghen de zhaohuan: Lei Feng jingshen shiji jiaoxiangqu*' ('The eternal summon: century symphony for the Lei Feng Spirit'). Available from: *http://cpc.people.com.cn/GB/64093/64387/17257301.html* [accessed 22 June 2013].

Li Kwok-sing (1995) *Glossary of Political Terms of the People's Republic of China* (translated by Mary Lok). Hong Kong, China: Chinese University Press.

Li Li (2012) 'Forever young Lei Feng: our times need the spirit of an altruist hero more than ever,' *Beijing Review*, 8 March 2012. Available from: *http://www.bjreview.com.cn/print/txt/2012-03/05/content_431750.htm* [accessed 20 May 2013].

Li Qiang (1999) 'Market transition and the generation's alteration of China's middle class,' *Strategy and Management*, 3, 35–44.

Li Yinhe and Evans, H (2001) '*Guanyu nvxing zhuyi de duihua*' ('Conversations about feminism'). *Sociology Research*, **4. Available from:** *http//www.socresonline.org.uk*

Li Zehou (1987) '*Man shuo Xiti Zhongyong*' ('Discussing Western learning as essence, Chinese learning for use'), *Kongzi yanjiu*, 1, 15–28.

Lian Hongning and Dong Wanyu (2009) '*Lei Feng ziliao quanguo zhi zui: Lei Feng zhanyou yisheng shoucang "Lei Feng"*' ('The largest Lei Feng material in China: Lei Feng's Comrade-in-arms collected "Lei Feng" throughout his life'), 17 February 2009. Available from: *http://news.xinhuanet.com/collection/2009-02/17/content_10831984.htm* [accessed 20 May 2013].

Liechty, M. (2003) *Suitably Modern: Making Middle Class Culture in a New Consumer Society*. Princeton, NJ: Princeton University Press.

Lin, J. (2011) *Fake Stuff: China and the Rise of Counterfeit Goods*. London: Routledge.

Ling Yang (2009) 'All for love: the Corn fandom, prosumers, and the Chinese way of creating a superstar,' *International Journal of Cultural Studies*, 12(527), 527–43.

Liu Jialin (2000) *Xinbian Zhongwai guanggaoshi (A New History of Chinese and Foreign Advertising)*. Guangzhou, China: Jinan daxue chubanshe.

Liu Libin (Ed.) (2004) *Zhongguo guanggao mengjinshi 1979–2003 (The Rapid History of Chinese Advertising)*. Beijing: Huaxia chubanshe.

Liu Yiqing (2010) '*Guanggao chuangyi zhong Zhongguo yuansu de yunyong*' ('Creative advertising using Chinese elements'), *Changjiang daxue xuebao (shehui kexue ban) (Yangtze University Social Sciences Edition)*, 33(3), 342–4.

Lu Xiaoya (1984) *The Girl in Red*. China: Emei Films.

Lu Xueyi (Ed.) (2002) *Research Report on the Social Strata in Contemporary China*. Beijing: Social Science Documentation Publishing House [in Chinese].

Lu Xueyi (Ed.) (2004) *Research Report on Social Mobility in Contemporary China*. Beijing: Social Science Documentation Publishing House [in Chinese].

Lu, S. (2001) *China, Transnational Visuality, Global Postmodernity*. Stanford, CA: Stanford University Press.

Lupton, D. (1997) 'Consumerism, reflexivity and the medical encounter,' *Social Science Medicine*, 45(3), 373–81.

Luyou Xiaobaike [Pocket Encyclopedia of Tourism], China: Shandong Youyi Shushe.

Lynch, D.C. (1999) *After the Propaganda State: Media, Politics and 'Thought Work' in Reformed China*. Stanford, CA: Stanford University Press.

Ma Jian (1987) *Stick Out Your Tongue*. Random House, London.

Mao Tse-tung (1919) 'The Women's Revolutionary Army.' In: S.R. Schram (Ed.), *Mao's Road to Power: Revolutionary Writings, 1912–1949, Vol. 1: The Pre-Marxist Period, 1912–1920*. New York: M.E. Sharpe.

Mao Tse-tung (1954) 'On new democracy,' *Selected Works of Mao Tse-tung*, Vol. III. London: Lawrence & Wishart, pp. 106–56

Mao Tse-tung (1976) *Quotations from Chairman Mao Tse-tung*. Beijing: Foreign Languages Press.

Martinsen, J. (2009) 'Lei Feng heritage for the whole world,' *Danwei* (blog site), 5 March 2009. Available from: *http://www.danwei.org/people/lei_feng_2009.php* [accessed 15 June 2013].

Marx, K. (1977) *Capital: A Critique of Political Economy*, Vol. 1. New York: Vintage Books.

McChesney, R.W. (2004) *The Problem of the Media: U.S. Communication Politics in the 21st Century*. New York: Monthly Review Press.

McKinsey & Company (2006) 'The value of China's middle class,' *McKinsey Quarterly*, 62–9.

McKinsey & Company (2009) Annual Chinese Consumer Study, Part II: One Country, Many Markets Targeting the Chinese Consumer with McKinsey. Available from: *https://solutions.mckinsey.com/insightschina/_SiteNote/WWW/Getfile.aspx?uri=/insightschina/default/en-us/aboutus/news/Files/wp2055036759/Insights_Cluster_FNL_web_4da74e92-e518-4a10-9528-862e75339b3b.pdf* [accessed 1 July 2013].

McKinsey & Company (2010) 'China's new pragmatic consumers,' *McKinsey Quarterly*. Available from: *http://www.mckinsey.com/insights/marketing_sales/chinas_new_pragmatic_consumers* [accessed 2 July 2013].

McLaughlin, K. (2012) 'Counterfeit medicine from Asia threatens lives in Africa,' *The Guardian*, 23 December 2012. Available from: *http://www.guardian.co.uk* [accessed 10 July 2013].

Meisner, M.J. (1977) *Mao's China: A History of the People's Republic*. London: Collier Macmillan.

Meisner, M.J. (1996) *The Deng Xiaoping Era: An Inquiry into the Fate of Chinese Socialism, 1978–1994*. New York: Hill & Wang.

Mencius (1970) Translated by D.C. Lau. London: Penguin Books.

MGI (2013) 'China's e-tail revolution: online shopping as a catalyst for growth.' Available from: *www.mckinsey.com/.../China%20e.../MGI_China_e-tailing_Full_report* [accessed 16 July 2013] [McKinsey Global Institute].

Milliard, C. (2013) 'Did you pocket Ai Weiwei's Sunflower Seeds? Now is your chance to own up,' *Blouin Art Info*, 11 February 2013. Available from: *http://uk.blouinartinfo.com/news/story/866166/did-you-pocket-ai-weiweis-sunflower-seeds-now-is-your-chance* [accessed 12 February 2013].

Minter, A. (2012) 'China infamous "Good Samaritan" case gets a new ending.' Available from: *http://www.bloomberg.com/news/2012-01-17/china-s-infamous-good-samaritan-case-gets-a-new-ending-adam-minter.html* [accessed 25 June 2013].

Mitchell, T. (Ed) (2000) *Questions of Modernity.* Minneapolis, MN: University of Minnesota Press.

Mittler, B. (2008) 'Popular propaganda? Art and culture in revolutionary China,' *Proceedings of the American Philosophical Society*, **152**(4), 466–89.

Moeller, H.G. (2006) *The Philosophy of the Daodejing.* New York: Columbia University Press.

Moore, M. (2011) 'China bans luxury advertising in Beijing,' *The Telegraph*, 22 March 2011. Available from: *http://www.telegraph.co.uk/news/worldnews/asia/china/8398097/China-bans-luxury-advertising-in-Beijing.html* [accessed 30 April 2013].

Mozi (2001) In: P.J. Ivanhoe and B.W. van Norden (Eds.), *Readings in Classical Chinese Philosophy*, Second Edition. Indianapolis, IN: Hackett.

Mueggler, E. (2002) 'Dancing fools: politics of culture and place in a "traditional nationality Festival",' *Modern China*, **28**(1), 3–38.

Nanfang Ribao (2003) 'Qiyejia cheng qingnian diyi ouxiang – xuan Lei Feng dang ouxiang de buzu yicheng [Youth say Lei Feng has become inadequate],' 17 March 2003 (written by Song Jihua, Yao Chuxiang, Cheng Jijing).

Ni Ning (2001) *Guanggaoxue jiaocheng (Advertising Textbook).* Beijing: Zhongguo renmin daxue chubanshe.

Nyiri, P. (2006) *Scenic Spots: Chinese Tourism, the State, and Cultural Authority.* Washington, DC: University of Washington Press.

Nyiri, P. (2010) *Mobility and Cultural Authority in Contemporary China.* Washington, DC: University of Washington Press, p. 62.

Oakes, T. (1988) *Tourism and Modernity in China.* London: Routledge.

Oakes, T. (2006) 'The village as theme park.' In: T. Oakes (Ed.), *Translocal China.* London: Routledge.

Oakes, T. (2011) 'Review of *Mobility and Cultural Authority in Contemporary China* by Pál Nyíri,' *China Journal*, **66**, 194–6.

Osnos, E. (2013) 'Ignoring Lei Feng: China's failed revolutionary biopics,' *New Yorker*, 13 March 2013. Available from: *http://www.newyorker.com/online/blogs/evanosnos/2013/03/lei-feng-communist-china-failed-films.html* [accessed 20 May 2013].

Palsson, G., Szerszynski, B., Sorlin, S., Marks, J., Avril, B., Crumley, C. et al. (2012) 'Reconceptualising the "anthropos" in the Anthropocene: integrating the social sciences and humanities in global environmental change research,' *Environmental Science & Policy*, **28**. Available from: *http://dx.doi.org/10.1016/j.envsci.2012.11.004* [accessed 2 May 2013].

Pang, L. (2012) *Creativity and Its Discontents: China's Creative Industries and Intellectual Property Rights Offenses*. Durham, NC: Duke University Press.

People's Daily (2001) 'Chinese youth provide 4.1-billion hours of volunteer service,' 23 August 2001. Available from: *http://english.people.com.cn/200108/23/eng20010823_78062.html* [accessed 22 June 2013].

People's Daily (2003) 'From model soldier Lei Feng to Bill Gates: China's new idols,' 28 January 2003. Available from: *http://english.peopledaily.com.cn/200301/28/eng20030128_110881.shtml* [accessed 23 June 2013].

People's Daily (2012) 'Forum held to honor Chinese ethics model,' 1 March 2012. Available from: *http://english.people.com.cn/90882/7744462.html* [accessed 20 June 2013].

Perdue, P. (n.d.) 'Rise and fall of the Canton Trade System III,' *MIT Visualizing Cultures*. Available from: *http://ocw.mit.edu/ans7870/21f/21f.027/rise_fall_canton_03/cw_essay01.html* [accessed 14 April 2013].

Platt, K. (2012) 'Zaha Hadid vs. the pirates: copycat architects in China take aim at the stars,' *Die Spiegel*, 28 December 2012. Available from: *http://www.spiegel.de* [accessed 12 June 2013].

Potter, J. and Potter, S. (1990) China's Peasants: The Anthropology of a Revolution. Cambridge: Cambridge University Press

Publisher's Note (1974) *Workers, Peasants and Soldiers Criticize Lin Piao and Confucius*. Beijing: Foreign Languages Press. Available from: *http://www2.kenyon.edu/Depts/Religion/Fac/Adler/Reln471/Criticize.htm* [accessed 11 April 2013].

Quinlan, M.B. and Quinlan, R.J. (2007) 'Modernization and medicinal plant knowledge in a Caribbean horticultural village,' *Medical Anthropology Quarterly*, **21**(2), 169–92.

Rabkin, A. (2012) 'Scenes from the Chinese consumerist revolution,' *The Cut*. Available from: *http://nymag.com/thecut/2012/08/scenes-from-the-chinese-consumerist-revolution.html* [accessed 2 May 2013].

Reed, G. (1991) 'The Lei Feng phenomenon in the PRC.' Unpublished dissertation, University of Virginia.

Reed, G. (1998) 'Is Lei Feng finally dead? The search for values in a time of reform and transition.' In: M. Agelasto and R. Adamson (Eds.), *Higher Education in Post-Mao China*. Hong Kong, China: Hong Kong University Press.

Renmin Ribao (1993) '*Lei Feng jingshen yong cun*' ('The Lei Feng spirit will always exist'), 5 March 1993.

Renmin Ribao (2003) '*Shidai xuyao Lei Feng jingshen: Fayang guangda Lei Feng jingshen*' ('The times are longing for the spirit of Lei Feng: further develop the spirit of Lei Feng and bring it to full expansion'), 5 March 2003.

Renmin Ribao (2013) '*Guoji shehui reqing zanyang Lei Feng jingshen*' ('The international community enthusiastically praises the Lei Feng spirit'), 5 March 2013, p. 3.

Rofel, L. (1999) *Other Modernities: Gendered Yearnings in China after Socialism*. Berkeley, CA: California University Press.

Rofel, L. (2007) *Desiring China: Experiments in Neoliberalism, Sexuality, and Public Culture*. Durham, NC: Duke University Press.

Rose, N. and Novas, C. (2005) 'Biological citizenship.' In: A. Ong and S.J. Collier (Eds.), *Global Assemblages: Technology, Politics, and Ethics as Anthropological Problems*. Malden, MA: Blackwell Publishing.

Rosen, S. (2009) 'Contemporary Chinese youth and the state,' *Journal of Asian Studies*, **68**(2), 359–69.

Salecl, R. (2011) *The Tyranny of Choice*. London: Profile Books.

Salecl, R. (n.d.a) 'Cartoon animation about choice.' Available from: *http://www.youtube.com/watch?v=1bqMY82xzWo* [accessed 1 June 2013].

Salecl, R. (n.d.b) 'The paradox of choice,' paper presented at *RSA (Royal Society for the encouragement of Arts, Manufactures and Commerce) Forum*. Available from: *http://www.youtube.com/watch?v=E4_HGRjJs9A* [accessed 10 June 2013].

Schell, O. (1988) *Discos and Democracy: China in the Throes of Reform*. New York: Anchor Books.

Schell, O. (1995) *Mandate of Heaven: A New Generation of Entrepreneurs, Dissidents, Bohemians and Technocrats Lays Claim to China's Future*. London: Warner Books.

Schoenhals, M. (1996) *China's Cultural Revolution: Not a Dinner Party*. Armonk, NY: M.E. Sharpe.

Schram, S.R. (Ed.) (1992) *Mao's Road to Power: Revolutionary Writings, 1912–1949 (Vol. 1: The Pre-Marxist Period, 1912–1920)*. New York: M.E. Sharpe.

Scott, C.J. (2010) *The Art of Not Being Governed: An Anarchist History of Southeast Asia*. New Haven, CT: Yale University Press.

Shang, D. (2012) 'Multiply it and fake it: on Ai Weiwei,' *Yishu*, **11**(2), March/April, 34–48.

Shanghai Daily (2006) 'Lei Feng becomes online game hero,' 16 March 2006. Available from: *http://news.xinhuanet.com/english/2006-03/16/content_4308138.htm* [accessed 20 July 2013].

Sheridan, M. (1968) 'The emulation of heroes,' *China Quarterly*, **33**, 47–72.

Shi Yonggang, Liu Qiongxiong, and Zhang Jun (2006) *Lei Feng: 1940–1962*, Second Edition 2012. Beijing: Shenghuo dushu xinzhi san lian shu dian.

Shi Yu and Lin Tao (2002) ' "*Lei Feng" yongyuan bu likai: liangbian daotan "Likai Lei Feng de rizi"* ' (' "Lei Feng" will never go: dialog about "The Day Lei Feng Left" '), *Dajiyuan (Epoch Times)*, 3 August 2002. Available from: *http://www.epochtimes.com/gb/2/3/8/n175208.htm* [accessed 28 May 2013].

Sigurðsson, G. (2012) 'Li, ritual and pedagogy: a cross-cultural exploration,' *Sophia*, **51**(2), 227–42.

Simmel, G. (1976) *The Metropolis and Mental Life*. New York: Free Press.

Smith, W.J. (2008) *China's Tibet?* Lanham, MD: Rowman & Littlefield.

Smythe, D. (1977) 'Communications: blindspot of Western marxism,' *Canadian Journal of Political and Social Theory*, **1**(3), 1–27

Song Shunqing (1983) *Shehui zhuyi guanggaoxue (The Discipline of Socialist Advertising)*. Taiyuan, China: Shanxi caijing xueyuan chubanshe.

Spalding, D. (2006) 'Eager paintings, empathetic products: Liu Ding's critical complicity,' *Yishu*, **5**(4), December, 69–72.

Spalding, D. (2010) 'Liu Ding: frameworks framed,' *Yishu*, **9**(1), January/February, 8–18.

Stanley-Baker, J. (1986) 'Forgeries in Chinese painting,' *Oriental Art*, **32**, Spring, 54–66.

Steen, A. (2013) ' "Voices of the mainstream": red songs and revolutionary identities in the People's Republic of China.' In: C. Utz and F. Lau (Eds.), *Vocal Music and Contemporary Identities: Unlimited Voices in East Asia and the West*. New York: Routledge.

Storrar, C. (2013) 'Lei Feng anniversary overshadowed by comrade's sudden death,' *China Times*, 8 March 2013. Available from: *http://www. wantchinatimes.com/ news-subclass-cnt.aspx?id=20130308000019&cid=1101* [accessed 20 May 2013].

Stross, R. (1990) 'The return of advertising in China: a survey of the ideological reversal,' *China Quarterly*, **123**, 485–502.

Studio Droog (n.d.) *The New Original*. Available from: *http://studio.droog.com/ projects/0/the-new-original* [accessed 23 April 2013].

Sun Jie (1990) *Tibet: Land of Mystery*. Buena Park, CA: Morning Glory Publishers.

Sun Shunhua (2007) *Zhongguo guanggaoshi (A History of Chinese Advertising)*. Jinan: Shandong daxue chubanshe.

Sweney, M. (2008) 'China steps up at Cannes Advertising Festival,' *The Guardian*, 18 June 2008. Available from: *http://www.guardian.co.uk/media/2008/jun/18/ advertising.chinathemedia* [accessed 30 April 2013].

Tao Te Ching (1989) Translated by D.C. Lau. Hong Kong, China: The Chinese University Press.

Tao Yongkuan, and Hu Zuyuan (1984) '*Shehui zhuyi guanggao conghengtan*' ('Talking about socialist advertising'), *Ningxia shehui kexue*, **2**, 38–42.

Taussig, M. (1993) *Mimesis and Alterity: A Particular History of the Senses*. London: Routledge.

Thompson, L.G. (1996) *Chinese Religion: An Introduction*. Belmont, CA: Wadsworth.

Thompson, M. (2010) 'Signals of virtue in Chinese consumerism and business,' *Journal of International Business Ethics*, **3**(2), 71–9.

Tian, K. and Dong, L. (2010) Consumer-citizens of China: The Role of Foreign Brands in the Imagined Future China. New York: Routledge

Tie Ning (1984) *The Red Shirt without Buttons*. Beijing: Zhongguo qingnian.

Tinari, P. (2010) 'Original copies.' In: G. Adamson (Ed.), *The Craft Reader*. London: Berg.

Tomba, L. (2004) 'Creating an urban middle class: social engineering in Beijing,' *China Journal*, **51**, January, 1–26

Tsai, K.S. (2002) *Back-Alley Banking: Private Entrepreneurs in China*. London: Cornell.

Tu, W. (1984) 'Confucian ethics and the entrepreneurial spirit in East Asia,' in *Confucian Ethics Today: The Singapore Challenge*. Singapore: Federal Publications.

Tu, W. (1996) 'Introduction,' *Confucian Traditions in East Asian Modernity: Moral Education and Economic Culture in Japan and the Four Mini-Dragons*. Cambridge, MA: Harvard University Press.

Tu, W., Hejtmanek, M., and Wachman, A. (1992) *The Confucian World Observed: A Contemporary Discussion of Confucian Humanism in East Asia*. Honolulu, HI: The East–West Center.

Turner, M. (1989) 'Early modern design in Hong Kong,' *Design Issues*, **6**(1), 79–91.

Valli, R. (2012) 'In need of new "hero" for young Chinese,' *Asia Calling*, 10 March 2012. Available from: *http://www.asiacalling.org/en/news/china/2554-in-need-of-new-hero-for-young-chinese* [accessed 27 June 2013].

Vancouver Sun (2005) 'Chinese firm "steals" art by painters here,' 29 December 2005. Available from: *http://www.canada.com/vancouversun*

Veblen, T. (1994, [1899]) *The Theory of the Leisure Class: An Economic Study of Institutions*. New York: Penguin Books.

Vogel, E. (2011) *Deng Xiaoping and the Transformation of China*. Cambridge, MA: Belknap Press.

Wainwright, O. (2013) 'Seeing double: what China's copycat culture means for architecture,' *Guardian*, 7 January 2013. Available from: *http://www.guardian.co.uk*

Wang Hui (2008) *Qu zhengzhihua de zhengzhi: duan ershi shiji de zhongjie yu jiushi niandai* (*Depoliticized Politics: The End of the Short Twentieth Century and the 1990's*). Beijing, China: Sheng huo, du shu, xin zhi san lian shu dian [in Chinese].

Wang Hui (2009) *The End of the Revolution: China and the Limits of Modernity*. London: Verso.

Wang Jian (2000) *Foreign Advertising in China: Becoming Global, Becoming Local*. Ames, IA: Iowa State University Press.

Wang Jing (2003) 'Framing Chinese advertising: some industry perspectives on the production of culture,' *Continuum: Journal of Media and Cultural Studies*, **17**(3), 247–70.

Wang Jing (2008) *Brand New China: Advertising, Media, and Commercial Culture*. London: Harvard University Press.

Wang Keping (2011). *Reading the Dao: A Thematic Inquiry*. London: Continuum.

Wang Lan and Huang Heshui (2005) '*Bu guifan guanggaoyu chutan*' ('Overview of advertising non-standard language'). In: Ding Junjie and Dong Lijin (Eds.), *Hexie yu chongtu: guanggao chuanbo zhong de shehui wenti yu chulu* (*Harmony and Conflict: Social Problems and Resolutions in Advertising*). Beijing: Zhongguo chuanmei daxue chubanshe.

Wang Zheng (2001) 'Call me *qingnian* (youth) but not *funü* (woman).' In: Bai Di, Zhong Xueping, and Wang Zheng (Eds.), *Some of Us: Chinese Women Growing Up in the Mao Era*. New Brunswick, NJ: Rutgers University Press.

Wang Zheng (2012) *Never Forget National Humiliation: Historical Memory in Chinese Politics and Foreign Relations*. New York: Columbia University Press.

Wang, C.J. and Lin, X. (2009) 'Migration of Chinese consumption values: traditions, modernization, and cultural renaissance,' *Journal of Business Ethics*, **88**, 399–409.

WB (2013) *World Development Indicators: Household Final Consumption Expenditure, etc. (% of GDP)*. Available from: *http://databank.worldbank.org/data/views/reports/tableview.aspx* [accessed: 4 May 2013] [World Bank].

Weber, M. (1930) *The Protestant Ethic and the Spirit of Capitalism* (translated by T. Parsons). London: HarperCollins Academic.

Weber, M. (1972) *Wirtschaft und Gesellschaft*. Tübingen, Germany: J.C.B. Mohr (Paul Siebeck) [in German].

Weber, M. (1988) 'Die Wirtschaftsethik der Weltreligionen,' *Gesammelte Aufsätze zur Religionssoziologie I.* Tübingen, Germany: J.C.B. Mohr (Paul Siebeck) [in German].

Wei Na (2013) 'No cap on Lei Feng profits,' *Global Times*, 4 March 2012. Available from: *http://www.globaltimes.cn/content/698540.shtml* [accessed 18 June 2013].

Wei Pengju (2004) 'Shizhuang: xiaofei shehui de shengti yuyan (Fashion: consumer society body language).' *Tianjin shehui kexue*, 3, 24–36.

Wen Fong (1962) 'The problem of forgeries in Chinese painting: Part 1,' *Artibus Asiae*, **25**(2/3), 95–140.

Whifield, S. (2006) 'East Asia: master forgers or innocent imitators?' In: R. London and M. Korey (Eds.), *Detecting the Text: Fakes, Forgeries, Fraud and Editorial Concerns* (Papers from the 40th Conference on Editorial Problems), November 2004, Toronto, Canada.

White, S. (1993) 'Medical discourses, Naxi identities, and the state: transformations in socialist China.' Doctoral dissertation, University of California, Berkeley.

White, S. (1998) 'From "barefoot doctor" to "village doctor" in Tiger Springs Village: a case study of rural health care transformations in socialist China,' *Human Organization*, **57**(4), 28 November, 480–90.

White, S. (2001) 'Medicines and modernities in socialist China: medical pluralism, Naxi identities, and the state in the Lijiang Basin.' In: L.H. Connor and G. Samuel (Eds.), *Healing Powers: Traditional Medicine, Shamanism, and Science in Contemporary Asia*. Westport, CT: Bergin & Garvey.

Williams, R. (1980) 'Advertising: the magic system.' In: R. Williams (Ed.), *Problems in Materialism and Culture*. London: Verso.

Willis, S. (1991) *A Primer for Daily Life*. London: Routledge.

Woeser, T. (2011) 'The media hype about Lhasa's "romance wall",' 27 May 2011. Available from: *http://woeser.middle-way.net/2011/05/blog-post_27.html* [accessed 27 May 2013].

Wong, E. (2013) 'In China, breathing becomes a childhood risk,' *New York Times*, 22 April 2013.

Wong, W. (2008) 'Framed authors: photography and conceptual art from Dafen Village,' *Yishu*, **7**(4), July/August, 32–43.

Wong, W. (2009) 'Xu Zhen's impossible is nothing: a discussion,' *Yishu*, **8**(3), May/June, 44–53.

Wright Mills, C. (1951) *White Collar: The American Middle Classes*. New York: Oxford University Press.

Xiaobing Tang (2002) 'The anxiety of everyday life in post-revolutionary China,' In: B. Highmore (Ed.), *The Everyday Life Reader*. London: Routledge.

Xiaomei Chen (1999) 'Growing up with posters in the Maoist era.' In: H. Evans and S. Donald (Eds.), *Picturing Power in the People's Republic of China: Posters of the Cultural Revolution*. Lanham, MD: Rowman & Littlefield.

Xin Wang (2008) 'Divergent identities, convergent interests: civic awareness of the rising middle-income Stratum in China,' *Journal of Contemporary China*, **17**(54), 53–69.

Xin Wang (2009) 'Seeking channels for engagement: media use in the political communication of the rising middle class in China,' *China: An International Journal*, **7**(1), March, 31–56.

Xinhua (2003) 'Chinese hero gets copyright protection,' 29 June 2003. Available from: *http://www.china.org.cn/english/culture/68407.htm* [accessed 20 May 2013].

Xinhua (2013a) 'China's ad industry rises to world's second: SAIC,' 26 April 2013. Available from: *http://news.xinhuanet.com/english/business/2013-04/26/c_132343074.htm* [accessed 30 April 2013].

Xinhua (2013b) 'SARFT bans "gift giving" TV, radio ads,' 5 February 2013. Available from: *http://news.xinhuanet.com/english/china/2013-02/05/c_132153230.htm* [accessed 30 April 2013].

Xu Baiyi (1988) *Guanggaoxue rumen (Advertising Basics)*. Shanghai, China: Shanghai wenhua chubanshe.

Xu Baiyi (1990) *Marketing to China: One Billion New Customers*. Lincolnwood, IL: NTC Business Books.

Xu Gang (1999) *Tourism and Local Development in China*. Richmond, VA: Curzon.

Xu Junji (2006) *Zhongguo guanggaoshi (A History of Chinese Advertising)*. Beijing: Zhongguo chuanmei daxue chubanshe.

Xu Min (2012) 'De-deification of Lei Feng will promote his appeal,' *People's Daily Online*, 27 February 2012. Available from: *http://english.people.com.cn/90780/7740949.html* [retrieved 20 June 2013].

Xunzi (1990) *A Translation and Study of the Complete Works* (translated by J. Knoblock). Stanford, CA: Stanford University Press, 2 volumes.

Yan Hui (2012) '*Yong Lei Feng jingshen yinling daxuesheng wangluo daode shilu*' ('On university students' network moral practice guided by Lei Feng spirit'), *Anhui gongye daxue xuebao (Journal of Anhui University of Technology)*, 29(6), 155–9.

Yan, Y. (2000) 'Of hamburger and social space: consuming McDonald's in Beijing.' In: S. Davis (Ed.), *The Consumer Revolution in Urban China*. Berkeley, CA: University of California Press.

Yang Baibing (1990) *Lei Feng riji xuan (Selected Diary of Lei Feng)*, Fourth Edition. Beijing: PLA Culture Publishing House.

Yang Yiyong (Ed.) (1997) *Equality and Efficiency: The Issue of Distribution of Income in Contemporary China*. Beijing: Today's China Publishing House [in Chinese].

Yang, G. (2005) 'Environmental NGOs and institutional dynamics in China,' *China Quarterly*, **181**, 46–66.

Yao Jie (2002) '*Xi WTO yu bentu guanggaoye de si da zhizhu*' ('On the four pillars of WTO and local advertising'). In: Qiao Jun, Cheng Zhuangzhuang, and Dong Lijin (Eds.), *Zhongguo guanggao hangye jingzhengli yanjiu (Research on China's Advertising Industry Competitiveness)*. Chengdu, China: Xinan caijing daxue chubanshe.

Yao Xi and Jiang Yibing (2006) *Jianming shijie guanggaoshi (A Brief History of World Advertising)*. Beijing: Gaodeng jiaoyu chubanshe.

Yao, P. (2005) 'Between truth and fiction: notes on fakes, copies, and authenticity in contemporary Chinese art,' *Yishu*, 4(2), June, 18–24.

Yao, S. (2002) *Confucian Capitalism: Discourse, Practice and the Myth of Chinese Enterprise*. London: RoutledgeCurzon.

Yeh, E.T. (2007) 'Tropes of indolence and the cultural politics of development in Lhasa, Tibet,' *Annals of the Association of American Geographers*, **97**(3), 593–612.

Young, M. (1989) 'Chicken Little in China: some reflections on women.' In: A. Dirlik and M. Meisner (Edss), *Marxism and the Chinese Experience: Issues in Contemporary Chinese Socialism*. Armonk, NY: M.E. Sharpe.

Yu Dan (2009) *Confucius from the Heart: Ancient Wisdom for Today's World*. London: Macmillan.

Yu Xuejun (1991) 'Government policies toward advertising in China (1979–1989),' *International Communication Gazette*, **48**, 17–30.

Yu, M. (2013) 'Inside China: Lei Feng and China's zeitgeist,' *Washington Times*, 14 March 2013. Available from: *http://www.washingtontimes.com/news/2013/mar/14/inside-china-lei-feng-and-chinas-zeitgeist/?page=all* [accessed 27 June 2013].

Yuan Dao (1998) *Tracing Dao to Its Source* (translated by D.C. Lau and R.T. Ames). New York: Ballantine Books.

Yue Xao Dong and Cheung Chau-kiu (2000) 'Selection of favourite idols and models among Chinese young people: a comparative study in Hong Kong and Nanjing,' *International Journal of Behavioral Development*, **24**(1), 91–8.

Yujie Zhu (2012a) 'Performing heritage: rethinking authenticity in tourism,' *Annals of Tourism Research*, **39**(3), 1495–1513.

Yujie Zhu (2012b) 'When the global meets the local in tourism: cultural performance in Lijiang as case studies,' *Journal of China Tourism Research*, **8**, 302–19.

Zhang Dongya (2010) 'What if Lei Feng served today?' *Beijing Today*, 26 March 2010. Available from: *http://www.beijingtoday.com.cn/tag/dai-xiang* [accessed 20 June 2013].

Zhang Kaining and Liu Xiangyuan (2007) *New Countryside New Family: The Population Health Promotion Program in the Larger Shangri-la Area*. Kunming, China: Yunnan Health & Development Research Association.

Zhang Nanzhou (1986) '*Jianli juyou Zhongguo tese de shehui zhuyi guanggaoye*' ('To build a socialist advertising with Chinese characteristics,' *Xiamen daxue xuebao*, **3**, 140–4.

Zhang Ran (2012) ' *"Lei Feng quanji" huanyuan zhenshi Lei Feng shoulu zhongduo shougao*' ('The "Complete Works of Lei Feng" return to the authentic Lei Feng and include numerous manuscripts'), *Renmin Wang*, 20 February 2012. Available from: *http://culture.people.com.cn/GB/22219/17156490.html* [accessed 18 June 2013].

Zhang Rui (2013) 'DreamWorks to make bestseller Tibet Code into film,' China.org.cn [accessed 22 April 2013].

Zhang Wen (2013) 'Locals forget Learn from Lei Feng Day,' *Global Times*, 6 March 2013. Available from: *http://www.globaltimes.cn/content/766113.shtml* [accessed 18 June 2013].

Zhang Zhidong (1900) *Quanxue pian (Exhortation to Study)* (tramslated by Samuel Woodbridge as *China's Only Hope*). New York: Fleming H. Revell Co.

Zhang Zhong (2012) '*Lei Feng pinpai zai wangluo shidai yu zou yu hong*' ('In the Internet age the Lei Feng brand becomes more and more popular'), *Zhongguo pinpai yu fangwei (China Brand and Anti-Counterfeiting)*, **3**, 33–4.

Zhao Chen (2005) *Zhongguo guanggaoshi (A History of Chinese Advertising)*. Beijing: Gaodeng jiaoyu chubanshe.

Zhao Yuezhi (1998) *Media, Market, and Democracy in China: Between the Party Line and the Bottom Line*. Chicago, IL: University of Illinois Press.

Zhao Yuji (1987) '*Shehui guanggao jiben lilun wenti tantao*' ('A discussion of the basic theoretical problems of socialist advertising,' *Beijing shehui kexue*, **1**, 107–13.

Zheng Yongnian (2013) 'China in 2012: troubled elite, frustrated society,' *Asian Survey*, **53**(1), 162–75.

Zhou Dunyi (2009) *Penetrating the Scripture of Change [Tongshu]* (translated by J.A. Adler). Available from: *http://www2.kenyon.edu/Depts/Religion/Fac/Adler/Writings/Tongshu.htm#33* [accessed 30 April 2013].

Zhou Ping (2013) 'A voluntrary sector to benefit all,' *Global Times*, 18 March 2013. Available from: *http://www.globaltimes.cn/content/768829.shtml#.Uc6vPJwXF9Y* [accessed 28 June 2013].

Zhou Xiaohong (Ed.) (2005) *Survey of the Chinese Middle Class*. Beijing: Social Sciences Academic Press.

Zhou Ying (2007) '*Zhongguo yuansu "san ren hang"*' ('Three protagonists of the Chinese elements'], *Chenggong yingxiao*, **3**, 54–5.

Zhou, L. and Hui, M.K. (2003) 'Symbolic value of foreign products in the People's Republic of China,' *Journal of International Marketing*, **11**(2), 36–58

Zhouyi Xinwen (2007) '*Nanzi chengfu shuaidao Lao tai fan beigao bei pan pei*' ('A man helped an elderly lady, became the accused and had to pay for compensation'), 6 September 2007. Available from: *http://news.163.com/07/0906/05/3NMDBNR600011229.html* [accessed 26 June 2013].

Zhu Min (2013) '*42 wan "Lei Feng" huoyue xing cheng*' ('City of 420.000 active Lei Feng stars'), *Renmin Wang*, 25 February 2013. Available from: *http://politics.people.com.cn/n/2013/0225/c1001-20589747.html* [accessed 20 June 2013].

Zhu Ying (2005) 'Yongzheng dynasty and Chinese primetime television drama,' *Cinema Journal*, **44**(4), 3–17

Zhu, J. (2010) 'Mothering expectant mothers: consumption, production, and two motherhoods in contemporary China,' *Ethos*, **38**(4), 406–21.

Zima, P. (1997) *Moderne/Postmoderne: Gesellschaft, Philosophie, Literatur*. Tübingen, Germany: A. Francke.

Zukin, S. and Smith-Maguire, J (2004) 'Consumers and consumption,' *Annual Review of Sociology*, **30**, 173–97.

Zuo, M. (2013) 'Lei Feng's spirit of serving others has lost its appeal,' *South China Morning Post*, 10 March 2013. Available from: *http://www.scmp.com/comment/insight-opinion/article/1187224/lei-fengs-spirit-serving-others-has-lost-its-appeal* [accessed 20 June 2013].

Index

Printed and bound by CPI Group (UK) Ltd, Croydon, CR0 4YY

08/05/2025

01864974-0002